Traditio

WORKBOOK FOR THE THIRD EDITION

Patricia A. Johnston

BRANDEIS UNIVERSITY PRESS
Waltham, Massachusetts

BRANDEIS UNIVERSITY PRESS
An imprint of University Press of New England
www.upne.com
© 1999 Patricia A. Johnston
Manufactured in the United States of America

For permission to reproduce any of the material
in this book, contact Permissions, University Press
of New England, One Court Street, Suite 250,
Lebanon NH 03766; or visit www.upne.com

Paperback ISBN: 978-1-61168-690-6
Ebook ISBN: 978-1-61168-714-9

5 4 3 2 1

Contents

How to Use This Workbook

The exercises and explanations in this workbook are intended to supplement the material in *Traditio: An Introduction to the Latin Language and Its Influence*, 3rd edition. Your instructor may choose to collect these exercises as you proceed through the text, either before or after you have corrected your work by comparing it to the answers in the Key at the end of each chapter. In any event, try to answer all the questions before consulting the Key, and then compare those answers with your own.

Make it a regular practice to learn all the paradigms by heart, by saying them aloud, by writing them out, and by using the Latin Software, "The Latin Tutor", which will drill you on the paradigms.

For Verbs, learn all four principal parts.

For Nouns, learn the Nominative, genitive, and gender.

For Adjectives, learn the Nominative Masculine, Feminine, and Neuter forms.

Adverbs, Prepositions, Conjunctions, and Interjections have only one form to be learned.

It is a good idea to make charts of case endings, verb patterns, and vocabulary cards with the English on one side and the Latin on the other. If you have a computer, you may find it helpful to build a vocabulary list, adding new vocabulary as you learn it. Such a list is helpful in alphabetic order (as you will find it at the back of *Traditio*), but you may also find it helpful to build lists which categorize words; for example, a list of all first declension words, another of second declension words, etc., or of verbs according to their conjugations. You may also want to group words according to their relationship, for example the verb "to love," *amō*, and its derivatives, e.g., the noun *amor*, the adjective *amābilis*, etc., or root verbs such as *teneō*, following by its compounds, such as *contineō*, *retineō*, *dētineō*, etc. Another helpful list would collect all the adverbs, or conjunctions, or prepositions (including such information as the case it governs). You will find that the mere act of creating these lists will help you to learn them well.

Finally, close attention to Latin derivatives in English words will not only help you to retain the meaning in Latin, but will also help in building your English vocabulary and spelling difficulties, since the Latin spelling tends to be retained in English.

I
The Verbal System

In this chapter we shall study both English and Latin verbs, with particular emphasis on the present, future and perfect tenses. All vocabulary and word forms will be based on the materials found in Chapter I of *Traditio*.

A. English Grammar Review: Verbs

A.1. Meaning. Verbs, whether English or Latin, indicate action (*put, see, think*), condition (*feel, be*), or process (*become, grow, die, change*).

Action:	Narcissus *saw* a face in the pool.
	He *put* his hand in the water.
	He *thought* he saw someone else.
Condition:	He *felt* great love for the boy in the water.
	The boy in the water *was* a reflection of Narcissus.
Process:	He *became* anxious.
	He *drowned* in the pool.
	After he *died*, Narcissus became a purple flower.

A.2. Subject and Predicate. All sentences in English contain a *subject* and a *predicate*. The *subject* is that part of the sentence which the sentence is about—it is the person or thing performing the action expressed by the verb when the voice of the verb is active (the passive voice will be discussed later). The *predicate* of the sentence contains the main verb, along with all its modifiers, objects, complements, and similar words.

Subject	Predicate
Narcissus	sighed.
Narcissus	sadly sighed.
Narcissus	saw a face.
The boy in the water	was a reflection of Narcissus.
Narcissus	became a purple flower after he died.

In the first example, the predicate is merely the verb of the sentence, which has no object or modifier (*sighed*). In the second example, the predicate is again the verb (*sighed*), which here has an *adverbial modifier* (*sadly*) which in this case tells *how* he sighed.

In the third example, the predicate is a verb (*saw*), which here has an object (*a face*). Unlike the verb in the first two sentences (*sighed*), which cannot take a direct object and is therefore called an *intransitive* verb, the verb of the third sentences does take a direct object (*a face*), and is therefore called a *transitive* verb, from the Latin **trāns** (*across*) and **itum** (*gone*): in other words, the action of the verb here has a direct impact upon its object.

1

The last two examples are *connecting verbs* (*was, became*) with their *complements* or *predicate nouns* (*a reflection; a flower*). Additionally, the last example has a modifier—in this case, in the form of a *dependent clause* (*after he died*). A dependent clause is one which does not, on its own, form a complete sentence, and hence relies on the main clause to give it meaning. Notice that a modifying clause (which tells *when* he became a flower) is not always next to the verb it modifies.

A.3. Sentences: Simple, Complex and Compound. Every sentence must have a *main clause*, which contains the main verb (he *saw* the boy). If it contains only one clause, it is known as a *simple sentence*. If it also contains one or more dependent clauses, it is known as a *complex sentence* (*when he turned, he saw the boy*). If it contains two or more independent clauses (that is, clauses, which can stand on their own), they are called *compound sentences* (he *saw* the boys and he *summoned* them.). Thus, in the sentence

He tried to touch the face which he saw,

the main clause is

He tried to touch the face.

This sentence is complete; it is an independent clause.

...which he saw.

describes the face, but it cannot stand as an independent sentence or clause. If the sentence read

He saw the face and he tried to touch it,

it would contain two independent clauses:

He saw the face. He tried to touch it.

and would be known as a *compound sentence*.

A.4. Verb Forms. You will have noticed that verbs in English do not contain a subject as the Latin verbs do. Even though the English verb does not include its subject, it does have to agree with its subject, and this agreement is reflected in the verbal endings:

Latin	English
videō	(I) see; (I) do see; (I) am seeing
videt	(he) sees; (he) does see; (he) is seeing
vidēbimus	(we) shall see; (we) shall be seeing
vidēbis	(you) will see, (you) will be seeing
vīdī	(I) saw; (I) did see; (I) have seen
vīdit	(he) saw; (he) did see; (he) has seen

In the above examples, some of the verbs consist of one or more *auxiliary verbs* (*do, does; am, is, shall be, have, have been, has been*, etc.) often combined with the *present* or *past participle* of the verb. The present participle usually ends in English with "-ing" (*seeing, calling, loving*). The form of the perfect participle is more varied (*seen; called; loved*). The first two verbs are in the *present tense*, but reflect different *aspects* of the present tense: *I see* and *he sees* are simple statements of the action; *I do see* and *he does see* represent the *emphatic aspect* of the verb, while *I am seeing* and *he is seeing* indicate an on-going activity and therefore represent the *continuous aspect* of the verb. Notice that these aspects also apply in the future tenses and in the past tenses (here, in the perfect tense). These various aspects of *tense* (the *time* of the action of the verb) occur in both English and in Latin.

A.5. Mood. In English, as in Latin, the possible moods of a verb are the Infinitive Mood, the Indicative Mood, the Imperative Mood, and the Subjunctive Mood.

The *Infinitive Mood* of a verb is the form of the verb which is *not* limited by person or number, **in** (*not*) **finītum** (*limited*). Hence *to speak* indicates the nature of the verbal action, but does not say who (in the singular or in the plural) is speaking.

The *Indicative Mood* of a verb represents a mere statement of fact: *he is speaking; he will speak, he will not speak, he spoke.*

The *Imperative Mood* is a command: *Speak! Don't speak!*

The *Subjunctive Mood,* **sub** (*under*) **iunctus** (*joined*), occurs most often in subordinate or dependent clauses. A purpose clause, for example, is a subordinate clause showing the intent or purpose of the subject: He came *to see me.*

A.6. Exercises: English Verbs. Indicate:

   i. which word is the subject,

  ii. which is the *main* verb of the following sentences.

 iii. indicate the *person* (first person [*I* or *we*], second person [*you*] or third person [*he, she, it,* or *they*] and the *number* [singular or plural] of the subject of the main verb, and its tense.

Example: Narcissus came to a pool to rest.

   i. Narcissus

  ii. came

 iii. 3rd person singular (Narcissus).

a. No woods, no goats, no cattle, no falling leaf troubled that glassy pool.

   i. *glassy pool*

  ii. *troubled*

 iii. *past tense / singular / 3rd person*

b. When he tried to quench his thirst in the pool, he saw an image in the pool.

   i. *He*

  ii. *saw or quench*

 iii. *3rd / singular / past*

c. A greater longing was growing in Narcissus.

   i. *Narcissus*

  ii. *longing*

 iii. *3rd / singular / ?unsure*

d. He looks in wonder, charmed by his reflection.

   i. *3rd*

  ii. *looks*

 iii. *3rd / singular / present*

e. Beautiful boy, please, come out, whoever you are!

   i. *boy*

  ii. *come out*

 iii. *3rd / singular / present*

B. Latin Verbs

B.1. Vocabulary Quiz. Translate the following into Latin, listing all four principal parts.

Example: love

Answer: **amō, amāre, amāvī, amātus**

  1. make a mistake

  2. understand

  3. see

4. capture
5. bite
6. prepare
7. give
8. be afraid of, fear
9. sing
10. think
11. hope
12. breathe
13. advise
14. hold

B.2. Tenses Based on Present Stem. Present and Future Tense Indicative Mood, and Present Tense Imperative Mood. Verbs of the present and future indicative tense and verbs of the imperative mood take their form from the stem of the present infinitive. The stem is obtained by dropping the final **-re** from the infinitive.

Conjugate the following verbs (that is, provide the singular and plural forms of the verbs) in the tense and mood indicated:

Example: **cantō cantāre,** *sing*

Present stem: **cantā**

Present tense: (present stem + personal ending)

person	singular	plural	translation	
1st	**cantō**	**cantāmus**	I sing	we sing
2nd	**cantās**	**cantātis**	you sing	you (pl.) sing
3rd	**cantat**	**cantant**	he/she/it sings	they sing

Future tense: (present stem + **bi** + personal ending)

person	singular	plural	translation	
1st	**cantābō**	**cantābimus**	I shall sing	we shall sing
2nd	**cantābis**	**cantābitis**	you will sing	you (pl.) will sing
3rd	**cantābit**	**cantābunt**	he/she/it will sing	they will sing

Imperative Mood (nothing added to present stem in singular; **-te** added in plural)

singular	plural	translation	
cantā	**cantāte**	sing!	sing!

Present Tense, Indicative Mood:

a. moneō, monēre, warn; advise

	singular	translation	plural	translation
1st person	___	___	___	___
2nd person	___	___	___	___
3rd person	___	___	___	___

b. optō, optāre, *want; wish*

	singular	translation	plural	translation
1st person	___	___	___	___
2nd person	___	___	___	___
3rd person	___	___	___	___

Future Tense, Indicative Mood:

c. cōgitō, cōgitāre, *think*

	singular	translation	plural	translation
1st person	_____	_____	_____	_____
2nd person	_____	_____	_____	_____
3rd person	_____	_____	_____	_____

d. videō, vidēre *see*

	singular	translation	plural	translation
1st person	_____	_____	_____	_____
2nd person	_____	_____	_____	_____
3rd person	_____	_____	_____	_____

Present Tense, Imperative Mood:

e. moneō, monēre *warn; advise*

	singular	translation	plural	translation
2nd person	_____	_____	_____	_____

f. optō, optāre *want; wish*

	singular	translation	plural	translation
2nd person	_____	_____	_____	_____

g. cōgitō, cōgitāre *think*

	singular	translation	plural	translation
2nd person	_____	_____	_____	_____

h. videō, vidēre *see*

	singular	translation	plural	translation
2nd person	_____	_____	_____	_____

B.3. Tenses Based on Perfect Stem. The perfect tense , which indicates past or completed action, is formed by adding perfect endings to the perfect stem of the verb; this stem is obtained by dropping the final **i** from the perfect stem and add the special personal endings which are used for the perfect tense only. The perfect endings are

Singular	Plural
-ī	**-imus**
-istī	**-istis**
-it	**-ērunt**

For *First Conjugation* verbs (that is, for verbs whose present infinitive ends in **-āre**), the third principal part will end in **-āvī**, e.g., **amāvī, sperāvī, cantāvī**. Thus the stem will end with **-āv-**. For *Second Conjugation* verbs (that is, for verbs whose present infinitive ends in **ēre**) the perfect stem will be less regular. The verbs you have learned so far have perfect stems ending **-uī** (**timēre, timuī; monere, monuī; tenēre, tenuī**) or they lengthen the vowel of the stem and **-ī** (**vidēre, vīdī**), or the first two letters are doubled (*reduplicated*) and **-ī** is added to the reduplicated stem (**mordēre, momordī**).

Example:
cantō, cantāre, **cantāvī**, cantātus, *sing*   videō, vidēre, **vīdī**, vīsus, *see*

Perfect stem **cantāv-**		Perfect stem **vīd-**	
	Translation		*Translation*
cantāvī	I sang/have sung	vīdī	I saw/ have seen
cantāvistī	you sang	vīdistī	you saw
cantāvit	he/she/it sang	vīdit	he saw
cantāvimus	we sang	vīdimus	we saw
cantāvistis	you (pl.) sang	vīdistis	you saw
cantāvērunt	they sang	vīdērunt	they saw

Conjugate the following verbs in the perfect tense:

a. **moneō, monēre, monuī, monitus,** *warn; advise*

	singular	translation	plural	translation
1st person				
2nd person				
3rd person				

b. **optō, optāre, optāvī, optātus,** *want; wish*

	singular	translation	plural	translation
1st person				
2nd person				
3rd person				

c. **mordeō, mordēre, momordī, morsus,** *bite; sting*

	singular	translation	plural	translation
1st person				
2nd person				
3rd person				

C. English Derivations From Latin

Although the direct ancestor of the English language is Anglo-Saxon, a Germanic language from which modern German is also derived, a very large proportion of English words are derived either directly from Latin, or indirectly through the modern Romance languages ÄFrench, Spanish, Italian, Roumanian),which are directly descended from Latin. A word is said to be *derived from* Latin if a Latin word is its source; for example, the adjective *amicable*, "friendly" is derived from the Latin adjective **amīcus**, "friend."

It has long been believed that there was once a common ancestor for all the Indo-European language groups, which include Slavic, Baltic, Celtic, Germanic, Italic, Greek, Iranian, and Sanskrit. The Italic languages were a group of dialects which included Latin, from which, in turn, the modern Romance languages are descended. Words are said to be *cognates* if they appear to share a common ancestor. Thus, there is believed to have been a common ancestor for the word meaning "mother" in the Indo-European group, to which many languages of Indo European ancestry have a word which is a *cognate*, for example:

Sanskrit	Iranian	Greek	Latin	Anglo-Saxon	Old Irish	Lithuanian
matar	*matar*	*meter*	*mater*	*moder*	*mathir*	*mote*

In each chapter of the *Traditio Workbook* you will be asked to identify English derivations based upon the new Latin vocabulary lists. You will find many more than one English derivation from the new Latin vocabulary words. Keep adding to your list as you proceed through the vocabulary lists in *Traditio*, and begin to notice how a word's meaning is changed by the individual *prefixes* (attached to the beginning of the word) and *suffixes* (attached to the end of the word). *-able* and *-ible* at the end of a word, for example, mean *able* or *capable of*, so that *amicable* means *capable of being loved*, and *provisional, pro-* (ahead), *vīsus* (seen), means *something done with a view to what lies ahead* or *is foreseen*. And since *ex* means *from, out, expire* will mean *breathe out* (usually for the last time) and hence *to die*. Look up new words in English dictionaries, which frequently will supply the Latin roots. Study the range of meaning these words have come to enfold. You will soon find you own vocabulary enlarging greatly, with increasing nuance in your expression, and you will also learn the pleasures of *etymology*, the study of the history of words, including their derivation.

Learn by heart the verbs in Chapter I of *Traditio*, and then identify the infinitive of the Latin verb from which the following English words are derived; then match the English word with its correct meaning:

English	Latin source		Meaning of English Word
Example:			
admonition	monēre	g.	a. fearful
conspiracy	_____	_____	b. pertaining to sight
dative	_____	_____	c. sarcastic
desperate	_____	_____	d. a divine influence
dedicated	_____	_____	e. repayment
erroneous	_____	_____	f. grammatical case for the indirect object in a sentence
erratic	_____	_____	g. a warning
incantation	_____	_____	h. to send by airwaves to a picture tube
inspiration	_____	_____	i. a secret agreement to do something together
mordant	_____	_____	j. the words uttered in magic ceremony
reparation	_____	_____	k. without hope
televise	_____	_____	l. mistaken
timid	_____	_____	m. wandering
visual	_____	_____	n. set apart in honor of some person or goal

D. Terminology Review

Explain what is meant by each of the following terms:

1. subject of the verb
2. indicative mood
3. imperative mood
4. present tense
5. future tense
6. perfect tense
7. principal parts of the Latin verb
8. infinitive
9. first conjugation

10. second conjugation
11. personal ending of the verb
12. derivative
13. suffix
14. present stem
15. perfect stem
16. dependent clause
17. independent clause
18. predicate
19. object of the verb
20. modifier
21. adverbial modifier
22. connecting verbs
23. transitive verb
24. intransitive verb

E. Translation

Review again all the vocabulary words in Chapter I, and then provide the correct Latin for the following expressions.

1. We made a mistake.
2. He often makes mistakes.
3. Don't (sing.) make a mistake!
4. Don't (plural) sing!
5. They are afraid.
6 Why are they afraid?
7. Give! (sing.)
8. Don't give! (plural)
9. They want to prepare.
10. Please, sing (sing.)
11. Don't (sing.) bite!
12. We don't want to make a mistake.
13. They captured.
14. We shall capture.
15. I don't understand
16. Why were you (plural) afraid?
17. Often I have been afraid.
18. Please, breathe (sing.)
19. We will hope.
20. They will sing

Key, Chapter I

A. English Grammar Review

A.6.

a.   i.   woods, goats, cattle, leaf.

     ii.   troubled

     iii.   3rd person plural

The plural subject here is known as a *compound subject* because it is a list of items which together comprise the subject; *no* and *no falling* describe the subjects, and thus are known as *adjectives*.

b.   i.   he

     ii.   saw

     iii.   3rd person singular

c.   i.   longing

     ii.   was growing

     iii.   3rd person singular

d.   i.   he

     ii.   looks

     iii.   3rd person singular

e.   i.   beautiful boy (you)

     ii.   come

     iii.   2nd person singular

The verb *come* is in the imperative mood—the beautiful boy is being spoken to. *Please!* is an exclamation (in Latin: **amābō tē**), *whoever you are* is a dependent clause, describing the person being addressed.

B.1.

1.   errō, errāre, errāvī, errātus

2.   videō, vidēre, vīdī, vīsus

3.   videō, vidēre, vīdī, vīsus

4.   captō, captāre, captāvī, captātus

5.   mordeō, mordēre, momordī, morsus

6.   parō, parāre, parāvī, parātus

7.   dō, dare, dedī, datus

8.   timeō, timēre, timuī, ——, (no fourth principal part)

9.   cantō, cantāre, cantāvī, cantātus

10.   cōgitō, cōgitāre, cōgitāvī, cōgitātus

11.   spērō, spērāre, spērāvī, spērātus

12.   spīrō, spīrāre, spīrāvī, spīrātus

13.   moneō, monēre, monuī, monitus

14.   teneō, tenēre, tenuī, tentus

B.2.

	singular	*translation*	*plural*	*translation*
a.	**moneō**	I warn or advise	**monēmus**	we warn
	monēs	you (s.)warn	**monētis**	you (pl.) warn
	monet	he,she,it warns	**monent**	they warn
b.	**optō**	I want	**optāmus**	we want
	optās	you (s.)want	**optātis**	you (plural) want
	optat	he,she,it wants	**optant**	they want.

c.	cōgitābō	I shall think	cōgitābimus	we shall think
	cōgitābis	you will think	cōgitābitis	you will think
	cōgitābit	he will think	cōgitābunt	they will think
d.	vidēbō	I shall see	vidēbimus	we shall see
	vidēbis	you will see	vidēbitis	you will see
	vidēbit	he will see	vidēbunt	they will see
e.	monē	warn! (sing.)	monēte	warn! (plural)
f.	optā	wish! (sing.)	optāte	wish! (plural)
g.	cōgitā	think! (sing.)	cōgitāte	think! (plural)
h.	vidē	see! (sing.)	vidēte	see! (plural)

B.3.

a.	monuī	monuistī	monuit
	I advised	you advised	he,she, it advised
	monuimus	monuistis	monuērunt
	we advised	you advised	they advised
b.	optāvī	optāvistī	optāvit
	I wanted	you wanted	he,she, it wanted
	optāvimus	optāvistis	optāvērunt
	we wanted	you wanted	they wanted
c.	momordī	momordistī	momordit
	I bit	you bit	he,she,it bit
	momordimus	momordistis	momordērunt
	we bit	you bit	they bit

C. ENGLISH DERIVATIONS FROM LATIN

English	Latin source		Meaning of English Word
admonition	monēre	g.	a warning
conspiracy	spīrāre	i.	a secret agreement to do something together
dative	dare	f.	grammatical case for the indirect in a sentence
desperate	spērāre	k.	without hope
dedicated	dare	n.	set apart in honor of some person or goal
erroneous	errāre	l.	mistaken
erratic	errāre	m.	wandering
incantation	cantāre	j.	the words uttered in magic ceremony
inspiration	spīrāre	d.	a divine influence
mordant	mordēre	c.	sarcastic
reparation	parāre	e.	repayment
televise	videō	h.	to send by airwaves to a picture tube
timid	timeō	a.	fearful
visual	videō	b.	pertaining to sight

D. TERMINOLOGY REVIEW

1. **subject of the verb:** the person or thing performing the action expressed by the verb(in the active voice).
2. **indicative mood:** a statement of fact.
3. **imperative mood:** expresses a command.
4. **present tense:** expresses what is happening at the present time.
5. **future tense:** expresses what will happen in the future.
6. **perfect tense:** expresses what has happened in the past
7. **principal parts of the Latin verb:** the first person singular present tense, the present infinitive, the first person singular perfect tense, and the perfect passive participle.
8. **infinitive:** the second principal part of the verb, translated *to [do something]*; is not limited by person or number, as finite verbs are.
9. **first conjugation:** verbs whose present active infinitive ends in **-āre.**

10. **second conjugation:** verbs whose present active infinitive ends in **-ēre.**
11. **personal ending of the verb:** first person (I, we), second person (you), third person (he, she, it, they).
12. **derivative:** a word formed from another word, by adding a suffix, prefix or in some way modifying the original word. This can happen between two languages, or within a single language.
13. **suffix:** one or more syllables added to the end of a word, thereby modifying the meaning of the original word.
14. **present stem:** the root of a verb, obtained by dropping -re from the end of the present infinitive.
15. **perfect stem:** the root of a verb, obtained by dropping -re from the end of the perfect infinitive.
16. **dependent clause:** a subordinate clause, which cannot on its own form a complete sentence.
17. **independent clause:** a clause which on its own forms a complete sentence.
18. **predicate:** the main verb of a sentence and all its modifiers, objects, complements, and similar words.
19. **object of the verb:** the noun or its substitute which is the goal of the action of the verb.
20. **modifier:** an adjective, adverb, or clause which limits or qualifies the sense of another word.
21. **adverbial modifier:** an adverb or clause which modifies an adjective, another adverb, or a verb.
22. **connecting verbs:** the various forms of intransitive verbs such as to be (am, is, are, etc.) and to become.
23. **transitive verb:** a verb which takes a direct object.
24. **intransitive verb:** a verb which, because of its meaning (e.g., be, become, grow, etc.) cannot take a direct object.

E. TRANSLATION

1. Errāvimus.
2. Saepe errat.
3. Nōlī errāre!
4. Nōlīte cantāre!
5. Timent.
6. Cūr timent?
7. Da!
8. Nōlīte dare!
9. Parāre optant.
10. Amabō tē, cantā!
11. Nōlī mordēre!
12. Errāre nōn optāmus.
13. Captāvērunt.
14. Captābimus.
15. Nōn videō.
16. Cūr timuistis?
17. Saepe timuī.
18. Amābō tē, spīrā
19. Spērābimus.
20. Cantābunt.

II
Nouns and Adjectives

In this chapter we shall study both English and Latin nouns and adjectives, as well as the adverbs which are derived from adjectives. All vocabulary and word forms will be based on the materials found in Chapter II of *Traditio*.

A. English Grammar Review: Nouns, Pronouns, and Adjectives

1. In English and in Latin, words are divided into eight Parts of Speech: Nouns, Adjectives (including Participles), Pronouns, Verbs, Adverbs, Prepositions, Conjunctions, and Interjections.

2. A *noun* (in Latin, **nomen**, or *name*) is the name of a person, place, or thing: *Narcissus, Greece, boy, love*. A noun can also be an abstract idea or quality: *idea, symbol, nation, event, narcissism, egotism*, etc.

The name of a person or place is known as a *proper noun,* and in English is capitalized: *Narcissus, Greece, Caesar, United States*.

Nouns not capitalized in English are known as *common nouns*: *boy, country, girl, love, idea*.

3. A *pronoun* is a word used in place of a proper or common noun. It distinguishes the person, place, thing, or idea, but does not name it. English and Latin have:

Personal Pronouns: *he, she we, you, they, it*.

Demonstrative Pronouns: *this, that, these, those*.

Relative Pronouns: *who, which, that*.

Interrogative Pronouns: *who? which? what?*

Reflexive Pronouns: in English, the reflexive or intensive pronoun plus *-self: myself, yourself, himself, themselves*.

Reciprocal Pronouns: *each other, one another*.

Numerical Pronouns: the cardinal numbers (one, two, three) and the ordinal numbers (first, second, third): *two* came to dinner; the *third* was absent.

4. An *adjective* gives some quality to a noun, and thus is said to *modify* a noun, for example, *good* manners, a *big* building, *tall* trees, a *brief* silence.

They placed *a delicious* meal on the banquet table.

The exhausted sailors quickly ate *the baked* bread and drank *the red* wine.

The adjective can be an *article* (a, the) in English; Latin does not have articles as English does, but does *use demonstrative adjectives* (*this, that*) when necessary.

The adjective can also be a *participle*, which is an adjective whose meaning is verbal (*exhausted, baked, steaming, steamed, collapsing, collapsed, collapsible* etc.) but which still agrees in case, number and gender with the noun it modifies. The verbal meaning can be active (*seeing*) or passive (*seen*), and can be in the present, future or past tense:

> They placed *a steaming* bowl of soup on *the* table.
> The bowl of *steamed* rice fell from *the collapsing* table.
> *No* bowls should be placed on *collapsible* tables.

The adjective can be *attributive*, that is, a simple modifier: a *steaming* bowl; *the collapsing* table; or it can be *predicative*, that is, part of the verbal part of the sentence when the verb is some form of "to be" or "to become":

> The bowl is *hot*; the food is *delicious* ; the table is *collapsible*.

5. An *adverb* modifies a verb or another adjective. In English, adverbs are often formed by adding *-ly* to an adjective:

> The waiter was *brooding* and *angry*. (adjectives)
> The waiter *angrily* placed a bowl of rice on the table. (adverb modifies verb)
> The *angrily* brooding waiter served the rice. (adverb modifies adjective)

Exercises: English Grammar

1. Identify the *nouns* in the following sentences, and indicate whether they are *common (C)* or *proper (P)*:

a. Narcissus saw the reflection of a beautiful boy in the pool.

_____(noun) _____(C or P); _____ _____;

_____ _____; _____ _____.

b. The nymphs pulled Narcissus down into the water.

_____ _____; _____ _____; _____ _____.

c. Narcissus was punished because he loved only himself.

_____ _____.

d. The nymph, Echo, loved him, and followed him everywhere.

_____ _____; _____ _____.

e. Echo was filled with sorrow when Narcissus rejected her love.

_____ _____; _____ _____; _____ _____;

_____ _____.

f. She wasted away until all that remained of her was her voice.

_____ _____; _____ _____.

2. Underline the *pronouns* in the following passage, and **indicate above it** what kind of pronoun it is (demonstrative = dem.; personal = P; relative = R; interrogative = I; reflexive = ref.; reciprocal = rec.; numerical = N.):

Narcissus saw himself reflected in the pool. He did not recognize that he was the

beautiful boy in the pool. He felt great love this beautiful boy, and tried to touch

him, but instead he fell into the pool and was drowned. The story of Narcissus is

the basis for the term, "narcissism", which we now use to describe self-love.

3. Underline the *adjectives* in the following passage, and **indicate above them** whether they are attributive (A), or predicative (P):

Narcissus was beautiful but vain. He was not able to reciprocate the love of

others. The gods decided to punish him for his self-love. One day he came to a beautiful, shady grove with a cool fountain in its midst. When he gazed into the fountain he saw his own reflection, but thought it was another boy. The boy was very beautiful. He felt great love for this boy, and tried to reach him, but instead fell into the pool and was drowned. The mountain nymphs wept at his death, and the gods caused a beautiful purple flower, which they named "narcissus," to grow in his memory.

B. Latin Nouns: First and Second Declension

All Latin nouns belong to one of five *declensions*, or patterns of case endings. In this chapter you are learning the patterns of case endings of the first declension, which is characterized by the letter **-a-**, and of the second declension, which is generally characterized by the letter **-o-**. While the nominative form may vary in each declension, the genitive singular form is fixed, and is what determines to which declension a noun belongs. Thus, the genitive singular of all nouns of the first declension end in **-ae**, and the genitive singular of all nouns in the second declension end in **-i**.

1. The Nominative case. Nouns and pronouns that are the subject of a verb will be in the nominative case. The adjectives modifying them and predicate adjectives will also be in the nominative case. Adjectives always have the same *gender, number* (singular or plural), and *case* as the word(s) they modify. They will not necessarily have the same declension ending, however— if the noun belongs to the first declension, and the gender is masculine, the ending on the adjective will come from the second declension. Here are the possible nominative endings that will be used for first and second declension nouns and adjectives:

	singular	plural
1st declension:	**-a**	**-ae**
2nd declension, masculine:	**-us, er**	**-ī**
2nd declension, neuter:	**-um**	**-a**

Identify, in the following passage, the nouns and adjectives which, in Latin, will be in the nominative case, and indicate the number and gender of their case endings:

Example: *Narcissus* was *beautiful* but *vain*. [all masculine, singular]

Narcissus was not able to return the love of others. Therefore the gods decided to punish him for his self-love. One day he came to a beautiful, shady grove with a cool fountain in its midst. When he gazed into the fountain he saw his own reflection, but thought it was another boy. The boy was very beautiful. He felt great love for this boy, and tried to reach him, but instead fell into the pool and was drowned. The mountain nymphs wept at his death, and the gods caused a beautiful purple flower, which they named "narcissus," to grow in his memory.

2. The Genitive case. The *genitive case* shows a relationship between two nouns; the most common of these relationships is that of possession: the *man's* dog, the *boy's* beauty, *Narcissus'* longing, etc. As you will learn later, however, the genitive case can show a number of other relationships between nouns. The genitive ending indicates ultimately to which declension a Latin noun begins. Here are the possible genitive endings that will be used for first and second declension nouns and adjectives:

	singular	plural
1st declension:	**-ae**	**-ārum**
2nd declension, masculine:	**-ī**	**-ōrum**
2nd declension, neuter:	**-ī**	**-ōrum**

Underline the words in this passage which will be in the genitive case:

Narcissus was not able to return the love of others. Therefore the gods decided to punish his self-love. One day he came to a forest's cool fountain, and when he gazed into its waters he saw his own reflection, but thought it was the face of another young boy. He was very moved by this boy's beauty, and tried to reach him, but instead fell into the pool and was drowned. The mountain nymphs wept at his death, and the gods caused a beautiful purple flower, which they named "narcissus," to grow in his memory.

3. The Dative case. The *dative case* indicates the indirect object of the verb, and nouns and pronouns in this case are usually translated *to* or *for* someone or something. The dative case indicates the person or thing to whom or which, or for whom or which, something is done.

Underline the words which will be in the dative case:

The nymph, Echo, tried to speak to Narcissus, but he gave her no attention. She followed him everywhere, but he was not kind to her. She had once been punished by the gods for speaking to them too much, and therefore could only repeat the last words anyone said to her. Therefore, when Narcissus told her "Non te amo!", Echo would tell him in response, "te amo." She was so overcome with sorrow when Narcissus died that she went deep into the forest and was not seen again. She wasted away until all that remained of her was her voice. If you call to her, she will answer you.

4. The Accusative case. Words in the *accusative case* are most often the direct object of the verb (other applications of the accusative case will be learned later). Which of the following words will be in the accusative case?

Narcissus loved only himself, not Echo. She followed him everywhere, but he was not kind to her. Because the gods had punished her, she could only repeat the last words of a sentence. When Narcissus died, she went into the forest. Her voice remained, however. If you call to her, you will hear her reply.

5. The Ablative case. The *ablative case* is an adverbial case, that is, a phrase in the ablative case often functions as an adverb would, modifying the action: He came *with me*. He spoke *with fervor*. He wrote *with a pencil*. These examples show accompaniment (with me), manner [how, in what manner, he spoke](with fervor), and instrument (with a pencil). The ablative can also show separation: We went *from the city*. A clown popped *out of the box*. How many ablatives of means/instrument (these two ablatives are the same), ablatives of manner, ablatives of accompaniment, and ablatives of separation can you find in the following passage?

Echo tried to be with Narcissus, and to share her love with him, but he was not moved by her love. She followed him everywhere, but she received no kindness from him. He hurt her feelings with his cruel words, but she loved him too much to be driven away by his words. When he died she was so overcome by sorrow that she went deep into the forest and was seen again by no one, but her voice will be heard by those who call her.

6. The Vocative case. The *vocative case* indicates the person being addressed. The case endings will be the same as the nominative except in the second declension, when the nominative ending of the noun is **-us**, in which case the singular vocative ending will be **-e**. The nominative plural and vocative plural are always the same.

Underline the words below that will be in the vocative case:

Do you know the story of Echo and Narcissus? Someone should say, "Echo, don't you realize Narcissus loves only himself? Don't waste your love on him!" But she would not listen. Perhaps, then, we should say, "Please, Narcissus, speak to Echo!" But all that Narcissus would have said to her was, "Echo, go away. **Nōn tē amō!**"

C. Latin Adjectives and Adverbs

Adjectives agree with the noun they modify in *case, number,* and *gender*. Adjectives of the first and second declension (ending in -**us**, -**a**, -**um** in the nominative singular) will tend to have the same ending as the first and second declension noun they modify except when a masculine noun belongs to the first declension, or a feminine noun belongs to the second declension. (e.g., **nauta bonus,** *the good sailor*).

First and second declension adjectives are formed by adding a long -**ē** to the stem of a first or second declension adjective (e.g., **pulchr-** + **ē,** beautifully). The stem of the adjective is found in the adjective's nominative singular feminine form: **pulchra.** The feminine ending -**a** is dropped and the adverbial ending is added: **pulchrē.**

As in English, the adjective in Latin can be *attributive, predicative,* or *substantive*: *attributive adjective* (agrees in case, number and gender with the noun it modifies):

> **Magnus vir fīliīs tuīs bona optat.**
> The great man wants *good things* for your sons.

predicative adjective (completes the meaning of the connecting verb and agrees in case, number, and gender with the noun it modifies:

> **Magnus est vir. (est = he/she/it is)**
> The man is *great.*

substantive adjective (it serves as a noun if the noun is implied but not stated; its number, gender and case agree with the noun that is implied):

> **Magnus fīliīs tuīs bona optat:**
> The *great man* wants *good things* for your sons.

Exercises: Declension of Noun/Adjective Phrases

C.1. Translate the following phrases into English, in the singular nominative, and then decline them in the singular and plural, all cases.

a. **puer parvus.** translation:_____

	Singular	Plural
Nom.	_____	_____
Gen.	_____	_____
Dat.	_____	_____
Acc.	_____	_____
Abl.	_____	_____
Voc.	_____	_____

b. **agricola noster.** translation:_____

	Singular	Plural
Nom.	_____	_____
Gen.	_____	_____
Dat.	_____	_____
Acc.	_____	_____
Abl.	_____	_____
Voc.	_____	_____

c. **bestia magna.** translation: _____

	Singular	Plural
Nom.	_____	_____
Gen.	_____	_____
Dat.	_____	_____
Acc.	_____	_____
Abl.	_____	_____
Voc.	_____	_____

d. **auxilium vestrum.** translation:_____

	Singular	Plural
Nom.	_____	_____
Gen.	_____	_____
Dat.	_____	_____
Acc.	_____	_____
Abl.	_____	_____
Voc.	_____	_____

C.2. Translate the following phrases into Latin, and then decline them in Latin, singular and plural, and translate the Latin phrases into English phrases which reflect their case endings:

a. *Our famous son.* translation: _____

	Singular	Plural
Nom.	_____	_____
Gen.	_____	_____
Dat.	_____	_____
Acc.	_____	_____
Abl.	_____	_____
Voc.	_____	_____

b. *the teacher's famous book.* translation: _____

	Singular	Plural
Nom.	_____	_____
Gen.	_____	_____
Dat.	_____	_____
Acc.	_____	_____
Abl.	_____	_____
Voc.	_____	_____

C.3. Translate the following sentences into Latin:

a. *The farmer is singing.*

b. *Sing, farmers!*

c. *We farmers sang.*

d. *She is singing beautifully.*

e. *We wanted beautiful things.*

f. *Have you seen my famous son?*

C.4. Translate the following sentences, and indicate whether the adjective is attributive (A), predicative (P), or substantive (S):

a. Magister stellās clārās in caelō vīdit.

b. Stella clāra est.

c. Puellae bona cantāvērunt.

d. Fīlius meus auxilium dedit.

e. Fīlius mala optat.

C.5. Translate the following sentences; then change the adjectives into adverbs, and translate the new sentence into English:

a. Puer miser cantāvit.

b. Bestia misera cibum captāvit.

c. Mē miseram vīdī.

d. Puella pulchra cantābit.

e. Dominus dōnum malum dedit.

D. Vocabulary Quiz: English to Latin/Latin to English

Indicate whether the following words are nouns (N) or adjectives (A); then list the nominative singular, genitive and gender of the Latin equivalent of the following nouns, and the nominative singular masculine, feminine, and neuter of the adjectives:

	N/A	Nom. Sing.	Genitive	Gender
star				
sky				
bright				
handsome				
famous				
beautiful				
boy				
girl				
man				
your (s.)				
your (pl.)				
our				
my				
book				
free				
word				
master				
teacher				
ruler				
jealousy				
friend				
farmer				
field				
small				
large				
road				

E. Derivations

English	Latin source	Meaning	Meaning of English Word
Liberia			a. desire to possess what others have
libretto			b. the overhead interior lining of a room
liberate			c. to bring into close association
library			d. express sorrow or sympathy for
celesta			e. a toroid containing plasma which is magnetically controlled and heated to about 100 million degrees C. to sustain a thermonuclear reaction.

magisterial _____ _____   f. a republic in West Africa founded in 1822 by freed American slaves.

magnanimous _____ _____   g. a place where books are kept

ceiling _____ _____   h. cultivation of the land

nautical _____ _____   i. the words or text of an opera

envy _____ _____   j. a musical instrument

affiliate _____ _____   k. set free

agriculture _____ _____   l. having to do with sailors, ships, or sailing

commiserate _____ _____   m. authoritative

stellarator _____ _____   n. generous in forgiving insult or injury

F. Terminology Review

Explain what is meant by each of the following terms:

1. noun
2. common noun
3. proper noun
4. adjective
5. attributive adjective
6. predicative adjective
7. substantive adjective
8. agreement of adjective
9. pronoun
10. adverb
11. case
12. nominative case
13. genitive case
14. dative case
15. accusative case
16. ablative case
17. vocative case
18. gender of nouns
19. declension
20. decline
21. noun stem
22. adjective stem

G. Translation

Translate the italicized words into Latin, making sure you use not only the correct noun, adjective, or noun-adjective combination, but the correct case, number, and gender of each Latin word.

ECHO AND NARCISSUS

god **dea, deae, f.**
goddess **deus, deī, m.**
nymph **nympha, nymphae, f.**

Echo was not a *woman* _____ nor a *girl* _____ nor the *daughter* _____ of any *man* _____. She was a *nymph* _____, that is, the *daughter* _____ of a god _____. She lived in the forest, where she used to spend many hours wandering. She had one problem, however: she talked too much. One day Echo angered the *goddess* _____ Juno, who grew angry and declared that from now on Echo would have only a tiny voice, and that she would not be permitted to speak to anyone until they spoke to her, and that even then she would only be permitted to repeat the last two *words*_____ spoken to her.

Thereafter *unhappy* _____ Echo wandered silently in the forests. One day she saw a *beautiful boy*_____. The name *of the boy* _____was Narcissus. Immediately she fell in love with him, but she could not speak *to the boy* _____ until he spoke to her. Wherever he went, she went, but he paid no attention to her. Finally, as the *boy* _____ sat in the woods, he heard her approach and he called out, "Who is it?" Echo replied softly, "Is it?" The *handsome boy* _____said, "Come here!" Echo repeated *the boy's* _____ words. When no one came, he called, "Are you avoiding me?" Echo replied "Me?" and ran eagerly toward him. But *the wicked boy*_____ felt no love for her. "It is not you that I love," he replied, and rudely ran away while Echo *miserably*_____ repeated, "I love." She remained there and her body slowly turned into stone. Now *the nymph's* _____ voice alone remains. If you speak to her, she will repeat *your* _____ last two *words* _____.

22

Key, Chapter II

A. Parts of Speech

1. *Nouns:*

1. **Narcissus**(P) saw the **reflection**(C) of a beautiful **boy**(C) in the **pool**(C).
2. The **nymphs**(C) pulled **Narcissus** (P) down into the **water**(C).
3. **Narcissus** (P)was punished because he loved only himself.
4. The **nymph**(C), **Echo**(P), loved him, and followed him everywhere.
5. **Echo** (P) was filled with **sorrow**(C) when **Narcissus**(P) rejected her **love**(C).
6. She wasted away until **all**(C) that remained of her was her **voice**(C).

2. *Pronouns:*

Narcissus saw **himself** (ref.) reflected in the pool. **He** (P) did not recognize that **he** (ref.) was the beautiful in the pool. **He** (P) felt great love for **this** (dem.) beautiful boy, and tried to touch **him** (P), but instead **he** (P) fell into the pool and was drowned. The story of Narcissus is the basis for the term "narcissism", which **we** (Pl) now use to describe self-love.

3. *Adjectives:*

Narcissus was **beautiful** (P) but **vain** (P). He was not **able** *(P) to reciprocate **the** (A) love of others. **The** (A) gods decided to punish him for his self-love. One day he came to **a beautiful** (A), **shady** (A) grove with a **cool** (A) fountain in its midst. When he gazed into **the** (A) fountain he saw his **own** (A) reflection, but thought it was **another** (A) boy. The boy was very **beautiful** (P). He felt **great** (A) love for **this** (A) boy, and tried to reach him, but instead fell into **the** (A) pool and was drowned. The **mountain** (A.) nymphs wept at his death, and **the** (A) gods caused a **beautiful** (A.) **purple** (A.) flower, which they named "narcissus," to grow in his memory.

Note: **able**: "was ...able" in Latin would be a single verb; in English, forms of "to be" ("was") plus a participle ("steaming", "collapsing"), are understood as a single verb in the imperfect tense,"was steaming" or "was collapsing."

B. Latin Nouns and Adjectives

1. Nominative case:

Narcissus [sing., masc.]was not able to return the love of others. Therefore **the gods**[1] [pl., masc.] decided to punish him for his self-love. One day **he** [masc., sing.] came to a beautiful, shady grove with a cool fountain in its midst. When **he** [masc., sing.] gazed into the fountain he [masc., sing.] saw his own reflection, but thought it was another boy. The **boy** [masc., sing.] was very **beautiful** [masc., sing.]. **He** [masc., sing.] felt great love for this boy, and tried to reach him, but instead fell into the pool and was drowned. **The mountain nymphs** [pl. fem. of **nympha, ae,** f.] wept at his death, and **the gods** [masc., pl.] caused a beautiful purple flower, which they named "narcissus," to grow in his memory.

2. Genitive case:

Narcissus was not able to return the love **of others**. Therefore the gods decided to punish **his** self-love. One day he came to a **forest's** cool fountain and when he gazed into **its** waters he saw **his** own reflection, but thought it was the face of **another young boy**. He was moved by **this boy's beauty**, and tried to reach him, but instead fell into the pool and was drowned. The mountain nymphs wept at **his** death, and the gods caused a beautiful purple flower, which they named "narcissus," to grow in **his** memory.

---

1   The gods could be all masculine, or a mix of masculine and feminine. Romans tended to treat groups of people (or gods) as masculine, unless, of course, they were all feminine goddesses.

3. Dative Case:

The nymph, Echo, tried to speak **to Narcissus**, but he gave **her** no attention. She followed him everywhere, but he was not kind **to her**. She had once been punished by the gods for speaking **to them** too much, and therefore could only repeat the last words anyone said **to her**. Therefore, when Narcissus told **her** (to her) "Nōn tē amō!", Echo would tell **him** (to him) in response, "tē amō." She was so overcome with sorrow when Narcissus died that she went deep into the forest and was not seen again. She wasted away until all that remained of her was her voice. If you call **to her**, she will answer **you** (to you).

4. Accusative case:

Narcissus loved **only himself**, not Echo. She followed **him** everywhere, but he was not kind to her. Because the gods had punished **her**, she could only repeat the **last words** of a sentence. When Narcissus died, she went into the forest. Her voice remained, however. If you call to her, you will hear **her reply**.

5. Ablative case:

Echo tried to be **with Narcissus**, (accompaniment) and to share her love **with him**, (accompaniment) but he was not moved **by her love** (means/instrument). She followed him everywhere, but she received no kindness **from him** (separation). He hurt her feelings **with** his **cruel words** (means/instrument), but she loved him too much to be driven away **by** his **words** (means/instrument). When he died she was so overcome **by sorrow** (means/instrument) that she went deep into the forest and was seen again **by no one** (agent), but her voice will be heard **by those** (agent) who call her.

6. Vocative case:

Do you know the story of Echo and Narcissus? Someone should say, "**Echo**, don't you realize Narcissus loves only himself? Don't waste your love on him!" But she would not listen. Perhaps, then, we should say, "Please, **Narcissus**, speak to Echo!" But all that Narcissus would have said to her was, "**Echo**, go away. Nōn tē amō!"

C.1.

	a. **puer parvus,** *little boy*	b. **agricola noster** *our farmer*	c. **bestia magna** *large animal*	d. **auxilium vestrum** *your (pl.) assistance*
		Singular		
Nom.	puer parvus	agricola noster	bestia magna	auxilium vestrum
Gen.	puerī parvī	agricolae nostrī	bestiae magnae	auxiliī vestrī
Dat.	puerō parvō	agricolae nostro	bestiae magnae	auxiliō vestrō
Acc.	puerum parvum	agricolam nostrum	bestiam magnam	auxilium vestrum
Abl.	puerō parvō	agricolā nostrō	bestiā magnā	auxiliō vestrō
Voc.	puer parvus	agricola noster	bestia magna	auxilium vestrum
		Plural		
Nom.	puerī parvī	agricolae nostrī	bestiae magnae	auxilia vestra
Gen.	puerōrum parvōrum	agricolārum nostrōrum	bestiārum magnārum	auxiliōrum vestrōrum
Dat.	puerīs parvīs	agricolīs nostrīs	bestiīs magnīs	auxiliīs vestrīs
Acc.	puerōs parvōs	agricolās nostrōs	bestiās magnās	auxilia vestra
Abl.	puerīs parvīs	agricolīs nostrīs	bestiīs magnīs	auxiliīs vestrōs
Voc.	puerī parvī	agricolae nostrī	bestiae magnae	auxilia vestra

C.2.

a. *Our famous son*

fīlius noster clārus	fīliī nostrī clārī
fīliī nostrī clārī	fīliōrum nostrōrum clārōrum
fīliō nostrō clārō	fīliīs nostrīs clārīs
fīlium nostrum clārum	fīliōs nostrōs clārōs
fīliō nostrō clārō	fīliīs nostrīs clārīs
fīlī noster clāre	fīliī nostrī clārī

b. *The teacher's famous books*

magistrī liber clārus	magistrī librī clārī
magistrī librī clārī	magistrīlibrōrum clārōrum
magistrī librō clārō	magistrī librīs clārīs
magistrī librum clārum	magistrī librōs clārōs
magistrī librō clārō	magistrī librīs clārīs
magistrī liber clāre	magistrī librī clārī

C.3.

a. Agricola cantat.

b. Cantāte, agricolae!

c. Agricolae cantāmus.

d. Pulchrē cantat.

e. Pulchra optāvimus.

f. Fīliumne meum clārum vīdistī?

C.4.

a. The teacher saw bright stars/constellations in the sky. (**stellās**) attributive.

b. The star/constellation is bright. (**clāra**) predicative.

c. The girls sang good things (or, They sang good things to the girl). **bona** (substantive).

d. My son gave assistance. (**meus**) attributive.

e. The son wants bad things. (**mala**) substantive.

C.5.

a. The miserable boy sang. **Puer miserē cantāvit.** The boy sang miserably.

b. The unhappy animal seized food. **Bestia miserē cibum captāvit.** The animal seized food unhappily.

c. I saw my unhappy self. **Mē miserē vīdī.** I unhappily saw myself.

d. The beautiful girl will sing. **Puella pulchre cantabit.** The girl will sing beautifully.

e. The master gave a bad gift. **Dominus donum male dedit.** The master gave a gift badly.

D. Vocabulary Quiz. English to Latin and Latin to English

star	N	stella, ae, f.
sky	N	caelum, ī, n.
bright	A	clarus, clara, clarum
handsome	A	pulcher, pulchra, pulchrum
famous	A	clarus, clara, clarum
beautiful	A	pulcher, pulchra, pulchrum
boy	N	puer, puerī, m.
girl	N	puella, puellae, f.
man	N	vir, virī, m.
your (s.)	A	tuus, tuua, tuum
your (pl.)	A	vester, vestra, vestrum
our	A	noster, nostra, nostrum
my	A	meus, mea, meum
book	N	liber, librī, m.
free	A	līber, lībera, līberum
word	N	verbum, verbi, n.
master	N	magister, magistrī, m., or dominus, dominī, m.
teacher	N	magister, magistrī, m.
ruler	N	dominus, dominī, m.
jealousy	N	invidia, invidiae, f.
friend	N	amīcus, amīcī, m. or amīca amīcae, f.
farmer	N	agricola, agricolae, m.
field	N	ager, agrī, m.
small	A	parvus, parva, parvum
large	A	magnus, magna, mangum
road	N	via, viae, f.

E. Derivations

English	Latin source	Meaning
Liberia	līber, lībera, līberum	f.
libretto	liber, librī, m.	i.
liberate	līber, lībera, līberum	k.
library	liber, librī, m.	g.
celesta	caelum, caelī, n.	j.
magisterial	magister, magistrī, m.	m.
magnanimous	magnus, magna, magnum	n.
ceiling	caelum, caelī, n.	b.
nautical	nauta, nautae, m.	l.
envy	invidia, invidiae, f.	a.
affiliate	fīlius, fīliī, m. or fīlia, ae, f.	c.
agriculture	agricola, agricolae, m.	h.
commiserate	miser, misera, miserum	d.
stellarator	stella, stellae, f.	e.

F. Terminology Review

1. *noun.* the name of a person, place or thing.
2. *common noun.* the general name of a person (*man, woman, etc.*), place (*house, town, city, etc.*), or thing.
3. *proper noun.* the name of a specific person or place
4. *adjective.* modifies a noun.
5. *attributive adjective.* a simple modifier.
6. *predicative adjective.* the adjective modifying the subject in the verbal part of the sentence (occurs with connecting verbs such as *to be, to become*).
7. *substantive adjective.* an adjective functioning as a noun. e.g., **bonum** a good (thing); **bona** if feminine, a good (woman); if neuter, good (things); **bonus** a good (man).
8. *agreement of adjective:* the ending of the adjective is in the same case, number, and gender (but not the same declension) as the noun it modifies.
9. *pronoun.* a word used in place of a noun, *he, she, you, them, etc.*
10. *adverb.* modifies a verb, another adverb, or an adjective. he spoke *well* (verb); your picture is *beautifully* painted (adjective, participle); he walked *painfully* slowly (adverb).
11. *case.* indicates the grammatical function of a noun within a sentence.
12. *nominative case.* indicates the subject of a sentence.
13. *genitive case.* indicates a relationship between two nouns, most commonly of possession.
14. *dative case.* indicates the indirect object of a verb.
15. *accusative case.* indicates the direct object of a verb; can also be the object of a preposition.
16. *ablative case.* indicates a number of adverbial functions; most commonly without a preposition indicates means or instrument by which something is done; frequently used with prepositions to indicate a number of functions, including accompaniment, separation, etc.
17. *vocative case.* indicates the person or thing addressed.
18. *gender of nouns.* masculine, feminine, or neuter. Sometimes obvious, at other times must be committed to memory.
19. *declension.* the pattern of endings affixing to a noun and its modifiers. There are a total of five declensions in Latin.
20. *decline.* to write or recite the pattern of endings appropriate to a noun and its modifiers.
21. *noun stem.* the root of the noun to which the case endings are affixed; obtained by dropping the genitive singular ending from the noun.
22. *adjective stem.* the root of the adjective to which the case endings are affixed; obtained by dropping the nominative feminine ending from the adjective.

G. Translation: Echo and Narcissus

Echo was not a *woman* (**fēmina**) nor a *girl* (**puella**) nor the *daughter* (**fīlia**) of any *man* (**virī**). She was a *nymph* (**nympha**), that is, the *daughter* (**fīlia**) *of a god* (**deī**). She lived in the forest, where she used to spend many hours wandering. She had one problem, however: she talked too much. One day Echo angered the *goddess* (**deam**) Juno, who grew angry and declared that from now on Echo would have only a tiny voice, and that she would not be permitted to speak to anyone until they spoke to her, and that even then she would only be permitted to repeat the last two *words* (**verba**) spoken to her.

Thereafter *unhappy* (**misera**) Echo wandered silently in the forests. One day she saw a *beautiful boy* (**puerum pulchrum**). The name *of the boy* (**puerī**)was Narcissus. Immediately she fell in love with him, but she could not speak *to the boy* (**puerō**) until he spoke to her. Wherever he went, she went, but he paid no attention to her. Finally, as the *boy* (**puer**) sat in the woods, he heard her approach and he called out, "who is it?" Echo replied softly, "is it?" The *handsome boy* (**puer pulcher**) said, "Come here!" Echo repeated *the boy's* (**puerī**) words. When no one came, he called, "Are you avoiding me?" Echo replied "Me?" and ran eagerly toward him. But *the wicked boy* (**puer malus**) felt no love for her. "It is not you that I love," he replied, and rudely ran away while Echo *miserably* (**miserē**) repeated, "I love." She remained there and her body slowly turned into stone. Now *the nymph's* (**nymphae**) voice alone remains. If you speak to her, she will repeat *your* (**tua**) last two *words* (**verba**).

III
Third and Fourth Conjugations

A. Third and Fourth Conjugations, Present, Future, and Perfect Tense

In the first chapter of *Traditio*, you learned the first and second conjugations, which are identified by the infinitive endings, **-āre** in the first conjugation, as in the pattern verb, **amāre**, *to love*, and in the second conjugation **ēre**, as in the pattern verb **tenēre**.

In this chapter you are learning the third and fourth conjugations, which are characterized by the infinitive endings **-ere** and **-īre**.

Fourth conjugation verbs have a long -i- in the infinitive, and so the verb stem ends in a long vowel, like verbs of the first and second conjugation: **audī- + -ō, -s, -t, -mus, -tis, -nt:** (note that the long ī shortens before another vowel.):

audiō, audīs, audit, audīmus, audītis, audiunt.

The stem of third conjugation verbs is found by dropping the entire infinitive ending, including the short **-e-**, which means that this stem has no vowel at the end. Third conjugation verbs are therefore said to have consonantal stems, instead of vowel stems. To conjugate these verbs, a vowel has to be supplied. In the present tense, third conjugation verbs add **-i-** for all persons except the first person singular, which adds **-o-**, and the third person plural, which adds **-u-: dūc- + ō, i+s, i+t, i+mus, i+tis, u+nt:**

dūcō, dūcis, dūcit, dūcimus, dūcitis, dūcunt.

A.1. Conjugate the following verbs in the present tense:

	pulsāre	dēbēre	mittere	appellāre
translation:	_____	_____	_____	_____
singular				
1st	_____	_____	_____	_____
2nd	_____	_____	_____	_____
3rd	_____	_____	_____	_____
plural				
1st	_____	_____	_____	_____
2nd	_____	_____	_____	_____
3rd	_____	_____	_____	_____

	agere	advenīre	dīcere	legere
translation:				
singular				
1st				
2nd				
3rd				
plural				
1st				
2nd				
3rd				

	petere	venīre	vīvere	cadere
translation:				
singular				
1st				
2nd				
3rd				
plural				
1st				
2nd				
3rd				

	scīre	sentīre	respondēre	invenīre
translation:				
singular				
1st				
2nd				
3rd				
plural				
1st				
2nd				
3rd				

A.2. There is a second category of third conjugation verbs which do have short **-i-** as a stem vowel. These verbs are identified by the combination of first principal part, which ends in **-iō**, and the second principal part; the infinitive, which, like regular third conjugation consonant-stem vowels, ends in a short **-ere**. These verbs are formed by adding **-i-** plus the personal endings to the consonant stem: **cap + i + ō, s, t, mus, tis, u + nt:**

capiō, capis, capit, capimus, capitis, capiunt.

Conjugate the following third conjugation i-stem vowels:

	accipere	facere	fugere	incipere
translation:				
singular				
1st				
2nd				
3rd				
plural				
1st				
2nd				
3rd				

A.3. While first and second conjugation verbs form the future tense by adding the marker, **-bi-** + the personal ending to the present stem of the verb, verbs of the third and fourth conjugation form the future tense by adding a long **-ē-** plus personal endings to the stem. The exception to this rule is the first person singular, which adds **-a-** + **m**. [**-m** is an alternate personal ending for the first person singular, which you will encounter again.]:

3rd: **dūc + ē + -s, -t, -mus, -tis, -nt:**

  dūcam, dūcēs, dūcet, dūcēmus dūcētis, dūcent

3rd-**iō:** **cap + i + ē + -s, -t, -mus, -tis, -nt:**

  capiam, capiēs, capiet, capiēmus, capiētis, capient,

4th: **audi + ē + -s, -t, -mus, -tis, -nt:**

  audiam, audiēs, audiet, audiēmus, audiētis, audient

Conjugate the following verbs in the future tense:

	pulsāre	**dēbēre**	**mittere**	**appellāre**
translation:				
singular				
1st				
2nd				
3rd				
plural				
1st				
2nd				
3rd				

	agere	**advenīre**	**dīcere**	**legere**
translation:				
singular				
1st				
2nd				
3rd				
plural				
1st				
2nd				
3rd				

	petere	**venīre**	**vīvere**	**cadere**
translation:				
singular				
1st				
2nd				
3rd				
plural				
1st				
2nd				
3rd				

	scīre	sentīre	rēspondere	invenīre
translation:	_____	_____	_____	_____
singular				
1st	_____	_____	_____	_____
2nd	_____	_____	_____	_____
3rd	_____	_____	_____	_____
plural				
1st	_____	_____	_____	_____
2nd	_____	_____	_____	_____
3rd	_____	_____	_____	_____

	accipere	facere	fugere	incipere
translation:	_____	_____	_____	_____
singular				
1st	_____	_____	_____	_____
2nd	_____	_____	_____	_____
3rd	_____	_____	_____	_____
plural				
1st	_____	_____	_____	_____
2nd	_____	_____	_____	_____
3rd	_____	_____	_____	_____

A.4. a. *The perfect tense* in all four conjugations is formed in the same way, by adding a *perfect ending* to the *perfect stem.*

List the perfect active endings:

	singular		*plural*
1st	_____	1st	_____
2nd	_____	2nd	_____
3rd	_____	3rd	_____

A.4. b. List the perfect stem for the following verbs, and categorize them according to their perfect stems:

   i.   **-āv** added to present stem

   ii.   **-īv** added to present stem

   iii.   **-u** added to present stem

   iv.   **-s** added and stem vowel lengthened

   v.   present stem vowel lengthened

   vi.   first two letters of present stem reduplicated

	Perfect stem	*category*	*Meaning of 1st person sing. perfect*
advenīre	_____	_____	_____
agere	_____	_____	_____
amāre	_____	_____	_____
appellāre	_____	_____	_____
cadere	_____	_____	_____
cantāre	_____	_____	_____

cōgitāre	_____	_____	_____
dare	_____	_____	_____
dēbēre	_____	_____	_____
dīcere	_____	_____	_____
invēnīre	_____	_____	_____
legere	_____	_____	_____
mittere	_____	_____	_____
monēre	_____	_____	_____
mordēre	_____	_____	_____
nescīre	_____	_____	_____
petere	_____	_____	_____
pulsāre	_____	_____	_____
respondēre	_____	_____	_____
sentīre	_____	_____	_____
timēre	_____	_____	_____
venīre	_____	_____	_____
vidēre	_____	_____	_____

A.5. Now conjugate the following verbs in the perfect tense. [Remember to drop the final -ī of the third principal part before adding the perfect endings]:

	mittere	cadere	nescīre	sentīre
translation:	_____	_____	_____	_____
singular				
1st	_____	_____	_____	_____
2nd	_____	_____	_____	_____
3rd	_____	_____	_____	_____
plural				
1st	_____	_____	_____	_____
2nd	_____	_____	_____	_____
3rd	_____	_____	_____	_____

	appellāre	respondēre	agere	advenīre
translation:	_____	_____	_____	_____
singular				
1st	_____	_____	_____	_____
2nd	_____	_____	_____	_____
3rd	_____	_____	_____	_____
plural				
1st	_____	_____	_____	_____
2nd	_____	_____	_____	_____
3rd	_____	_____	_____	_____

	dīcere	legere	petere	venīre
translation:	_____	_____	_____	_____
singular				
1st	_____	_____	_____	_____
2nd	_____	_____	_____	_____
3rd	_____	_____	_____	_____
plural				
1st	_____	_____	_____	_____
2nd	_____	_____	_____	_____
3rd	_____	_____	_____	_____

B. Imperative Mood, Third and Fourth Conjugations

The second person singular imperative mood of fourth conjugation verbs consists of the present stem of the verb.

4th: **audī!** *Listen!* **mēaudi!** *Hear me!, Listen to me!*

The second person singular imperative mood of third conjugation verbs is formed by adding a short **-e** to the consonant stem. The exception to this rule is:

3rd: **lege!** *Read!* **librum lege!** *Read the book!*

3rd **-iō:** **cape!** *Seize!* **virum cape!** *Seize the man!*

There are four verbs which provide exceptions to this rule. The second person singular imperative of **dūcere, dīcere, facere,** and an irregular verb which you will learn later, ferre, consist of the consonant stem without any additional vowel:

dūcere, to lead	**dūc virōs!**	*Lead the men!*
dīcere, to speak	**dīc puellae!**	*Speak to the girl!*
facere, to do, make	**bona fac!**	*Do good things!*
ferre, to carry, bring	**dōna fer!**	*Bring gifts!*

The second person plural imperative of the fourth conjugation is formed by adding **-te** to the present stem of the verb. The second person plural imperative of the third conjugation is formed by adding **-ite**. There are no exceptions in the plural.

4th:	**audīte!**	*Listen!*	**mē audīte!**	*Hear me!, Listen to me!*
3rd:	**legite!**	*Read!*	**librum legite!**	*Read the book!*
	dūcite virōs!	*Lead the men!*	**dīcite puellae!**	*Speak to the girl!*
	bona facite!	*Do good things!*		
3rd **-iō:**	**capite!**	*Seize!*	**virum capite!**	*Seize the man!*

Form the second person singular and plural imperative of the following verbs:

	pulsāre	dēbēre	mittere	invenīre
2nd singular	_____	_____	_____	_____
translation	_____	_____	_____	_____
2nd plural	_____	_____	_____	_____
translation	_____	_____	_____	_____

	appellāre	respondēre	agere	advenīre
2nd singular	_____	_____	_____	_____
translation	_____	_____	_____	_____
2nd plural	_____	_____	_____	_____
translation	_____	_____	_____	_____

	cōgitāre	monēre	petere	venīre
2nd singular				
translation				
2nd plural				
translation				

	vīvere	cadere	scīre	sentīre
2nd singular				
translation				
2nd plural				
translation				

	accipere	errāre	spīrāre	incipere
2nd singular				
translation				
2nd plural				
translation				

C. sum, esse

The irregular verb *to be* in the present tense takes its stem from the first principal part in three instances, and from the second principal part in the other three instances:

1st person sing.	**su + m**	*I am*
1st person pl.	**su + mus**	*We are*
3rd person pl.	**su + nt**	*They are*

2nd person sing.	**es**	*you (s.) are*
2nd person plural	**es + tis**	*you (pl.) are*
3rd person sing.	**es +t**	*he/she/it is*

The irregular verb **possum, posse,** to be able, is a compound of **pot-** plus the verb **sum, esse.** Before the letter **-s-**, the **-t** in **pot-** becomes **-s-:**

1st person sing.	**pos + su + m**	*I am*
1st person pl.	**pos + su + mus**	*We are*
3rd person pl	**pos + su + nt**	*They are*

2nd person sing.	**pot + es**	*you (s.) are*
2nd person plural.	**pot + es + tis**	*you (pl.) are*
3rd person sing.	**pot + es +t**	*he/she/it is*

The future tense of **sum** and its compounds is based on the stem **eri-** [first person singular **erō**]. There is no imperative form of these verbs in classical Latin (they do, however, exist in archaic and medieval Latin).

C.1. Conjugate **sum** and **possum** in the present and future tenses:

	Present tense:		Future Tense:	
	sum	possum	sum	possum
translation: singular				
1st				
2nd				
3rd				

34

plural				
1st	_____	_____	_____	_____
2nd	_____	_____	_____	_____
3rd	_____	_____	_____	_____

The verb *to be*, in English and in Latin, is known as a connecting verb, or *copula*. It is intransitive by nature, that is, it cannot take a direct object. Consequently nouns connected by this verb will always be in the same case. Compare:

I (subject) will read the book (object of the verb).	**librum legam.**
My life (subject) is a book (predicate noun).	**vīta mea liber est.**

In the first example, the book is in the accusative case because it is the direct object of the verb—I am doing something to the book. In the second example the book and my life are equivalent, and so both are in the same case, in this example, the nominative case; **vīta mea** is the subject, and **liber** is the predicate nominative, which means it too is in the nominative case, but it is the complement of the subject rather than the subject itself. If we make **esse** a complementary infinitive—that is, an infinitive which complements or completes the meaning of the verb possum—the same principle will apply.

I will be able to read the book.	**librum legere poterō.**
My life can be a book.	**vīta mea liber esse potest.**

liber remains in the nominative case, because the subject to which it is equated by **esse** is in the nominative case. When **possum** is complemented by a transitive verb such as **legere**, the object remains accusative. **Possum** is rarely used without a complementary infinitive. Other verbs that govern a complementary infinitive, such as **dēbēre**, by contrast, can also function as regular transitive verbs:

We ought to speak (*complementary infinitive*).	**Dīcere dēbēmus.**
He owes his life (*direct object*) to the master.	**Vītam dominō dēbet.**

C.2. Translate the following phrases into English:

1. Puerō dōna dabō (dedī).
2. Puerō dōna dare dēbeō (dēbēbō, dēbui).
3. Meō fīliō dōna dare potes (poteris, potuistī).
4. Ager agricolae dōna dēbet (dēbuit).
5. Echō respondere nōn poterit (potuit).
6. Narcissus fugere nōn dēbet (dēbuit).
7. Echō Narcissī verba miserē dīcet (dīcit).
8. Magister puerōs accipīt (accipiet, accipere poterit).

D. Prepositions in English and the Latin Ablative Case

A preposition is a word which shows the relationship between a noun, pronoun, or clause to some other element of a sentence. The word comes from the Latin **prae** (*before*) + **positio** (*placement*): it is thus a word *placed before the noun* to show the relationship of that noun to some element of the sentence. The sound of music; far *from* home; a gift *for* you; he came *with* alacrity (*how*), I came *with* my friend (*accompaniment*). The noun following the preposition in English is called the *object of a prepostion*. *Music, home, you, alacrity, friend* in the above examples are objects of the prepositions *of, from, for, with* and *with*. English has about fifty commonly used prepositions.

The most common of the English prepositions are *at, by, for, from, in, of, on, to,* and *with*. In Latin six of the equivalents of these prepositions govern the ablative case. Nouns or phrases governed by prepositions are often identified as *adverbial phrases* or, if a complete clause, *adverbial clauses*. Like all adverbs, they modify a verb, an adjective, another adverb, or a whole clause. They tell a) *how*, b) *when or in what order*, c) *where*.

In Latin these ideas and more are expressed by adverbs or by one or more nouns in the ablative case governed sometimes by a preposition, and sometimes without a preposition.

a) *with*:

  i. **cum** + ablative : accompaniment:

    cum amīcīs meīs — *with my friends*

  ii. **cum** + ablative: how (manner):

    cum cura — *with care, carefully*
    magnā (cum) cūrā — *with great care, very carefully*
    [**cum** may be omitted in this use if noun is modified]

  iii. no preposition: (means or instrument)

    vinculō — *with a chain, by means of a chain*
    magnīs vinculīs — *with large chains, by means of large chains*

b) *when*:

    unā horā — *within one hour; at one o'clock*

c) *where*:

    in agrō — *in the field*
    [Compare…*in agrum*] — *into the field - (accusative case shows motion into or toward)*
    in caelō — *in the sky*

d) *separation*:

  from, out of: — **ab, dē, or ex + ablative:**
    dē caelō — *down from the sky*
    ab iānuā — *away from the door*
  without: — **sine (+ ablative)**
    sine amīcīs — *without friends*

E. Vocabulary Quiz: English to Latin

Translate the following into Latin, listing the four principal parts of verbs; nominative, genitive and gender of nouns; masculine, feminine, and neuter nominative singular of adjectives; and the indeclinable forms of pronouns, adverbs, conjunctions, and propositions:

English Verbs:	Four principal parts of Latin equivalent:
seize	
receive	
begin	
make	
spend	
avoid	
come	
find	
arrive at	
to know	
not to know	

ask (for) _____

answer _____

fall _____

perish _____

drink _____

Nouns: *Nominative, Genitive, gender:*

door _____

worry _____

gratitude _____

land _____

life _____

Adjectives: *Masculine, feminine, and neuter nominative singular of adjectives:*

which one of two _____

neither _____

Latin _____

any _____

none _____

Other (adverbs and prepositions):

what? _____

why? _____

us _____

here _____

there _____

where? _____

because _____

with _____

without _____

from _____

F. Derivations

You have learned nine adjectives whose genitive (**-ius**) singular and dative (**-i**) singular forms are different from regular first and second declension adjectives. Using a dictionary, indicate from which of these the following words are derived:

English	Latin source	Meaning of Latin Word	Meaning of English Word
1. solipsism			
2. neutralize			
3. alibi			
4. alter			
5. total			
6. totipalmate			
7. nullify			
8. neutron			

9. alien _____ _____ _____
10. desolate _____ _____ _____
11. unite _____ _____ _____

G. Terminology Review

Give examples in Latin of the following terms and translate your examples into English:

1. ablative of separation

_____

2. ablative of accompaniment

_____

3. ablative of instrument

_____

4. copula

_____

5. predicate nominative

_____

6. complementary infinitive

_____

7. preposition

_____

8. perfect stem

_____

9. consonant stem

_____

H. Translation

Translate the italicized words into Latin, making sure you use not only the correct verb, noun, adjective, etc., but also he correct endings for each word.

PHAETHON'S WILD RIDE

volō, volāre *to fly*
dē + ablative *down from, from, out of*

Phaethon *was the son* _____ of the Sun, but he had never met his father. His mother therefore decided it was time for Phaethon to visit his father. *"It will not be* _____ difficult for you to find him," *she said.* _____ "He lives in the East. *You go alone* _____ and visit him and get to know him." Phaethon excitedly rushed out; he crossed *the land* _____ of his own people, the Ethiopians, and *he arrived* _____ in the land of the fiery sun and approached the place from which his father rises.

He climbed the steep path and entered his father's palace, but stood far from the father, whose light *he could not* _____ bear at too close a range. The Sun turned his eyes to Phaethon and warmly *received* _____ his *son* _____. *"Come, now, my son!* _____ Tell me: *Why have you come?* _____ _____" Phaethon *responded* _____ that he wanted to know if the Sun really was his father. The Sun replied, *"Ask* _____ any favor you wish. *I will grant* _____ it to you to prove you are my son." Phaethon thereupon *asked for* _____ permission to ride his father's chariot for one whole day. The Sun replied *unhappily* _____, *"Another thing* _____ I would

gladly grant you, but in this one request I would like *to be able* _____ to persuade you to withdraw. The thing you desire is too great for a mortal; it is more great
than *I can give to a god* _____. Even Jupiter, the greatest *of the gods*
_____, *will not ask to drive* _____ this chariot. Still, a promise must be
kept." He *carefully* _____ instructed his *son* _____ how to control the
chariot. "*Do not fly* [to fly = *volāre*] _____ too low, nor too high. The middle way
is safest. *Hold your course* [course = *via*] _____ between the
coiling Serpent and the low-lying Altar. The rest I leave to Fortune."

   There were no stars in the sky _____ when Phaethon climbed
into the chariot. But the horses quickly realized that their burden *was* _____ too light. Just
as ships toss about if they are not carrying their full cargo, so this chariot leaped into the air
and was thrown about as if it were empty. Their driver *did not know* _____ how to
control the horses. The fierce constellations frightened the boy as he drew near to them;
when he drew near to poisonous Scorpio, *he was frightened* _____ to such
a degree that he dropped the reins, and the horses raced out of control. The earth caught
fire, meadows turned grey, and withered crops burned. Great cities perished and the woods
on the mountains *were* _____ aflame. Finally Jupiter hurled a thunderbolt, knocking Phaethon *from the sky* _____ and to his death. His sisters wept for him and
their tears were turned into drops of amber.

Key, Chapter III

A.1. PRESENT TENSE:

	pulsāre	**dēbēre**	**mittere**	**appellāre**
trans.	*to strike*	*to owe*	*to send*	*to call*
Singular				
1st	pulsō	dēbeō	mittō	appellō
2nd	pulsās	dēbēs	mittis	appellās
3rd	pulsat	dēbet	mittit	appellat
Plural				
1st	pulsāmus	dēbēmus	mittimus	appellāmus
2nd	pulsātis	dēbētis	mittitis	appellātis
3rd	pulsant	dēbent	mittunt	appellānt

	agere	**advenīre**	**dīcere**	**legere**
trans.	*to do*	*to arrive*	*to speak*	*to read*
Singular				
1st	agere	adveniō	dīcō	legō
2nd	agis	advenīs	dīcis	legis
3rd	agit	advenit	dīcit	legit
Plural				
1st	agimus	advenīmus	dīcimus	legimus
2nd	agitis	advenītis	dīcitis	legitis
3rd	agunt	adveniunt	dīcunt	legunt

	petere	**venīre**	**vīvere**	**cadere**
trans.	*to seek*	*to come*	*to live*	*to fall*
Singular				
1st	petō	veniō	vīvō	cadō
2nd	petis	venīs	vīvis	cadis
3rd	petit	venit	vīvit	cadit
Plural				
1st	petimus	venīmus	vīvimus	cadimus
2nd	petitis	venītis	vīvitis	caditis
3rd	petunt	veniunt	vīvunt	cadunt

	scīre	**sentīre**	**respondēre**	**invenīre**
trans.	*to know*	*to feel*	*to respond*	*to discover*
Singular				
1st	sciō	sentiō	respondeō	inveniō
2nd	scīs	sentīs	respondēs	invenīs
3rd	scit	sentit	respondet	invenit
Plural				
1st	scīmus	sentīmus	respondēmus	invenīmus
2nd	scītis	sentītis	respondētis	invenītis
3rd	sciunt	sentiunt	respondent	inveniunt

A.2. 3RD -IO PRESENT TENSE:

	accipere	**facere**	**fugere**	**incipere**
trans.	*to receive*	*to make*	*to flee*	*to begin*
Singular				
1st	accipiō	faciō	fugiō	incipiō
2nd	accipis	facis	fugis	incipis
3rd	accipit	facit	fugit	incipit

Plural

1st	accipimus	facimus	fugimus	incipimus
2nd	accipitis	facitis	fugitis	incipitis
3rd	accipiunt	faciunt	fugiunt	incipiunt

A.3. FUTURE TENSE:

	pulsāre	**dēbēre**	**mittere**	**appellāre**
trans.	*to strike*	*to owe*	*to send*	*to call*
Singular				
1st	pulsābō	dēbebō	mittam	appellābō
2nd	pulsābis	dēbebīs	mittēs	appellābis
3rd	pulsabit	dēbebit	mittet	appellabit
Plural				
1st	pulsābimus	dēbēmus	mittēmus	appellābimus
2nd	pulsabītis	dēbētis	mittētis	appellābitis
3rd	pulsabunt	dēbebunt	mittent	appellābunt

	agere	**advenīre**	**dīcere**	**legere**
trans.	*to do*	*to arrive*	*to speak*	*to read*
Singular				
1st	agam	adveniam	dīcam	legam
2nd	agēs	adveniēs	dīcēs	legēs
3rd	aget	adveniet	dīcet	leget
Plural				
1st	agēmus	adveniēmus	dīcēmus	legēmus
2nd	agētis	adveniētis	dīcētis	legētis
3rd	agent	advenient	dīcent	legent

	petere	**venīre**	**vīvere**	**cadere**
trans.	*to seek*	*to come*	*to live*	*to fall*
Singular				
1st	petam	veniam	vīvam	cadam
2nd	petēs	veniēs	vīvēs	cadēs
3rd	petet	veniet	vīvet	cadet
Plural				
1st	petēmus	veniēmus	vīvēmus	cadēmus
2nd	petētis	veniētis	vīvētis	cadētis
3rd	petent	venient	vīvent	cadent

	scīre	**sentīre**	**respondēre**	**invenīre**
trans.	*to know*	*to feel*	*to respond*	*to discover*
Singular				
1st	sciam	sentiam	respondēbō	inveniam
2nd	sciēs	sentiēs	respondēbis	inveniēs
3rd	sciet	sentiet	respondēbit	inveniet
Plural				
1st	sciēmus	sentiēmus	respondēbimus	inveniēmus
2nd	sciētis	sentiētis	respondēbitis	invenietis
3rd	sciunt	sentiunt	respondēbunt	invenient

	accipere	**facere**	**fugere**	**incipere**
trans.	*to receive*	*to make*	*to flee*	*to begin*
Singular				
1st	accipiam	faciam	fugiam	incipiam
2nd	accipiēs	faciēs	fugiēs	incipiēs
3rd	accipiet	faciet	fugiet	incipiet

Plural

1st	accipiēmus	faciēmus	fugiēmus	incipiēmus
2nd	accipiētis	faciētis	fugiētis	incipiētis
3rd	accipient	facient	fugient	incipient

A.4. a.

	singular		plural
1st	-ī	1st	-imus
2nd	-istī	2nd	-istis
3rd	-it	3rd	-ērunt

A.4. b.

	Perfect stem	category	Meaning of 1st person sing.perfect
advenīre	advēn-	v) *stem lengthened*	I have come
agere	ēg-	v) *stem lengthened*	I have done
amār-e.	amāv-	i) *-āv*	I have loved
appellāre	appellāv-	i) *-āv*	I have addressed, called
cadere	cecid-	vi) *reduplicated*	I have fallen
cantāre	cantāv-	i) *-āv*	I have sung
cōgitāre	cōgitāv-	i) *-āv*	I have thought
dare	ded-	vi) *reduplicated*	I have given
dēbēre	dēbu-	iii) *-u*	I have owed, been obligated
dīcere	dīx-	iv) *-s*	I have spoken, said
invenīre	invēn-	v) *stem lengthened*	I have discovered
legere	lēg-	v) *stem lengthened*	I have read, gathered
mittere	mīs-	iv) *-s*	I have sent
monēre	monu-	iii) *-u*	I have advised, warned
mordēre	momord-	vi) *reduplicated*	I have bitten
nescīre	nescīv-	ii) *-īv*	I did not know
petere	petīv-	ii) *-īv*	I have sought, asked
pulsāre	pulsāv-	i) *-āv*	I have beaten
respondēre	respond-	v) *stem lengthened**	I have replied
sentīre	sēns-	iv) *-s*	I have felt, sensed
timēre	timu-	iii) *-u*	I feared, have been afraid
venīre	vēn-	v) *stem lengthened*	I have come, I came
vidēre	vīd-	v) *stem lengthened*	I saw, have seen

*Although **respondēre** follows the principle of category v.), the stem does not actually lengthen because the vowel **-o-** is followed by two consonants, and therefore is already naturally long.

A.5. Perfect tense

	mittere	**cadere**	**nescīre**	**sentīre**
trans.	*to send*	*to fall*	*not to know*	*to feel*
Singular				
1st	mīsī	cecidī	nescīvī	sēnsī
2nd	mīsistī	cecidistī	nescīvistī	sēnsisti
3rd	mīsit	cecidit	nescīvit	sēnsit
Plural				
1st	mīsimus	cecidimus	nescīvimus	sēnsimus
2nd	mīsistis	cecidistis	nescīvistis	sēnsistis
3rd	mīsērunt	cecidērunt	nescīvērunt	sēnsērunt

	apellare	respondere	agere	advenire
trans.	*to call*	*to respond*	*to do*	*to arrive*
Singular				
1st	appellāvī	respondī	ēgi	advēnī
2nd	appellāvistī	respondistī	ēgistī	advēnistī
3rd	appellāvit	respondit	ēgit	advēnit
Plural				
1st	appellāvimus	respondimus	ēgimus	advēnimus
2nd	appellāvistis	respondistis	ēgistis	advēnistis
3rd	apellavērunt	respondērunt	ēgērunt	advēnērunt

	dīcere	legere	petere	venīre
trans.	*to speak*	*to read*	*to seek*	*to come*
Singular				
1st	dixī	lēgī	petīvī	vēni
2nd	dixistī	lēgistī	petīvistī	vēnistī
3rd	dixit	lēgit	petīvit	vēnit
Plural				
1st	diximus	lēgimus	petīvimus	vēnimus
2nd	dixistis	lēgistis	petīvistis	vēnistis
3rd	dixērunt	lēgērunt	petīvērunt	vēnērunt

B. Imperative forms:

	pulsāre	dēbēre	mittere	invenīre
2nd singular	pulsā	dēbē	mitte	invenī
2nd plural	pulsāte	dēbēte	mittite	invenīte
translation	*strike!*	*owe!*	*send!*	*find!*

	appellāre	respondēre	agere	advenīre
2nd singular	appellā	respondē	age	advenī
2nd plural	appellāte	respondēte	agite	advenīte
translation	*call! address!*	*respond!*	*come! lead!*	*come!*

	cōgitāre	monēre	petere	venīre
2nd singular	cōgitā	monē	pete	venī
2nd plural	cōgitāte	monēte	petite	venīte
translation	*think!*	*warn! advise!*	*seek! ask!*	*come!*

	vīverē	cadere	scīre	sentīre
2nd singular	vīve	cade	scī	sentī
2nd plural	vīvite	cadite	scīte	sentīte
translation	*live!*	*fall!*	*know!*	*feel! sense!*

	accipere	errāre	spīrāre	incipere
2nd singular	accipe	errā	spīrā	incipe
2nd plural	accipite	errāte	spīrāte	incipite
translation	*accept!*	*wander!*	*breathe!*	*begin!*

C.1. sum and possum:

	Present tense:		*Future Tense:*	
	sum	possum	sum	possum
trans.	*I am*	*I can*	*I will be*	*I will be able*
Singular				
1st	sum	possum	erō	poterō
2nd	es	potes	eris	poteris
3rd	est	potest	erit	poterit

Plural

1st	sumus	possumus	erimus	poterimus
2nd	estis	potestis	eritis	poteritis
3rd	sunt	possunt	erunt	poterunt

C.2.

1. I will give (I have given) the child (boy) a gift.
2. I ought (I will be obligated, I have been obligated) to give the child a gift.
3. You can (you will be able, you have been able) to give my son gifts.
4. The field owes (owed) gifts to the farmer.
5. Echo will not be able (was not able) to reply.
6. Narcissus ought not to flee (shouldn't have fled).
7. Echo will unhappily speak (unhappily speaks) Narcissus' words.
8. The teacher welcomes/receives (will welcome, can welcome) the children.

E. VOCABULARY QUIZ: ENGLISH TO LATIN

English Verbs	*Latin*
seize	capiō, -ere, cēpī, captus
receive	accipio, -ere, accēpī, acceptus
begin	incipiō, -ere, incēpī, inceptus
make	ago, agere, -ēgi, -actus *or* faciō, facere, fēcī, factus
spend	ago, agere, -ēgi, -actus
avoid	fugiō, -ere, fūgī, fugitum
come	veniō, -īre, vēnī, ventum
find	inveniō, -īre, invēnī, inventum
arrive at	adveniō, -īre, advēnī, adventum
to know	sciō, scīre, scīvī, scītus
not to know	nesciō, nescīre, nescīvī, nescītus
ask (for)	petō, -ere, petīvī, petītus
answer	respondeō, -ēre, respondī, respōnsus
fall	cadō, -ere, cecidī, cāsus
perish	occidō, -ere, occidī, occāsus
drink	bibō, -ere, bibī,————

Nouns	
door	iānua, -ae, f.
worry	cūra, -ae, f.
gratitude	grātia, -ae, f.
land	terra, -ae, f.
life	vīta, -ae, f.

Adjectives	
which one of two	uter, utra, utrum
neither	neuter, neutra, neutrum
Latin	Latīnus, -a, -um
any	ūllus, -a, -um
none	nūllus, -a, -um

Other	
what?	quid
why?	cūr
us	nōs
here	hīc
there	ibi
where?	ubi
because	quod
with	cum (+ ablative)
without	sine (+ ablative)
from	ā, ab (+ ablative)

44

F. DERIVATIONS:

	English	Latin source	Meaning	Meaning of English Word
1.	solipsism	sōlus	alone	the theory that nothing but the self exists
2.	neutralize	neuter	neither of two	to render ineffective
3.	alibi	alius + ubi	elsewhere	excuse (noun)
4.	alter	alter	other	change
5.	total	tōtus	entire	entire
6.	totipalmate	tōtus + palma	entire + hand	having all four fingers fully webbed
7.	nullify	nūllus	no, none	to render ineffective, futile
8.	neutron	neuter	neither of two	a neutral particle
9.	alien	alius	other	foreign
10.	desolate	sōlus	alone	barren, devastated, deserted
11.	unite	unus	one	to join into one connected whole

G. TERMINOLOGY REVIEW

1. ablative of separation: This came *from books*: **ex librīs**
2. ablative of accompaniment: We came *with friends*: **cum amīcīs**
3. ablative of instrument: We hit him *with a book*: **librō**
4. copula: My friend is a good man. Meus amīcus **est** vir bonus.
5. predicate nominative: My friend is *a good man*. Meus amīcus est **vir bonus.**
6. complementary infinitive: We are able to read your book. Librum tuum **legere** possumus.
7. preposition: **ex** librīs, **cum** amīcīs
8. perfect stem: Third principal part, without the personal ending -ī
9. consonant stem: Present stem of regular third conjugation verbs: **dūc-, dīc-, ag-,** etc.

H. TRANSLATION: PHAETHON'S WILD RIDE

Phaethon *was the son* (**fīlius erat**) of the Sun, but he had never met his father. His mother therefore decided it was time for Phaethon to visit his father. *"It will not be* (**Nōn erit**) difficult for you to find him," *she said* (**dixit**) "He lives in the East. *You go alone* (**Tū sōle**) and visit him and get to know him." Phaethon excitedly rushed out; he crossed *the land* (**terram**) of his own people, the Ethiopians, and *he arrived* (**advēnit**) in the land of the fiery sun and approached the place from which his father rises.

He climbed the steep path and entered his father's palace, but stood far from the father, whose light *he could not* (**nōn potuit**) bear at too close a range. The Sun turned his eyes to Phaethon and warmly *received* (**accēpit**) his *son* (**fīlium**). *"Come, now, my son!* (**Agedum, mī fīlī!**) Tell me: *Why have you come?* (**Cūr vēnistī**)?" Phaethon *responded* (**respondit**) that he wanted to know if the Sun really was his father. The Sun replied, *"Ask* (**Pete**) any favor you wish. *I will grant* (**Dabō**) it to you to prove you are my son." Phaethon thereupon *asked for* (**petīvit**) permission to ride his father's chariot for one whole day. The Sun replied *unhappily* (**miserē**), *"another thing* (**aliud**) I would gladly grant you, but in this one request I would like *to be able* (**posse**) to persuade you to withdraw. The thing you desire is too great for a mortal; it is more great than *I can give to a god* (**deō dare possum**) Even Jupiter, the greatest *of the gods* (**deōrum**), *will not ask to drive* (**agere nōn petet**) this chariot. Still, a promise must be kept." He *carefully* (**cum cūrā**) instructed his *son* (**fīliō**) how to control the chariot. *"Do not fly* (**Nōlī volāre**) too low, nor too high. The middle way is safest. *Hold your course* (**tenē viam tuam**) between the coiling Serpent and the low-lying Altar. The rest I leave to Fortune."

There were no stars in the sky (**nūllae stellae in caelō fuērunt**) when Phaethon climbed into the chariot. But the horses quickly realized that their burden *was* (**fuit**) too light. Just as ships toss about if they are not carrying their full cargo, so this chariot leaped into the air and was thrown about as if it were empty. Their driver *did not know* (**nescīvit**)how to control the horses. The fierce constellations frightened the boy as he drew near to them; when he drew near to poisonous Scorpio, *he was frightened* (**timuit**) to such a degree that he dropped the reins, and the horses raced out of control. The earth caught fire, meadows turned grey, and withered crops burned. Great cities perished and the woods on the mountains *were* (**fuērunt**) aflame. Finally Jupiter hurled a thunderbolt, knocking Phaethon *from the sky* (**dē caelō**) and to his death. His sisters wept for him and their tears were turned into drops of amber.

IV
The Subjunctive Mood;
The Dative Case

In this chapter you will learn the *present and imperfect tenses* of verbs in the *subjunctive mood* in Latin. You will also learn two major uses of the subjunctive, namely, to express a *command*, and to show *purpose* . As you will see here and in later chapters, the subjunctive mood occurs most frequently in dependent clauses. In Chapter V you will encounter the remaining forms of the subjunctive and additional uses of the subjunctive mood. You will also encounter the imperfect tense in the indicative mood in Chapter V.

The reason the imperfect tense in the indicative mood is delayed is to help you comprehend a statement which will be often repeated:

> The *tenses of the subjunctive mood*—the *times* when
> they take place—*are not based on linear chronology.*

Tenses in the *indicative mood* reflect whether they take place in past, present or future time. By contrast, the tenses in the *subjunctive mood* can only be understood *in relation to the time of the verb to which they are subordinated* in a dependent clause, and in relation to the time of some implicitly subordinating verb in the case of independent clauses. Thus the present tense of the subjunctive would be happening at the same time as the main verb of the sentence (which could be in the present or future), and the imperfect tense of the subjunctive would be happening at the same time as the main verb (which would be in a past tense). This principle is known as the *rule of sequence of tenses*, which you will encounter more fully in Chapter V.

You will also learn some important uses of the *Dative Case.*

A. The Subjunctive Mood

Unlike the Indicative Mood, the Subjunctive Mood indicates something other than fact. It may express a wish or a command, an opinion or intention, the result of another action, or the anticipation of what may happen in the future or a conjecture of what could happen in the present or could have happened in the past but did not—all sorts of conjectures and nuances are expressed in the subjunctive mood. This is just as true in English as in Latin, although contemporary speakers and writers tend to try to avoid such statements.

Consider what would be the mood of the verb in the following examples:

> *I'll be darned!*
> *Heaven forbid!*
> *Suffice it to say...*

Be that as it may...

or of a song:

Let me be the one!

Clearly these are not statements of fact, and consequently they are not in the indicative mood, but rather are examples of the subjunctive in an independent clause. The subjunctive is used in English more formally, too; for example, in recommendations, resolutions, demands, and legal expressions, etc.

It is required *that every member inform* himself or herself...

We hereby request *that the citizenry keep watch* over....

I ask *that you participate* in making this decision.

I strongly recommend *that she be accepted* into this program....

Be it resolved *that hereafter no mortal be declared a god*....

In future chapters we shall encounter the different uses of the subjunctive which would capture expressions such as these. A very basic application of the subjunctive, in English as well as in Latin, is to express purpose. English employs an *adverbial clause of purpose* to express someone's intention or purpose; this kind of clause is commonly expressed in English by *so that*, or more formally, *by that*:

The Sun permitted Phaethon to ride his chariot
so that he could prove he was Phaethon's father.

I am permitting you to ride my chariot *that I may prove* I am your father.

Another common way to express purpose in English is to use an infinitive in place of the subordinating conjunction. (Latin never uses an infinitive this way):

The Sun permitted Phaethon to ride his chariot *to prove* he was
Phaethon's father.

Increasingly, the subjunctive has fallen out of use in English, as writers and speakers try to avoid it, but they do so at the cost of a range of nuance in their speech. A mastery of the subjunctive mood, however little or much you choose to use it in English, will add enormously to your ability to expand the nuance of your expression.

B. The Subjunctive Mood in Latin

B.1. In Latin the subjunctive occurs frequently. It is used in independent clauses, but more commonly in dependent clauses. It is used four different ways in independent clauses:

i. Jussive or Hortatory Subjunctive
ii. Deliberative Subjunctive
iii. Potential Subjunctive
iv. Optative Subjunctive

In this chapter, we are concerned with the first of these, the *jussive* or *hortatory* subjunctive. This use expresses a command, and is often used in place of imperative forms of verbs; one advantage to this subjunctive is that is can be used in all three persons, singular and plural, including the first person (when it is called the *hortatory* subjunctive). Consider the examples in section A, above. They are all indirect commands or requests of one sort or another. The original commands would be something like:

Let every member inform himself or herself....

Let us keep watch over....

Participate in making this decision.

Let her be accepted into this program....(or)Accept her into this program....

Hereafter let no mortal be declared a god....

Notice that only the third example fits the second person command, to "you." To capture the sense of the other four subordinated commands, English needs to add "Let," In Latin, these four commands would tend to be expressed by the jussive subjunctive.

B.2. Formation of the Present Subjunctive

1. As demonstrated in *Traditio*, in the first conjugation the stem vowel -ā- changes to -ē- to form the present subjunctive.

Present Indicative	Translation	Present Subjunctive	Translation
appellō	*I am calling*	**appellem**	*Let me call*
appellās	*you are calling*	**appellēs**	*Call!*
appellat	*(s)he is calling*	**appellet**	*Let her/him call (etc.)*

In the second, third, and fourth conjugations, -ā- is the sign of the present subjunctive; in the second and fourth conjugations it is added to the stem, while in the third conjugation it is added to the consonant stem.

The verb **sum** (and hence its compound **possum**) is quite regular: the personal endings are added to its subjunctive stem **si-**.

B.2. a. Translate the following verbs, and then change them to the present subjunctive in Latin, retaining the person and number of the original form:

Indicative	translation	Subjunctive
dēbeō		
dēbēs		
dēbēmus		
dēbētis		
agit		
agunt		
agimus		
agis		
sumus		
est		
potest		
sunt		
potes		

B.2. b. Now translate the following verbs as jussive subjunctive; then change the Latin verbs from the subjunctive to the indicative, and translate the indicative form of the verbs:

Subjunctive	translation	Indicative	translation
veniās			
petat			
vīvat			
vīvāmus			
dūcant			
dīcant			
fugiat			
appellēmus			
agātis			

faciātis	_____	_____	_____
adsīmus	_____	_____	_____
cēdāmus	_____	_____	_____
dēmōnstrem	_____	_____	_____
pōnāmus	_____	_____	_____
quaerās	_____	_____	_____

B.3. The Imperfect Subjunctive is formed by adding a personal ending to the infinitive. Change the following verbs to the imperfect subjunctive, retaining the person and number of the original verb. (Do not attempt to translate the imperfect subjunctive—out of context it will not make sense.):

Present Subjunctive	Imperfect Subjunctive
veniās	_____
petat	_____
vīvat	_____
vīvāmus	_____
dūcant	_____
dīcant	_____
fugiat	_____
appellēmus	_____
agātis	_____
faciātis	_____
adsīmus	_____
cēdāmus	_____
dēmōnstrem	_____
pōnāmus	_____
quaerās	_____

B.4. Subjunctive in Dependent Clauses: Clauses of Purpose. While the jussive subjunctive is the most common occurrence in independent clauses, one the most common occurrence of the subjunctive in a dependent clause shows the intention or purpose of the person (or thing) in doing something.

  i. He is sending gifts _so that we will consider Caesar our friend._
 ii. Caesar will send aid _so that we shall be well._
iii. We came _in order to hear her words._
 iv. You brought aid _so that we would survive._

The main clauses are complete ideas: he is sending gifts, Caesar will send aid, we came, and you brought aid. Each of the dependent clauses will be introduced by **ut** and its verb will be in the sujunctive mood. The tense of the subjunctive will depend on whether the tense of the main verb governs _primary sequence_ or _secondary sequence_: the basic rule is that when the main verb is in the present or future tense it will govern the present tense of the subjunctive in the dependent clause, and when the main verb is in a past tense, it will govern the imperfect tense of the dependent clause. The _actual time_ of the subjunctive clause in these cases will be the same as the time of the main verb—it will be _contemporaneous or future_ with respect to the time of the main verb.

Thus in the first example, Caesar sends gifts now, with the hope that we will consider him our friend when those gifts arrive and thereafter. In the second example, the time when we shall be well will presumably begin when aid arrives and continue threafter. So too in the third and fourth examples. But in the first two examples the *tense* of the subordinated (subjunctive) verb will be *present*, while tense of the last two will be *imperfect*:

    i. Dōna mittit **ut** Caesārem nostrum amīcum **habeāmus.**

    ii. Caesar auxilium **mittet ut salveāmus.**

    iii. **Vēnimus ut** verba **audīrēmus.**

    iv. Auxilium **mīsistī ut superessēmus.**

When the purpose is negative, the dependent clause is introduced by **nē** insteadof ut:

    i. Nūlla dōna mittit **nē** Caesārem nostrum amīcum **habeāmus.**

    ii. Caesar auxilium nōn **mittet nē salveāmus.**

    iii. **Fūgimus nē** verba **audīrēmus.**

    iv. Auxilium nūllum **mīsistī nē superessēmus.**

B.4. a. Translate the following sentences into English:

1. Veniās mēcum.

2. Tēcum veniam ut amīcōs tuōs videam.

3. Ubi sunt convīvae tuās? Convīvae meae fugient nē tē videant.

4. Bene vīvātis! Fēmina dōna mittit ut bene vīvātis.

5. Fēmina dōna ante iānuam pōnet ut puerī (dōna) inveniant.

6. Cēdēmus ad iānuam ut virum appellēmus.

7. Agedum! Dīc virō ut respondeat.

8. Cētera dēmōnstrābō. Cētera demonstrā! Cētera dēmōnstrem.

B.4. b. Change the underlined verb to the perfect tense, indicative mood, and make the necessary tense change in the subordinate clause; then translate the new sentence:

1. Tēcum <u>veniam</u> ut amīcōs tuōs videam.

2. Convīvae meae <u>fugient</u> nē tē videant.

3. Fēmina dōna <u>mittit</u> ut bene vīvātis.

4. Fēmina dōna ante iānuam <u>pōnet</u> ut puerī (dōna) inveniant.

5. <u>Cēdēmus</u> ad iānuam ut virum appellēmus.

C. Dative Constructions

C.1. Indirect Object: In Chapter II you learned that the most common use of the Dative Case is to indica*te* an indirect object. While English employs a preposition (*to* or *for*) to indicate the person or thing indirectly affected by the verb, *Latin never uses a preposition with the Dative Case*. Some verbs in both English and in Latin automatically govern an indirect object:

        speak (to):   **Tibi dīcō.**

        give (to):   **Tibi dōnum dō.**

        show (to),   **Tibi dōnum meum dēmōnstrō.**

Other verbs, such as *listen* (to) do not govern the dative in Latin: **Tē audiō**, *I am listening to you* (accusative). Here the Latin is saying, literally, *I am hearing you; I hear you*. In learning new vocabulary words, therefore, it is important to make note of the particular constructions these words govern. In the new vocabulary for Chapter IV, the verbs **adsum**, **cēdō**, and **dēsum** are all intransitive, and therefore cannot take a direct object, but do frequently occur with a noun or pronoun in the dative case. The meaning of such verbs will sometimes be affected by the dative construction. **adsum** alone means *to be present*:

Hīc adsum, *I'm here! Here I am!*

When it governs the dative case, it means, in effect, *to be present for the benefit of someone else*, and hence *to assist* or *give assistance to* someone:

Tibi adsum. *I am giving assistance to you.*

Similar constructions apply to **dēsum**, *to be absent*, and hence with the dative, *to fail someone*, or *to let someone down* or *to disappoint them*:

Vestrīs amīcīs numquam dēfuistis. *You have never disappointed your friends.*

Cēdō as an intransitive verb with no indirect object simply means to go, move, depart, and even to yield, as in an argument. But with the dative it means to *submit to* someone, *to yield to* someone, etc. These and the other datives you are learning in this book all ultimately boil down to a category of *reference* or *respect*: I speak, give a gift, yield, give thanks, am present or absent—all *with reference to* someone, *for their benefit or disadvantage* (both are possible). The dative case is basically a case of reference, which can have positive, neutral, or negative overtones.

C.1. Translate the following into Latin:

1. Thank you.
2. I came to thank you.
3. Will they thank me?
4. No one will thank you.
5. Show me your friends.
6. I will show you my friends so that they can thank you.
7. I want to help you.
8. Did you come to help me?
9. You let me down.
10. Don't let me down!
11. Why didn't you respond to me?
12. Show me the way!

C.2. Dative of Possession: The dative of possession is used only with forms of the verb *to be*. In essence, it says, *x belongs to me*, or *I have*. By contrast, the genitive of possession or the possessive pronoun merely indicates that *a* belongs to *b*. Both constructions are found in Latin, with somewhat different implications.

Compare:

Cōnsīlium est mihi.
I have a plan.

Cōnsīlium meum est...
My plan is....

Cōnsīlium est fēminae (dative)
The woman has a plan.

Cōnsīlium fēminae (genitive) **bonum est.**
The woman's plan is good.

C.3. Datives of Purpose and Reference: The *dative of purpose* serves to link two nouns which are not quite equal. In English, we may say *the animal is a friend*, whereas in Latin the expression is more likely to be, the animal *serves as/functions as* a friend. In effect the dative of purpose avoids saying two things are completely equal, but that there is a close link between them. The dative of purpose is almost always accompanied by a second dative, which shows *with reference to whom or what* this link exists: the animal is a friend *with reference to you*: **Tibi bestia amīcō est.** The combination of these two datives is therefore known as a *double* dative construction.

C.4. Translate the following phrases into English, and indicate whether the underlined word(s) indicate a dative of Indirect Object (IO), Possession (Poss), Purpose (Pur), or Reference (R) :

1. <u>Amīcīs nostrīs</u> adsimus.
2. <u>Tibi</u> cēdō
3. Cōnsilium meum <u>virō magnō</u> dēmōnstrābō.
4. Cōnsilium meum <u>tibi auxiliō</u> sit.
5. <u>Agricolae auxiliō</u> est ager magnus.
6. Tua verba erunt <u>mihi malō</u>.
7. Dōna <u>tibi</u> dabō ut <u>mihi</u> altera dōna dēs.
8. Dōna ante iānuam posuit ut essent <u>auxiliō aliīs</u>.
9. Potuitne dōnum nostrum esse <u>auxiliō tibi</u>?

D. Derivations and Vocabulary Quiz

English	Latin source	Latin Meaning	Meaning of English Word
cause			
monster			
demonstrate			
cognition			
deposit			
inquiry			
inquest			
vocation			
invocation			
jussive			
proceed			
accede			
recede			
ambulatory			
inanimate			
animation			
counsel			
impecunious			
satisfy			
insanity			
molest			

E. Terminology Review

Explain what is meant by each of the following terms:

1. adverbial clause of purpose

2. the rule of sequence of tenses in adverbial clauses of purpose

3. jussive subjunctive

4. hortatory subjunctive

5. What is the sign of the subjunctive mood, present tense in

    i.   the first conjugation?

    ii. the second conjugation?

    iii. the third conjugation?

    iv. the fourth conjugation?

6. What is the sign of the subjunctive mood, imperfect tense in all conjugations?

7. double dative

F. Translation:

VULCAN AND VENUS

Venus, the goddess, was the wife of the unattractive, limping god, Vulcan, the god of fire and the blacksmith-deity who, assisted by his one-eyed assistants, the Cyclopes, forged weapons for the gods, in particular the thunderbolt with which Jupiter ruled the races of men and gods. It was a curious marriage—the most beautiful and desirable of the goddesses and the least attractive of the gods. Venus, being who she was, was frequently unfaithful to her husband. One of her amours was Mars, the god of war. When Vulcan learned of their affair, he put his craft to work to punish the lovers: he made great chains which were invisible, and set them up so that when the two lovers were together the chains fell down upon them and locked them in their embarrassing, tell-tale position. Then all the gods came and stared and laughed at them, and through their shame they were justly punished for their misbehavior.

This story was very popular in antiquity. When poets depicted sea-nymphs or women at the loom, the subject of their conversation was frequently the tale of the love affair of Mars and Venus. In the chapter IV passage in *Traditio*, when the cook is preparing a seductive meal for Erotium and Menaechmus,the cook waxes poetic, perhaps intending to allude to the steamy marriage of the god of fire and the unfaithful goddess who was the embodiment of love (Eros): "I shall place the food near the violence of Vulcan and I shall summon Erotium": **cibum ad Vulcānī violentiam pōnam et Erōtium vocābō.**

Vocabulary:
deus, deī, *m*; **dea, deae,** *f. a god*
Vulcānus, ī, *m. Vulcan, the god of fire*
oculus, ī, *m. eye*
Venus (nominative); **Venerem** (accusative), *Venus*
Mars (nominative); **Martem** (accusative), *Mars*
tandem (adverb), *finally*
levia (neuter, accusative, plural) *lightweight*
fortia (neuter, accusative, plural) *strong*
Bellum, -ī, *n. War*
extemplō (adverb), *immediately*
rīdeō, rīdēre, rīsī, rīsus *to laugh, to smile*
diū (adverb) *for a long time*

nōtissimus, -a, -um *most famous*
fābula, -ae, *f. tale, story*
haec (nom. sing. feminine demonstrative adjective, agreeing with **fābula**) *this*

Translate the following sentences:

1. Ūnus deōrum vēnit ad Vulcānum et dixit, "Vīdī oculis meīs: Venus Martem amat."

2. Vulcānus, miser, respondēre nōn potuit.

3. Sōlus cōgitāvit, "Quid facere possum?"

4. Tandem vincula levia sed fortia fēcit.

5. Nūllus vincula vidēre potuit.

6. Vulcānus vincula fēcit ut Venerem et Martem caperet.

7. Deus Bellī et dea pulchra vincula nōn vīdērunt.

8. Extemplō Vulcānus pulsāvit vincula et vincula in duōs deōs cecidērunt.

9. Tum Vulcānus aliōs deōs vocāvit ut duōs deōs in vinculīs vidērent.

10. Deī aliī rīsērunt. Diū haec fuit nōtissima fābula in tōtō caelō.

Key, Chapter IV

B.2. a.

Indicative	translation	Subjunctive
dēbeō	I owe	dēbeam
dēbēs	you owe	dēbeās
dēbēmus	we owe	dēbeāmus
dēbētis,	you (pl) owe	dēbeātis
agit	he, she, it does leads, drives, spends, etc.	agat
agunt	they do, lead, drive, etc.	agant
agimus	we do, etc.	agāmus
agis	you (s) do, etc.	agās
sumus	we are	sīmus
est	he, she, it is	sit
potest	he, she, it is able	possit
sunt	they are	sint
potes	you are able	possīs

B.2. b.

Subjunctive	translation	Indicative	translation
veniās	Come!	venīs	You are coming.
petat	Let him seek.	petit	He is seeking.
vīvat	Let him live.	vīvit	He is living.
vīvāmus	Let us love.	vīvimus	We live, are alive.
dūcant	Let them lead.	dūcunt	They are leading.
fugiat	Let him flee.	fugit	He is fleeing.
appellēmus	Let us address	appellāmus	We are addressing.
agātis	Do!	agitis	You are doing.
faciātis	Make!	facitis	You are making.
adsīmus	Let us help.	adsumus	We are helping, we are present.
cēdāmus	Let us go!	cēdimus	We are going.
dēmōnstrem	Let me show	dēmōnstrō	I am showing.
pōnāmus	Let us put, place	pōnimus	We are placing, putting.
quaerās	Ask! Inquire!	quaeris	You are asking.

B.3.

Present Subjunctive	Imperfect Subjunctive
veniās	venīrēs
petat	peteret
vīvat	vīveret
vīvāmus	vīverēmus
dūcant	dūcerent
dīcant	dīcerent
fugiat	fugeret
appellēmus	appellārēmus
agātis	agerētis
faciātis	facerētis
adsīmus	adessēmus
cēdāmus	cēderēmus
dēmōnstrem	dēmōnstrārem
pōnāmus	pōnerēmus
quaerās	quaererēmus

B.4. a.

1. Come with me.
2. I will come with you so that I may see your friends.

3. Where are your dinner companions? My dinner companions will run away in order not to see you.
4. May you live well! The woman is sending gifts so that you may live well.
5. The woman will place gifts before the door so that children may find them.
6. We shall go to the door to speak to the man.
7. Come now! Speak to the man so that he will answer.
8. I shall show the remaining things. Show the remaining things! Let me show the rest.

B.4. b.

1. Tēcum *vēnī* ut amīcōs tuōs vidērem. *I came with you to see your friends.*
2. Convīvae meae *fūgērunt* nē tē vidērent. *My companions fled in order not to see you.*
3. Fēmina dōna *mīsit* ut bene vīverētis. *The woman sent gifts so that you would live well.*
4. Fēmina dōna ante iānuam *posuit* ut puerī (dōna) invenīrent. *The woman placed gifts before the door so that the children would find (them).*
5. *Cessimus* ad iānuam ut virum appellārēmus. *We went to the door to call the man.*

C.1.

1. Tibi grātiās agō.
2. Vēnī ut tibi grātiās agerem.
3. Mihi grātiās agent?
4. Nūllus tibi grātiās aget.
5. Tuōs amīcōs mihi mōnstrā. (or) Vestrōs amīcōs mihi mōnstrāte.
   Tuōs amīcōs mihi mōnstrēs. (or) Vestrōs amīcōs mihi mōnstrētis.
6. Tibi meōs amīcōs mōnstrābō ut tibi grātiās agant.
7. Tibi auxilium dare optō. (or) Tibi adesse optō.
8. Vēnistīne ut mihi adessēs? (or) ut mihi auxilium darēs?
   Vēnistisne ut mihi adessētis? (or) ut mihi auxilium darētis?
9. Mihi dēfuistī. (or) Mihi dēfuistis.
10. Nē mihi dēsit! (or) Nē mihi dēsītis!
    Nōlī mihi dēesse! (or) Nōlīte mihi dēesse!
11. Cur mihi nōn respondistī? (respondistis)
12. Viam mihi mōnstrā! (mōnstrāte)

C.4.

1. Let us assist our friends. (IO)
2. I yield to you. (IO)
3. I will show the great man my plan. (IO)
4. Let my plan be a help (Pur) to you (R).
5. A large field is a help (Pur) to the farmer (R).
6. Your words will be a bad thing(Pur) for me(R).
7. I will give you (IO) gifts so that you will give other gifts to me (IO).
8. (S)he placed gifts before the door so that they would be a help (Pur) to others (R).
9. Was our gift able to be a help (Pur) to you (R)? [Was our gift able to help you?]

D. DERIVATIONS AND VOCABULARY QUIZ

English	Latin source	Latin Meaning	English Meaning
cause	causa	cause, reason; legal case	reason
monster	mōnstrāre	show	an abnormal, horrifying creature
demonstrate	mōnstrāre	show	show
cognition	cognoscere	learn, recognize	perception
deposit	dē + pōnere	put, place + down	to put down; a security payment
inquiry	quaerere	look for, seek	an investigation
inquest	quaesītus	look for, seek	a legal inquiry
vocation	vocāre	call, summon	a particular occupation or profession
invocation	vocāre	call, summon	a prayer or entreaty to a greater power
jussive	iubēre	to order, command	expressing a mild command
proceed	prō + cēdere	to go + forward	to go forward

accede	**ad + cēdere**	to go + toward	to consent or agree to
recede	**re + cēdere**	to go + again	to go backwards
ambulatory	**ambulāre**	to walk	capable of walking
inanimate	**in + animus**	not + soul, spirit	not alive
animation	**animus**	soul, spirit	give life to something
counsel	**cōnsilium**	advice	advice
impecunious	**in + pecūnia**	not + money	without money
satisfy	**satis + facere**	enough + make	to fulfill the needs or expectations
insanity	**in + sānus**	not + of sound mind	unsoundness of mind
molest	**molestus**	annoying	to interfere with, injuriously

E. TERMINOLOGY REVIEW

1. **Adverbial clause of purpose:** A dependent clause, introduced by **ut** if the clause is positive, and by **nē** if the clause is negative, whose verb is subjunctive, which shows the purpose or intent of the subject of the main verb.

2. **Sequence of tenses:** In adverbial clauses of purpose, the subjunctive verb will be in the present tense if the the main verb is in the present or future tense, and will be in the imperfect tense if the main verb is in a past tense.

3. **Jussive subjunctive:** An independent use of the subjunctive, which gives a command.

4. **Hortatory subjunctive:** The same as #3, except that *hortatory* refers to commands of the first person (*Let me...*, *Let us...*,) whereas *jussive* refers to commands of the second and third persons.

5. **Sign of the subjuncitve mood:**
    i. First conjugation: the vowel **-ē-** replaces the stem vowel **-ā-**
    ii. Second conjugation: the vowel **-ā-** is added to the stem vowel **-ē-**
    iii. Third conjugation: the vowel **-a-** is added to the consonant stem, and for **-iō** verbs **-ia** is added to the consonant stem.
    iv. Fourth conjugation: the vowel **-ā-** is added to the stem vowel **-ī-**

6. **Sign of imperfect subjunctive in all conjugations:** personal endings are added directly to the infinitive.

7. **Double dative:** The combination of the dative of Purpose and the dative of Reference.

F. TRANSLATION: VULCAN AND VENUS

1. One of the gods came to Vulcan and said, "I saw with my own eyes: Venus loves Mars."
2. Vulcan, unhappy, was not able to respond.
3. Alone, he thought, "What can I do?"
4. Finally he made lightweight but strong chains.
5. No one was able to see the chains.
6. Vulcan made chains in order to capture Venus and Mars.
7. The god of War and the beautiful goddess did not see the chains.
8. Suddenly Vulcan struck the chains and the chains fell onto the two gods.
9. Then Vulcan summoned the other gods so that they could see the two gods in chains.
10. The other gods laughed. For a long time this was the most famous story in the entire sky.

V
Remaining Tenses of the Indicative and Subjunctive Moods; Conditions; Potential Subjunctive

A. Remaining Tenses of the Indicative Mood

Latin, like English, has six tenses in the indicative: the present, the imperfect, the future, the perfect, the pluperfect, and the future perfect. The first three are based on the present stem and the last three are based on the perfect stem of the verb. To these stems are added the appropriate tense signs and the personal endings:

amō, amāre, amāvī, amātus

Present stem: **amā-**	*tense marker*	*personal ending*
Present tense:	**amā-** (no additional)	**ō, s, t, mus, tis, nt**
Imperfect tense	**amā-** **bā**	**m, s, t, mus, tis, nt**
Future tense	**amā-** **bi**	**ō, s, t, mus, tis, nt**
Perfect stem: **amāv-**	*tense marker*	*personal ending*
Perfect tense	**amav-** (no additional)	**ī, istī, it, imus, istis, erunt**
Pluperfect tense	**amāv-** **erā**	**m, s, t, mus, tis, nt**
Future Perfect tense	**amāv-** **eri**	**ō, s, t, mus, tis, nt**

Notice that there are some parallels between the signs of imperfect tense and the pluperfect tenses: **a** in both tense signs (compare English *was*), and the same set of personal endings (specifically, the **-m** in the first person). There are similar parallels between the signs of the future tense and the future perfect tenses: **i** in both tense signs (compare English *will*), and the same set of personal endings (specifically, the **-ō** in the first person).

The Latin indicative tenses are like the English indicative tenses:

English Tense	English Example	Latin Tense	Latin Example
present	*The slave is distracting the horse.*	present	**Servus equum distrahit.**
past	*The slave was distracting the horse.*	imperfect	**Servus equum distrahēbat.**
future	*The slave will distract the horse.*	future	**Servus equum distrahet.**
perfect	*The slave has distracted the horse.*	perfect	**Servus equum distraxit.**
past perfect	*The slave had distracted the horse.*	pluperfect	**Servus equum distraxerat.**
future perfect	*The slave will have distracted the horse.*	future perfect	**Servus equum distraxerit.**

Notice that the *English past tense* is usually defined as a time gone by or an action or state of being completed or in progress at a former time, as opposed to the English perfect tense, which refers to an action or state of being completed at the time it is being referred to. Like the Latin imperfect tense, the English past tense does not make clear whether or when the past action was completed: *He asked, he was asking, he did ask.* The perfect tense, by contrast, indicates that he is no longer asking: *He has asked, he has been asking.*

To express the past perfect tense, which is the equivalent of the Latin pluperfect, English always employs the auxiliary verb, *had: He had asked, He had been asking.* While the perfect tense indicates that something has been completed prior to some event in the present, the pluperfect indicates that it was completed prior to some event in the past.

A.1. Conjugate the following verbs in all tenses:

cōgitō

maneō

cōgō

iaciō

adsum

possum

A.2. Now write a complete Synopsis, Active Voice, of each of the above verbs, in the person and number indicated:

a. **cōgitō**, 1st person singular

Principal Parts _____, _____, _____, _____

Tenses	Indicative Mood	Translation	Subjunctive Mood
Present	_____	_____	_____
Imperfect	_____	_____	_____
Future	_____	_____	N/A
Perfect	_____	_____	_____
Pluperfect	_____	_____	_____
Future Perfect	_____	_____	N/A

b. **maneō**, 2nd person singular

Principal Parts _____, _____, _____, _____

Tenses	Indicative Mood	Translation	Subjunctive Mood
Present	_____	_____	_____
Imperfect	_____	_____	_____
Future	_____	_____	_____
Perfect	_____	_____	_____
Pluperfect	_____	_____	_____
Future Perfect	_____	_____	_____

c. **cōgō**, 3rd person singular

Principal Parts _____, _____, _____, _____

Tenses	Indicative Mood	Translation	Subjunctive Mood
Present	_____	_____	_____
Imperfect	_____	_____	_____
Future	_____	_____	_____
Perfect	_____	_____	_____
Pluperfect	_____	_____	_____
Future Perfect	_____	_____	_____

d. **iaciō**, 1st person plural

Principal Parts _____, _____, _____, _____

Tenses	Indicative Mood	Translation	Subjunctive Mood
Present	_____	_____	_____
Imperfect	_____	_____	_____
Future	_____	_____	_____
Perfect	_____	_____	_____
Pluperfect	_____	_____	_____
Future Perfect	_____	_____	_____

e. **adsum**, 2nd person plural

Principal Parts _____, _____, _____, _____

Tenses	Indicative Mood	Translation	Subjunctive Mood
Present	_____	_____	_____
Imperfect	_____	_____	_____
Future	_____	_____	_____
Perfect	_____	_____	_____
Pluperfect	_____	_____	_____
Future Perfect	_____	_____	_____

f. **possum**, 3rd person plural

Principal Parts _____, _____, _____, _____

Tenses	Indicative Mood	Translation	Subjunctive Mood
Present	_____	_____	_____
Imperfect	_____	_____	_____
Future	_____	_____	_____
Perfect	_____	_____	_____
Pluperfect	_____	_____	_____
Future Perfect	_____	_____	_____

As you probably discovered in the process of practicing conjugations both ways, you are now now at a point in learning Latin where writing out synopses rather than full conjugations may be a more effective way to test yourself on these verbs—a more intensive, focusing exercise. Try testing yourself both ways from now on, choosing whichever method you find more challenging, so that the learning process will continue to hold your full attention.

A.3. Fill out the following chart:

TENSE MARKERS AND PERSONAL ENDINGS, ACTIVE VOICE

	INDICATIVE	*SUBJUNCTIVE*

Present Stem Ends in:

1st conj.:	_____
2nd conj.:	_____
3rd conj.:	_____
3rd **iō**:	_____
4th conj.:	_____

Present tense: *personal endings:* _____

1st conj.:	_____	1st conj.:	_____
2nd conj.:	_____	2nd conj.:	_____
3rd conj.:	_____	3rd conj.:	_____
3rd **iō**:	_____	3rd **iō**:	_____
4th conj.:	_____	4th conj.:	_____

Imperfect tense: *personal endings:* _____

1st conj.:	_____	1st conj.:	_____
2nd conj.:	_____	2nd conj.:	_____
3rd conj.:	_____	3rd conj.:	_____
3rd **iō**:	_____	3rd **iō**:	_____
4th conj.:	_____	4th conj.:	_____

Future tense: *personal endings:* _____

1st conj.:	_____	
2nd conj.:	_____	*N*
3rd conj.:	_____	*O*
3rd **iō**:	_____	*N*
4th conj.:	_____	*E*

	INDICATIVE	*SUBJUNCTIVE*

PERFECT STEM: _____

Perfect Tense:	_____	**Perfect Tense:**	_____
personal endings:	_____	*personal endings:*	_____
Pluperfect Tense:	_____	**Pluperfect Tense:**	_____
personal endings:	_____	*personal endings:*	_____
Future Perfect:	_____		*NONE*
personal endings:	_____		

B. Conditions in English versus Latin

In English grammar, Conditions are usually divided into simple conditions, less-vivid conditions, and contrary-to-fact conditions. English still uses the subjunctive in conditions, at least in the *if*-clause, when there is doubt about the fulfillment of the clause:

> If I *should win* the lottery,....
>
> If *you were getting an 'A' in this course*,....
>
> If *I had taken that flight*, ...

Often English will imply a subjunctive in the *if*-clause, for example

> What would you do *if I sang out of tune?*

If is the most usual conjunction for conditional clauses. Its negatives are *if not, unless* (= *if not*), and *whether* (= *if...if, if...or if*). In formal writing, however, *in case, provided, provided that, on condition that, in the event that,* and other phrases are also used to express a conditional clause.

B.1. Simple Conditions in English state (in the *if*-clause) a condition or action necessary for the truth or occurrence of the main statement (the *then*-clause) of a sentence. The indicative verb forms (as in Latin) are used:

> *If the semaphore arm is horizontal*, you know that a train is in that block of track.
>
> He will be there *unless something happens to his car.*
> *Whether he comes or not*, I shall go to the concert.

An older type of condition survives in some proverbs:

> *Spare the rod* and spoil the child. (*If you spare the rod*, you will spoil the child.)

In speech, we often express a condition by a compound sentence:

> *You just try that* and you'll be sorry. (*If you try that*, you will be sorry.)

[In Latin, this will be expressed by the indicative mood.]

B.2. Less-vivid conditions (theoretical or hypothetical but still possible—compare Latin ideal conditions) are usually made with *should...would* or with the past tense:

> *If he should raise his offer another $100*, I would take it.
> Or: *If he raised his offer*, I would take it.
>
> *If you revised your papers carefully*, your writing would improve and you would receive a higher grade.

[In Latin, this will be expressed by an Ideal condition; also known as less-vivid condition; both verbs will be in the present tense, subjunctive mood.]

B.3. Contrary-to-Fact Conditions: conditions that cannot be met, contrary-to-fact conditions formerly were expressed with the subjunctive and still are in formal writing (sometimes even with a rather archaic inversion). The indicative is increasingly used in this type of condition.

> General: *If I was going to be there, I'd be glad to help.*
>
> Formal: *If I were going to be there, I would be glad to help.*

[In Latin, this would be a present contrary-to-fact condition, expressed by the imperfect subjunctive]

> General: *If I had known what I know now, I should [I'd] never have let him go.*
> *If he had known what he knows now, he would [he'd] never have let us go.*
>
> Formal: *Had I known what I now know, I should never have let him go.*
> *Had he known what he now knows, he would never have let us go.*

62

[In Latin, this would be past contrary-to-fact, expressed by the pluperfect subjunctive: si scivīssem...., numquam permisissem....; si scīvisset......, numquam permīsisset...]

Latin Conditions—Summary

	General Conditions (*Indicative*)			*Subjunctive* Conditions	
Condition:	If,	then	Condition: If,		then
Present	present tense	present tense	*Present Contrary-to-fact*		
			imperfect tense		imperfect tense
			"were,		would"
Future	future tense	future tense	*Ideal or Less-Vivid*:		
			present tense		present tense
			"should,		would"
Past	any past tense	any past tense	*Past Contrary-to-fact*		
			pluperfect tense		pluperfect tense
			"had,		would have"

Potential Subjunctive (negative: non:)
"Then"-clause (no "if" clause)...

Opinion of Speaker in Present or Future Time — present or perfect "would"

Opinion of Speaker in Past Time — imperfect (or pluperfect) "would have"

B.4. Indicate what kind of condition is called for in the following sentences, and change the italicized words to the appropriate Latin form.

1. If *you were* my son, *I would not entrust* you to a clever slave.
2. *I would entrust you* to a clever slave.
3. *I would not have entrusted you* to a clever slave.
4. If *you had been* my son, *I would have sent* you to a different school.
5. If *I send* a rose to you for every time you make me blue, *you'll have* a room full of roses.
6. If *I sent* a rose to you for every time you made me blue, *you'd have* a room full of roses.
7. If *I should send* a rose to you for every time you made me blue, *you would have* a room full of roses.
8. *You would't have* a room full of roses *unless I had sent* them to you.
9. *If I have lived* wisely and well, my father *was* the reason.
10. *He guided me* with words and examples *if he wanted* me to do something.
11. *He would guide me* with examples *if he wanted / if he should want* me to do something.

B.5. Identify the condition and translate:

1. Mihi satis est sī vītam fāmamque tuam servāre possum.
2. Mihi satis fuisset sī vītam fāmamque tuam servāre potuissem.
3. Discipulus poētās nōn intellegat nisi stellās et philosophiam discat.
4. Vitia tua fugerem sī possem.
5. Sī vitia tua fugere possim, nōnne vir bonus et magnus sim?

C. Latin Vocabulary Quiz

Identify the form and meaning of the following and translate into English; if it is a verb, list its principal parts; if a noun, list its nominative, genitive, and gender:

traxerit _____

extrahās _____

distrahēs _____

dēlīberāverāmus _____

cūrēmus _____

coēgērunt _____

valeāmus _____

iacit _____

cēlāverit _____

crēdiderat _____

laudāvisset _____

mānserat _____

remanēret _____

remedia _____

integrum _____

aequum _____

equum _____

quantum _____

invītum _____

num _____

ad _____

ex _____

de _____

-que _____

-ne _____

cum _____

tot _____

enim _____

fortūnae _____

nīl _____

sententiam _____

audāciīs _____

nuptiīs _____

modīs _____

D. Terminology Review

Define the following terms:

1. protasis

2. apodosis

64

3. Ideal condition

4. Present contrary-to-fact condition

5 Past contrary-to-fact condition

6. Potential subjunctive

7. Pluperfect tense

8. Imperfect tense

E. Translation

Translate the following into English:

DAEDALUS AND ICARUS

Daedalus, ī, m, Daedalus (a master craftsman)
Icarus, ī, m, Icarus (son of Daedalus)
Sōl, Sōlis, m Sun
volō, āre, āvi, ātus, to fly

Daedalus ex insulā[1] Crētā[2] excēdere optāvit, sed fugere nōn poterat. Ergo multās pennās[3] lēgit et ā parvīs ad magnās pennās cērā[4] iunxit,[5] ut super undās[6] volāret. Puer Icarus pennās vidēbat inque cērīs ludēbat,[7] sed cōnsilium[8] patris nescīvit.

Tum pater Icarum instruit[9]: "Icare, tē in mediō cēdere iubeō nē unda pennās capiat, sī demissius (*too low*) volēs. Sī celsius (*too high*) volēs, Sōl tē adūrat[10]. Cum mē carpē[11] viam mediam! Dat oscula[12] nātō[13] et ante[14] volat puerōque[15] timet. Pater filiusque volābant super undās, sed subitō[16] Icarus, caelī cupidus[17], Daedalum deseruit[18]. Celsius viam carpsit, et Sōl cērās, pennārum vincula, mollīvit[19]. Nuda[20] bracchia[21] quatit[22] sed undae puerum accipunt. Pater, nec pater, "Icare," dixit, "ubi es?"

E.1. Identify the following conditions, and translate accordingly.

1. Sī Icarus celsius volābit, pater nōn laetus[23] erit.

2. Sī Icarus celsius volet, pater nōn laetus sit.

3. Sī Icarus celsius volāret, pater nōn laetus esset.

1	**insula, -ae,** *f* = island
2	**Crēta, -ae,** *f* = the island Crete
3	**penna, -ae,** *f* = feather
4	**cēra, -ae,** *f* = wax
5	**iungō, -ere, iunxī, iunctus** = join
6	**unda, -ae,** *f* = wave; **super undās** = above the waves
7	**lūdō, -ere, lūsī, lūsus** = play
8	**cōnsilium, -ī** *n* = plan
9	**instruō, -ere, instruxī, instructus** instruct
10	**adūrō, -ere, adussī, adustum** set on fire
11	**carpō, -ere, carpsī, carptus** pluck, gather, enjoy. (here, "make your way, *viam,*")
12	**osculum, -ī,** *n* kiss
13	**nātus, -ī** *m* son
14	**ante,** prep before
15	**-que** enclitic conjunction (attached to the second word in a series) and
16	**subitō,** *adv* suddenly
17	**cupidus, -a, -um** (objective genitive) "longing for"
18	**deserō, -ere, -uī, desertus** abandon, desert
19	**mollio, -īre, -īvī, -ītus** soften
20	**nūdus, -a, -um** bare, naked
21	**bracchium, -ī** *n* arm
22	**quatiō, -ere, —, quassus** shake, beat
23	**laetus, -a, -um,** happy

4. Sī Icarus celsius volāvisset, pater nōn laetus fuisset.

5. Pater laetus fuisset nisi Icarus celsius volāvisset.

E.2. Potential subjunctive. Translate:

1. Pater laetus esset.

2. Pater laetus fuerit.

3. Pater laetus fuisset.

4. Pater laetus sit.

5. Icarus demissius nōn volet.

6. Icarus demissius nōn volāret.

7. Icarus demissius nōn volāverit.

8. Icarus celsius volāre velit.

9. Sōl cērās molliat.

10. Sōl pennārum vincula mollīverit.

KEY, Chapter V

A.1.

cōgitō INDICATIVE

Present	Imperfect	Future	Perfect	Pluperfect	Fut. Perf.
cōgitō	cōgitābam	cōgitābō	cōgitāvimus	cōgitāveram	cōgitāverō
cōgitās	cōgitābās	cōgitābis	cōgitāvistī	cōgitāverās	cōgitāveris
cōgitat	cōgitābat	cōgitābit	cōgitāvit	cōgitāverat	cōgitāverit
cōgitāmus	cōgitābāmus	cōgitābimus	cōgitāvimus	cōgitāverāmus	cōgitāverimus
cōgitātis	cōgitābātis	cōgitābitis	cōgitāvistis	cōgitāverātis	cōgitāveritis
cōgitant	cōgitābant	cōgitābunt	cōgitāvērunt	cōgitāverant	cōgitāverint

SUBJUNCTIVE

Present	Imperfect	Perfect	Pluperfect
cōgitem	cōgitārem	cōgitāverim	cōgitāvissem
cōgitēs	cōgitārēs	cōgitāverīs	cōgitāvissēs
cōgitet	cōgitāret	cōgitāverit	cōgitāvisset
cōgitēmus	cōgitārēmus	cōgitāverīmus	cōgitāvissēmus
cōgitētis	cōgitārētis	cōgitāverītis	cōgitāvissētis
cōgitent	cōgitārent	cōgitāverint	cōgitāvissent

maneō INDICATIVE

Present	Imperfect	Future	Perfect	Pluperfect	Fut. Perf.
maneō	manēbam	manēbō	mansī	manseram	manserō
manēs	manēbās	manēbis	mansistī	manserās	manseris
manet	manēbat	manēbit	mansit	manserat	manserit
manēmus	manēbāmus	manēbimus	mansimus	manserāmus	manserimus
manētis	manēbātis	manēbitis	mansistis	manserātis	manseritis
manent	manēbant	manēbunt	mansērunt	mansērant	manserint

SUBJUNCTIVE

Present	Imperfect	Perfect	Pluperfect
maneam	manērem	manserim	mansissem
maneās	manērēs	manserīs	mansissēs
maneat	manēret	manserit	mansisset
maneāmus	manērēmus	manserīmus	mansissēmus
maneātis	manērētis	manserītis	mansissētis
maneant	manērent	manserint	mansissent

cōgō INDICATIVE

Present	Imperfect	Future	Perfect	Pluperfect	Fut. Perf.
cōgō	cōgēbam	cōgam	coēgī	coēgeram	coēgerō
cōgis	cōgēbās	cōgēs	coēgistī	coēgerās	coēgeris
cōgit	cōgēbat	cōget	coēgit	coēgerat	coēgerit
cōgimus	cōgēbāmus	cōgēmus	coēgimus	coēgerāmus	coēgerimus
cōgitis	cōgēbātis	cōgētis	coēgistis	coēgerātis	coēgeritis
cōgunt	cōgēbant	cōgent	coēgērunt	coēgerant	coēgerint

SUBJUNCTIVE

Present	Imperfect	Perfect	Pluperfect
cōgam	cōgerem	coēgerim	coēgissem
cōgās	cōgerēs	coēgerīs	coēgissēs
cōgat	cōgeret	coēgerit	coēgisset
cōgāmus	cōgerēmus	coēgerīmus	coēgissēmus
cōgātis	cōgerētis	coēgerītis	coēgissētis
cōgant	cōgerent	coēgerint	coēgissent

iaciō INDICATIVE

Present	Imperfect	Future	Perfect	Pluperfect	Fut. Perf.
iaciō	iaciēbam	iaciam	iēcī	iēceram	iēcerō
iacis	iaciēbās	iaciēs	iēcistī	iēcerās	iēceris
iacit	iaciēbat	iaciet	iēcit	iēcerat	iēcerit
iacimus	iaciēbāmus	iaciēmus	iēcimus	iēcerāmus	iēcerimus
iacitis	iaciēbātis	iaciētis	iēcistis	iēcerātis	iēceritis
iaciunt	iaciēbant	iacient	iēcērunt	iēcerant	iēcerint

SUBJUNCTIVE

Present	Imperfect	Perfect	Pluperfect
iaciam	iacerem	iēcerim	iēcissem
iaciās	iacerēs	iēcerīs	iēcissēs
iaciat	iaceret	iēcerit	iēcisset
iaciāmus	iacerēmus	iēcerīmus	iēcissēmus
iaciātis	iacerētis	iēcerītis	iēcissētis
iaciant	iacerent	iēcerint	iēcissent

adsum INDICATIVE

Present	Imperfect	Future	Perfect	Pluperfect	Fut. Perf.
adsum	aderam	aderō	adfuī	adfueram	adfuerō
ades	aderās	aderis	adfuistī	adfuerās	adfueris
adest	aderat	aderit	adfuit	adfuerat	adfuerit
adsumus	aderāmus	aderimus	adfuimus	adfuerāmus	adfuerimus
adestis	aderātis	aderitis	adfuistis	adfuerātis	adfueritis
adsunt	aderant	aderint	adfuērunt	adfuerant	adfuerint

SUBJUNCTIVE

Present	Imperfect	Perfect	Pluperfect
adsim	adessem	adfuerim	adfuissem
adsīs	adessēs	adfuerīs	adfuissēs
adsit	adesset	adfuerit	adfuisset
adsīmus	adessēmus	adfuerīmus	adfuissēmus
adsītis	adessētis	adfuerītis	adfuissētis
adsint	adessent	adfuerint	adfuissent

possum INDICATIVE

Present	Imperfect	Future	Perfect	Pluperfect	Fut. Perf.
possum	poteram	poterō	potuī	potueram	potuerō
potes	poterās	poteris	potuistī	potuerās	potueris
potest	poterat	poterit	potuit	potuerat	potuerit
possumus	poterāmus	poterimus	potuimus	potuerāmus	potuerimus
potestis	poterātis	poteritis	potuistis	potuerātis	potueritis
possunt	poterant	poterint	potuērunt	potuerant	potuerint

SUBJUNCTIVE

Present	Imperfect	Perfect	Pluperfect
possim	possem	potuerim	potuissem
possīs	possēs	potuerīs	potuissēs
possit	posset	potuerit	potuisset
possīmus	possēmus	potuerīmus	potuissēmus
possītis	possētis	potuerītis	potuissētis
possint	possent	potuerint	potuissent

A.2. SYNOPSES

a. cōgitō
Principal Parts **cōgitō, cōgitāre, cōgitāvī, cōgitātus**

	Indicative Mood	*Translation*	*Subjunctive Mood*
Present	**cōgitō**	I think	**cōgitem**
Imperfect	**cōgitābam**	I used to think	**cōgitārem**
Future	**cōgitābō**	I shall think	———
Perfect	**cōgitāvī**	I thought	**cōgitāverim**
Pluperfect	**cōgitāveram**	I had thought	**cōgitāvissem**
Future Perfect	**cōgitāverō**	I shall have thought	———

b. maneō
Principal Parts **maneō, manēre, manuī, mānsus**

	Indicative Mood	*Translation*	*Subjunctive Mood*
Present	**manēs**	you are waiting	**maneās**
Imperfect	**manēbās**	you were waiting	**manērēs**
Future	**manēbis**	you will wait	———
Perfect	**manuistī**	you waited	**manueris**
Pluperfect	**manuerās**	you had waited	**manuissēs**
Future Perfect	**manueris**	you will have waited	———

c. cōgō
Principal Parts **cōgō, cōgere, cōegī, coactus**

	Indicative Mood	*Translation*	*Subjunctive Mood*
Present	**cōgit**	he compels	**cōgās**
Imperfect	**cōgēbat**	he was compelling	**cōgerēs**
Future	**cōget**	he will compel	———
Perfect	**cōegit**	he has compelled	**coēgerit**
Pluperfect	**cōegerat**	he had compelled	**coēgisset**
Future Perfect	**cōegerit**	he will have compelled	———

d. iaciō
Principal Parts **iaciō, iacere, iēcī, iactus**

	Indicative Mood	*Translation*	*Subjunctive Mood*
Present	**iacimus**	we are throwing	**iaciāmus**
Imperfect	**iaciēbāmus**	we were throwing	**iacerēmus**
Future	**iaciēmus**	we shall throw	———
Perfect	**iēcimus**	we threw	**iēcerīmus**
Pluperfect	**iēcerāmus**	we had thrown	**iēcerāmus**
Future Perfect	**iēcerimus**	we shall have thrown	———

e. adsum
Principal Parts **adsum, adesse, adfuī, adfutūrus**

	Indicative Mood	*Translation*	*Subjunctive Mood*
Present	**adestis**	you (*pl.*) support	**adsītis**
Imperfect	**aderātis**	you were supporting	**adessētis**
Future	**aderitis**	you will support	———
Perfect	**adfuistis**	you supported	**adfuerītis**
Pluperfect	**adfuerātis**	you had supported	**adfuissētis**
Future Perfect	**adfueritis**	you will have supported	———

f. possum
Principal Parts **possum, posse, potuī, ———**

	Indicative Mood	*Translation*	*Subjunctive Mood*
Present	**possunt**	they are able	**possint**
Imperfect	**poterant**	they were able	**possent**

Future	**poterunt**	they will be able	————
Perfect	**potuērunt**	they were (have been) able	**potuerint**
Pluperfect	**potuerant**	they had been able	**potuissent**
Future Perfect	**potuerint**	they will have been able	————

A.3.

TENSE MARKERS AND PERSONAL ENDINGS, ACTIVE VOICE

INDICATIVE		*SUBJUNCTIVE*

Present Stem Ends in:

	1st conj.:	**ā**
	2nd conj.:	**ē**
	3rd conj.:	consonant stem
	3rd **iō**:	consonant stem
	4th conj.:	**ī**

Present tense: *personal endings:* ō, s, t, mus, tis, nt

1st conj.:	**ā**	1st conj.:	**ē**
2nd conj.:	**ē**	2nd conj.:	**e + ā**
3rd conj.:	shortened stem + **i**	3rd conj.:	shortened stem + **ā**
3rd **iō**:	shortened stem + **i**	3rd **iō**:	shortened stem + **iā**
(except 3rd pl: + **i** +**unt**)		————————	
4th conj.:	**ī**	4th conj.:	**iā**

Imperfect tense: *personal endings:* m, s, t, mus, tis, nt

		Present infinitive + personal endings:	
1st conj.:	**ābā**	1st conj.:	**ārē**
2nd conj.:	**ēbā**	2nd conj.:	**ērē**
3rd conj.:	**ēbā**	3rd conj.:	**erē**
3rd **iō**:	**iēbā**	3rd **iō**:	**erē**
4th conj.:	**iēbā**	4th conj.:	**īrē**

Future tense: *personal endings:* ō or m, s, t, mus, tis, nt

1st conj.:	**ābi**	*N*
2nd conj.:	**ēbi**	*O*
3rd conj.:	**ē**	*N*
3rd **iō**:	**iē**	*E*
4th conj.:	**iē**	

PERFECT STEM: varies: **āv-, ū-, s-** *lengthened stem; reduplicated stem*

INDICATIVE	*SUBJUNCTIVE*
Perfect Tense: perfect stem + *personal endings:* ī, istī, it, imus, istis, ērunt	**Perfect Tense:** perfect stem + **eri** + *personal endings:* m, s, t, mus, tis, nt
Pluperfect Tense: perfect stem + **erā** + *personal endings:* m, s, t, mus, tis, nt	**Pluperfect Tense:** perfect stem + **isse** + *personal endings:* m, s, t, mus, tis, nt
Future Perfect: perfect stem + **eri** *personal endings:* ō, s, t, mus, tis, nt	*N O N E*

B.4.

1. present contrary-to-fact: **essēs, nōn commendārem.**
2. present potential: **commendem/ commendāverim.**
3. past potential: **nōn commendārem.**
4. past contrary-to-fact: **fuissēs, mīsissem.**
5. general, future: **mittam, habēbis.**

6. ideal (less vivid): **mittam, habeās.**
7. ideal (less vivid): **mittam, habeās.**
8. past, contrary to fact: **nōn habuissēs, nisi mīsissem.**
9. past general: **sī vixī, (pater) erat/fuit (causa).**
10. past general: **mē dūcēbat, sī optābat/volēbat.**
11. ideal (less vivid): **mē dūcat, sī velit/optet.**

B.5.

1. It is enough for me if I am able to save your life and your reputation. (general condition, future indicative)
2. It would have been enough for me if I had been able to save your life and your reputation. (past contrary-to-fact, pluperfect subjunctive)
3. The student would not understand the poets if he should not/if he didn't learn the constellations and philosophy. (ideal/less vivid, present subjunctive)
4. I would avoid your vices/faults if I were able. (present contrary-to-fact, imperfect indicative).
5. If I should be able to avoid your vices/faults, I would be a great and good man, wouldn't I? (ideal/less vivid, present subjunctive)

C. Latin Vocabulary Quiz

traxerit	3rd sing. fut. perf. indic. or perf. subjunctive, *to drag*, **trahō, trahere, traxī, tractus**
extrahās	2nd sing. pres. subj., *to drag out*, **extrahō, extrahere, extraxī, extractus**
distrahēs	2nd sing. fut. indic., *to tear into pieces*, **distrahō, distrahere, distraxī, distractus**
dēlīberāverāmus	1st pl. plupf. indic., *consider carefully*, **dēlīberō, -āre, -āvī, -ātus**
cūrēmus	1st pl. pres. subj., *care for*, **cūrō, cūrāre, cūravī, cūrātus**
cōegērunt	3rd pl. perf. indic., *compel*, **cōgō, cōgere, coēgī, coāctus**
valeāmus	1st pl. pres. subj., *to be well*, **valeō, valēre, valuī, valitūrus**
iacit	3rd sing. pres. indic., *to throw*, **iaceō, iacēre, iacuī, iactus**
cēlāverit	3rd sing. fut. perf. indic. or perf. subj., *to cover, conceal*, **cēlō, cēlāre, cēlāvī, cēlātus**
crēdiderat	3rd sing. plpf. indic., *to believe*, **crēdō, crēdere, crēdidī crēditus**
laudāvisset	3rd sing. plpf. subj., *to praise*, **laudō, laudāre, laudāvī, laudātus**
mānserat	3rd sing. plpf. indic., *to remain*, **maneō, manēre, mānsī, mānsus**
remanēret	3rd sing. imperf. subj., *to remain*, **remaneō, remanēre, remānsī, remānsus**
remedia	nom. or acc. pl., *remedy, cure*, **remedium, -ī,** *n.*
integrum	accus. sing. masc., or nom. or accus. sing. neuter, *whole, untouched*, **integer, -gra, -grum**
aequum	accus. sing. masc., or nom. or accus. sing. neuter, *equal, fair*, **aequus, -a, -um**
equum	accus. sing. masc., *horse*, **equus, -ī,** *m.*
quantum	accus. sing. masc., or nom. or accus. sing. neuter, *how great*, **quantus, -a, -um**
invītum	accus. sing. masc., or nom. or accus. sing. neuter, *unwilling*, **invītus, -a, -um**
num	interrogative particle, expecting a negative answer
ad	preposition, with accusative, *to, towards*
ex	preposition, with ablative, *from, out of*
dē	preposition, with ablative, *from, down from, concerning*
-que	enclitic conjunction, *and*
-ne	enclitic interrogative particle, attaches to the end of the first word of a clause, asks a question.
cum	preposition, with accusative
tot	indeclinable adjective, *so many*
enim	postpositive conjunction, *for, indeed, for indeed, truly*
fortūnae	gen. sing., dat. sing., voc. sing., or nom. *pl., fortune*, **fortūna, fortūnae,** *f.*
nīl	indeclinable noun or adverb, shortened form of **nihil**, *nothing*
sententiam	acc. sing., *opinion*, **sententia, sententiae,** *f.*
audāciīs	abl. pl. or dat.pl., *courage, boldness*, **audācia, audāciae,** *f.*
nuptiīs	abl. pl. or dat. pl., *marriage*, **nuptiae, nuptiārum,** *f.*
modīs	abl. pl. or dat.pl., *manner, method, way*, **modus, modī,** *m.*

D. Terminology Review

1. **Protasis:** the "then" clause of a condition.
2. **Apodosis:** the "if" clause of a condition.
3. **Ideal condition:** present subjunctive in both clauses, translates "If... (I) should..., then... (I) would...
4. **Present contrary-to-fact condition:** imperfect subjunctive in both clauses, translates "If... (I) were..., then... (I) would..."
5. **Past contrary-to-fact condition:** pluperfect subjunctive in both clauses, translates "If... (I) had..., then... (I) would have..."
6. **Potential subjunctive:** Indicates the possibility of something happening, with the implicit "if" clause suppressed.
7. **Pluperfect tense:** equal to the English past perfect; took place before something in the past took place.
8. **Imperfect tense:** took place in the past or was happening in the past; not clear whether or not it was completed in the past.

E. Translation: Daedalus and Icarus

Daedalus wanted to depart from the island, Crete, but was not able to escape. Therefore he gathered many feathers and joined the feathers with wax, from the small ones to the large ones, so that he would fly above the waves. The child Icarus saw (this) and played in the wax, but he did not know (his) father's plan.

Then the father instructed Icarus, "Icarus, I order you to go in the middle so that the wave will not seize the feathers, if you should fly too low. If you should fly too high, the Sun would burn you. Seize the middle path with me!" He gives kisses to his son and flies before (him) and fears for the child. The father and the son were flying above the waves, but suddenly Icarus, eager for the sky, abandoned Daedalus. Too high, he took a path, and the Sun softened the wax, the chains (connections) of the feathers. He shakes (his) naked arms but the waves receive the child. The father, (who is now) not a father, said, "Icarus, Where are you?"

E.1.

1. If Icarus flies too high, the father will not be happy.	*simple future*
2. If Icarus should fly too high, the father would not be happy.	*ideal*
3. If Icarus were flying too high, the father would not be happy.	*present contrary-to-fact*
4. If Icarus had flown too high, the father would not have been happy.	*past contrary-to-fact*
5. The father would have been happy if Icarus had not flown too high.	*past contrary-to-fact*

E.2.

Potential Subjunctive

1. Father would have been happy.
2. Father would be happy.
3. Father would have been happy.
4. Father would be happy.
5. Icarus would not fly too low.
6. Icarus would not have flown too low.
7. Icarus would not fly too low.
8. Icarus would want to fly too high.
9. The Sun would melt the wax.
10. The Sun would melt the connections of the feathers.

VI
Relative Pronouns; Interrogative Pronouns; Questions; Sequence of Tenses; Volō, Nōlō, Mālō

A. English Grammar: That, Which, What, Who, Whom.

A.1. These words are often a source of confusion in English because they fall into a number of different grammatical categories and numbers, and if not used correctly there can be uncertainty as to what they refer to. *What* can be an adjective or a pronoun. It is always interrogative but it can be singular or plural:

What Daedalus made was *a pair* of wings.	(singular)
What Daedalus bound with wax *were feathers*.	(plural)

Which can be an interrogative adjective or pronoun, or a relative pronoun:

Which path did Icarus choose?	(interrogative adjective)
Which of the paths did Icarus choose?	(interrogative pronoun)
The path *which* Icarus chose was fatal.	(relative pronoun)
We know *which* path Icarus chose.	(interrogative adjective)

Who and *whom* are interrogative pronouns or relative pronouns:

Who flew too close to the sun?	(interrogative pronoun)
We know *who* flew too close to the sun.	(interrogative pronoun)
Icarus is the boy *who* flew too close to the sun.	(relative pronoun)

That can be an adjective, an adverb, a conjunction, or a relative pronoun:

That boy flew too close to the sun.	(adjective, singular)
Those wings disintegrated when the wax melted.	(adjective, plural)
He shouldn't have flown *that* high.	(adverb)
Daedalus made wings so *that* they could escape.	(conjunction)
Icarus discovered *that* the sun had melted the wax.	(conjunction)

As a relative pronoun, *that* is equivalent to *who, whom*, or *which*:

> The wings *that* (*which*) he had made disintegrated.
> The boy *that* (*who*) fell from the sky was Icarus.
> The boy *that* (*whom*) he saw falling was Icarus.

Whom is a declined form of English *who*, equivalent to any of the cases in Latin except the nominative (*of whom, to whom, whom* accusative, *with whom*). *Whom*, like *who*, can be singular or plural. *Whose* is the genitive singular or plural, used when the preposition *of* is omitted: *The man whose son fell from the sky was Daedalus. Of* should never be used with *whose* in English, since that would be equivalent to saying the same thing twice ("of whom of whom"). *That* and *which* do not decline in English.

A.2. Relative and Interrogative Pronouns in Latin

The main difference between a relative and and interrogative pronoun, in English as well as in Latin, is that an interrogative pronoun has no antecedent:

i. *Who* fell from the sky? (interrogative)
   Quis dē caelō cecidit?
ii. *What* fell from the sky? (interrogative)
   Quid dē caelō cecidit?
iii. The boy *who* fell from the sky was Icarus. (relative)
   Puer *qui* dē caelō cecidit erat Icarus.
iv. The boy *whom* he saw was Icarus. (relative)
   Puer *quem* vīdit erat Icarus.
v. The boy *whose* father was Daedalus fell from the sky. (relative)
   Puer *cuius* pater erat Daedalus dē caelō cecidit.

In the first example, the only thing that is known about the person who fell from the sky is that it was a single person, since *quis* is masculine or feminine. In the second example, it was a single *thing* that fell, since *quid* is neuter. An interrogative pronoun has no *antecedent* to refer back to.

In the last three examples, by contrast, the relative pronouns refer clearly back to the boy or **puer**, who is the antecedent. In example iii., he is the subject of **cecidit**, the verb of the relative clause, and hence is in the nominative case. In example iv., he is the direct object of **vīdit**, the verb of the relative clause, and so the relative pronoun is in the accusative case. In example v., the subject of the relative clause is his father, **pater**, and so the genitive case of the relative pronoun indicates the relationship between the **puer** and the **pater**.

A pronoun is one of several important means for subordinating one or more clauses within a sentence, producing a complex sentence with any number of subordinated clauses. Complex sentences with a number of subordinated clauses are know as *periodic sentences*. Although students are now encouraged to write short sentences with relatively few subordinated clauses, the ability to create fine periodic sentences and to use them at a rhetorically effective moment is a skill worth developing. Examine, for example, some of the great speeches of recent as well as earlier historical moments and you will find much of their power based in the judicious use of finely crafted, periodic sentences. In the following sentence relative pronouns subordinate a series of related statements will illustrate

Daedalus ...... | *created* **wings**
who was a great craftsman | in **which** he joined feathers with wax in order to escape from Crete.

Daedalus ...... | **alās** fecit
quī erat magnus artifex | **in quibus** pennās cērā iunxit ut ex insulā Crētā excēderet.

The first relative pronoun refers back to Daedalus. The second refers back to the wings, which are the direct object of **fēcit** and are therefore in the accusative case, plural, feminine gender.

> Relative prounouns always agree with their antecedent in number and gender, but their case is always determined by their function in their own clause.

A.3. a.

Decline the relative pronoun **qui, quae, quod** from memory:

	Singular			*Plural*		
	Masc.	Fem.	Neuter	Masc.	Fem.	Neuter
Nom.	_____	_____	_____	_____	_____	_____
Gen.	_____	_____	_____	_____	_____	_____
Dat.	_____	_____	_____	_____	_____	_____
Acc.	_____	_____	_____	_____	_____	_____
Abl.	_____	_____	_____	_____	_____	_____

A.3. b. Translate the italicized words into the correct Latin:

feathers:	**penna, ae**, *f.*
wing:	**ala, ae**, *f.*
wax:	**cēra, ae**, *f.*
wave:	**unda, ae**, *f.*

He arranged the *feathers,*_____ from the small ones, *which*_____ were on the bottom, to the large ones, *which* _____ he placed on the top, into the shape of a *wing,* _____ with *which* _____ he would fly above the waves. His child Icarus saw the *wings which* _____ his father was creating and played in the *wax,*_____ with *which* _____ his father was gluing the feathers, but he did not know his father's plan.

Then *Daedalus,*_____ who _____ had tested the wings himself, prepared his son to fly. Instructing his *son,*_____ *whom*_____ he had fitted with wings, he said, "Icarus, I warn you to follow the *path*_____ which_____ I take, midway between heaven and earth. If you fly too low, the *waves*_____ which _____ touch your wings will make them heavy, and if you fly too high, the Sun will burn them. Stick to my course!" He gave kisses to his *son,* _____ for *whom* _____ he trembled with fear.

B. Questions

Latin Interrogative Words. In Chapter VI of *Traditio* is a list of Latin interrogative words, words that "interrogate" or ask a question. Interrogative pronouns (*Who* did this? *What* are you reading? *Whose* dog is barking?) and interrogative adjectives (*Which* book are you reading? *Which* dog is barking?) are similar in form. Interrogative adjectives in Latin are the same as the relative pronouns. The interrogative pronoun does not ordinarily have separate feminine forms in the singular (although the ablative singular feminine sometimes does appear in manuscripts); and the nominative singular (**quis, quid**) and the accusative singular neuter (**quid**) have separate forms. Otherwise the forms are essentially the same.

There are some other interrogative adjectives which also appear as exclamatory adjectives or in correlative constructions: **Quantus, -a, -um** and **Quot** are good examples of this category. **Quantus** means *how great, how large.* It is equivalent in meaning to the exclamatory and interrogative adverb **quam,** *how!* plus **magnus**: *how great! how great? how large! how large?* Ordinarily, Latin will use **quantus** rather than **quam magnus**:

Quantus est Caesar? Quantus est Caesar!
How great is Caesar? or *How great Caesar is!*

Often **quantus** will be "correlated" or balanced with **tantus**:

> **Tantus erit Caesar quantās terrās vincet.**
>> Caesar will be *as great as* the lands he conquers.

Quot, which can also be interrogative or exclamatory, means *how many*, and is often correlated with **tot**, *so many*:

> **Quot pennās alīs erant, tot dē caelō cecidērunt.**
>> As *many* feathers *as* his wings had fell from the sky.

Interrogative Adverbs. The English question mark (with inverted word order) would fit into this category. The Latin enclitic **-ne**, which is attached to the end of the first word in a question, would be the equivalent of the inverted order plus question mark in English. **Nōnne** and **num** (at the beginning of a clause) expect a positive and a negative answer, respectively. Closely related to the enclitic **-ne** is an, which appears at the beginning of a clause, sometimes alone, at other times paired with **-ne**. A double question can also be introduced by **utrum**, paired with **an**:

> **Poteratne Icarus volāre?**   (a simple question)
>> *Was Icarus able to fly?*

> **An Icarus volāre poterat?**   (a simple question)
>> *Was Icarus able to fly?*

> **Daedalusne an Icarus volāre poterat?**   (a double question)
>> *Was Daedalus or Icarus able to fly?*

> **Utrum Daedalus an Icarus volāre poterat?**   (a double question)
>> *Was Daedalus or Icarus able to fly?*

> **Nōnne Icarus volāre poterat?**   (expecting a "yes" answer)
>> *Icarus was able to fly, wasn't he?*

> **Num Icarus volāre poterat?**   (expecting a "no" answer)
>> *Icarus wasn't able to fly, was he?*

The question *Why?* is expressed by **cūr**, **quāre**, or **quam ob rem**.

> **Cūr Icarus volāvit?**   *Why did Icarus fly?*
> **Quāre cecidit?**   *Why did he fall?*

How? is expressed by a phrase which means "in what manner":

> **Quō modo alās fēcit?**   *How did he make wings?*

Ubi? asks *Where?* and **Unde?** *From where? When?* is asked by **quandō**? It should be noted, however, that when these three words are not used in a question, they function as relative conjunctions:

ubi   *where?* or (*at the time*) *when, at the place where*

> Ubi Icarus cecidit?   *Where did Icarus fall?*
> Ubi Icarus cecidit, Daedalus lacrimāvit.   *When Icarus fell, Daedalus wept.*

quandō   *when?* or (*at the time*) *when*

> Quandō tē vidēbō?   *When will I see you?*
> Quandō tē vidēbō, laetus erō.   *When I see you I will be happy.*

unde   *from where?* or (*the place*) *from where*

> Unde vēnisti?   *From where did you come?*
> Locum unde vēnērunt est Crēta.   *The place they came from is Crete.*

B.1. Decline the interrogative pronoun from memory: **quis, quid**

	Singular		Plural		
	M. & F.	Neuter	Masc.	Fem.	Neuter
Nom.	_____	_____	_____	_____	_____
Gen.	_____	_____	_____	_____	_____
Dat.	_____	_____	_____	_____	_____
Acc.	_____	_____	_____	_____	_____
Abl.	_____	_____	_____	_____	_____

B.2. Translate the following questions, and indicate whether the interrogative word is a pronoun, adjective, or adverb:

1. Quid fēcit Daedalus?
2. Quot pennās parvās in alīs Daedalus posuit?
3. Quantās pennās in alīs Daedalus posuit?
4. Quandō Daedalus alās fēcit?
5. Quis alās fēcit?
6. Cui puerō alās fēcit?
7. Unde vēnērunt Daedalus et Icarus?
8. Quō modo pater alās feit?

Direct, Deliberative, and Indirect Questions. In English, direct questions can begin with an interrogative word or with an inversion of word order of a direct statement, usually by moving the verb to the beginning of the sentence:

Who is my friend?	(interrogative word)
Why are you here?	(interrogative word)
Are you my friend?	(inverted word order) (direct statement: you are my friend)
Are you here?	(inverted word order) (direct statement: you are here)

Direct questions in Latin are also introduced by interrogative words. Since word order is not as important in Latin as in English, inverted word order in Latin is not suffficent to indicate a question. Hence Latin will frequently use the enclitic **-ne** or the alternative constructions listed above to indicate that a question is being asked:

Quis est amīcus meus?

Cūr vēnistī?

Amīcus*ne* meus es?

Vēnistī*ne*?

Deliberative questions, in English and in Latin, are also known as *rhetorical questions*, since they ask a question which doesn't really anticipate an answer.

What could Daedalus do?

Would any father have acted differently?

Where could he go?

In Latin, the verb of a deliberative question will be in the subjunctive. The present subjunctive reflects what is happening in the present or future, rather like the verb of an ideal condition, which is also in the present subjunctive even though it refers to something (albeit unlikely) in the future.

Quid Daedalus faciat?	*What can Daedalus do?*
Num alius pater aliter agat?	*Would any father act differently?* (**aliter**, adv., differently)
Ubi cēdat?	*Where would he go?*

If the question is referring to something in the past, the verb will be in the imperfect:

Quid Daedalus faceret?	*What could he have done?*
Num alius pater aliter ageret?	*Would any father have acted differently?*
Ubi cēderet?	*Where could he have gone?*

The tenses of the deliberative subjunctive, as you can see, follow the same pattern that the tenses of the potential subjunctive follow:

	Present action	Past action
Deliberative subjunctive	present subj.	imperfect subj.
Potential subjunctive	present subj.	imperfect subj.

Like the potential subjunctive, the negative of the deliberative subjunctive is also expressed by **nōn**.

Indirect Questions. Any question, statement, or command can be subordinated, so that it becomes an indirect question, an indirect statement, or an indirect command. In this chapter you are working with indirect questions. In chapter VII you will work with indirect statements, and in chapter XIII you will encounter indirect commands. One rule which you will encounter repeatedly in working with subordinated clauses is the rule of sequence of tenses, which applies to every subjunctive verb in a dependent clause. Study carefully the explanation in Chapter VI of the complete rule of sequence of tenses. The basic distinction to make is between primary sequence and secondary sequence:

If the main verb is in the *present* or *future* tense, it governs *primary sequence* in the subordinated clause, and if it is in a *past* tense, it governs *secondary sequence* in the subordinated clause.

How to recognize an indirect question? Basically, a subordinated clause which begins with an interrogative word will be an indirect question. Do not confuse indirect questions with relative clauses, whose introducing pronoun always has an antecedent: an interrogative word has no antecedent. Compare:

How many feathers fell?	(direct question)
I know *how many feathers fell.*	(indirect question)
I saw the feathers *which fell.*	(relative clause)

In Latin:

Quot pennae cecidērunt?	(direct question)
Sciō *quot pennae ceciderint.*	(indirect question, primary sequence)
Scīvī *quot pennae cecidissent.*	(indirect question, secondary sequence)
Vīdī pennās *quae cecidērunt.*	(relative clause)

B.3. Translate the following sentences, which are based on the new vocabulary (Verba Tenenda) in Chapter VI, and indicate whether the sentence contains a direct question, a deliberative question, an indirect question, or no question.

1. Quid est remedium cūrae?
2. Agitābō mēcum quid sit remedium.
3. Scīsne remedium quod petō?
4. Nesciō quod remedium petitūrus sīs.
5. Quis sciat tantum remedium?
6. Quis scīret tantum remedium?
7. Num quis tantum remedium invenīre possit?
8. Tantumne remedium invenīre velis?
9. Rogāvī quis cūrās malās āmittere māllet.
10. Meminī quantās cūrās Aenēās habēret. (**Aenēas**, hero of Vergil's epic poem, the *Aeneid*)

11. In hōc lūdō discēs quid sit sapientia et quid sit vitium.

12. Puer rogavit quae essent elementa.

13. Ibi līberī ēlementa canticō didicēbant.

14. Paedagōgus puerīs, quandō quantum esset ūnus et ūnus nesciēbant, aderat.

15. Scīsne fābulam dē Arachnē?

16. Fābulam nesciō, sed quid dē Arachnē nōveris audīre velim.

17. Nesciō quam fābulam dēclāmātūrus sīs.

C. Irregular Verbs: Volō, Nōlō, Mālō

Identify the following forms and change to the present indicative, retaining the person and number of the original, and translate the present indicative form.

	Form	Pres. Indic.	Translation
1. velim			
2. nōlueris			
3. voluisset			
4. māluissēmus			
5. māluit			
6. māluerās			
7. vīs			
8. mālēmus			
9. vōletis			
10. vellēs			
11. nōllem			
12. voluerātis			

D. Derivations

Using a dictionary, indicate from which Latin words the following English words are derived:

English	Latin source	Latin Meaning	Meaning of English Word
amiss			
declamation			
defamatory			
delicious			
describe			
didactic			
dignitary			
disputatious			
dissolution			
exercise			
fame			

formative			
impurities			
interrogate			
laboratory			
mutation			
nonfiction			
ostentatious			
proposal			
scripture			
scholarly			
sedentary			
unnatural			
vicinity			
vitiate			
volition			

E. New Terminology

Define or explain the following terms:

1. relative pronoun
2. antecedent
3. future active participle
4. interrogative pronoun
5. relative clause
6. indirect question
7. rhetorical question
8. interrogative adverbs
9. primary sequence
10. secondary sequence

F. Translation

ARACHNE AND MINERVA

Arachne was an unusually skilled weaver. So great was her skill that Minerva herself, the goddess of arts and skills, came disguised as an old woman, to see what Arachne was weaving. "You must have been taught by Minerva herself," said the old woman. Arachne was offended at the suggestion that she had been taught by anyone, no matter how great that teacher might be. "Let Minerva come and contend with me!" she exclaimed. "I will defeat her!"

But the old woman said to Arachne, "Some things that come with old age are desirable: we grow more experienced with advancing years. Take my advice: be satisfied to be called the best mortal weaver, but yield to the goddess, and apologize for your words. She will forgive you if you ask."

Arachne rudely rejected her warnings. "I don't need the advice of an old lady. I can take care of myself. Why doesn't Pallas come and accept my challenge?" "She has come!" cried the goddess, throwing off her disguise. Others trembled, but Arachne was not frightened.

Immediately the two began their contest. Minerva wove a tapestry with stories telling how she had defeated Mars in order to become the deity of Athens. She showed humans who were now icy mountains, and others who were now birds, and others who were now a temple. They had been punished for their insults to the gods.

Arachne wove a tapestry with stories showing how the gods deceived mortals: Europa and Antiope and Leda and Danae were Jupiter's victims. Neptune and Apollo were there, too. Minerva could find no fault in the tapestry. With anger and jealousy she destroyed the tapestry which showed the crimes of the gods and she struck Arachne. Arachne, miserable, placed a noose around her neck to hang herself, but Minerva took pity on her. She sprinkled Arachne with the juice of Hekate's herb, and immediately Arachne's hair, and ears, and nose dropped off. Her head shrank to almost nothing and her whole body became tiny. Her fingers were attached to her sides, as legs, and the rest of her was belly. From her belly she now spins her thread and is busy with her web, as a spider.

Special Vocabulary:

antīquus, -a, -um old, ancient
Arachnē (nominative); **Arachnēs** (genitive); **Arachnem** (accusative), *f.*
    the mortal spinstress, Arachne
arānea, -ae, *f.* spider
aureus, -a, -um, golden, gold-colored
contendō, -ere, contendī, contentus, compete, contend
dea, -ae, *f.* goddess
deus, -ī, *m.* god
fīlum, -ī, *n.* thread, yarn
fulvus, -a, -um, reddish-yellow
lāna, -ae, f. wool
lānaria, -ī, *m.* worker in wool
lānificus, -a, -um, working in wool
Minerva, -ae, *f.* ,The goddess Minerva (equivalent to the Greek goddess Pallas Athena)
nimis, adverb, too much, excessively
rubeus, -a, -um, red
tēla, -ae, *f.* web, tapestry

Translate the following sentences and explain why the bold verbs are in the subjunctive mood.

1. Dea Minerva quō modo Arachnē **florēret** audīvit.

2. Minerva vēnit ut **vidēret** quid **faceret** Arachnē.

3. "Es bona lānaria," dixit fēmina antīqua, et rogāvit quis Arachnem **docuisset**.

4. Fēmina antīqua rogat Minervane Arachnem **instituerit**.

5. Fēmina antīqua rogābat quis Arachnem **instituisset**.

6. Fēmina antīqua rogābit ubi Arachnē lānarius esse **didicerit**.

7. Nūlla dea nec alter magister mē instituit quō modo tēlam meam **factūra essem**.

8. Minerva **veniat** ut **videat** quam pulchram tēlam facere **possim**!

9. Ubi Arachnē rogāvit cūr Minerva nōn **venīret**, Dea dixit, "Advēnit!"

10. Aliī timuērunt, sed Arachnē et Minerva contendere **incēpērunt**.

11. Quis fila fulva rubeaque aureaque imbuerat quae et Dea et Arachnē **lēgērunt**?

12. Nesciō quis fīla **imbuerit**.

13. Quis fābulās quās Minerva scrīpsit nōn **sciat**?

14. Num Arachnē sciēbat quid Minerva saevīs fābulīs **monēret**?

15. Arachnē in tēlā scrīpsit quō modo deī hūmānōs miserōs **lūsissent**.

16. Tēla Arachnēs erat nimis pulchra, nimis bona.

17. Invidia Minervam cēpit quandō tēlam fēminae parvae vīdit, et fēminam pulsāvit, et dē fēminā in arāneam mūtāvit.

18. Nunc cēteram Arachnem venter (*venter*, nom. sing., *belly*) habet, dē quō fīlum mittit, et antīquās exercet arānea tēlās.

Key, Chapter VI

A.3. a.

	Singular M.	F.	N.	Plural M.	F.	N.
Nom.	quī	quae	quod	quī	quae	quae
Gen.	cuius	cuius	cuius	quōrum	quārum	quōrum
Dat.	cui	cui	cui	quibus	quibus	quibus
Acc.	quem	quam	quod	quōs	quās	quae
Abl.	quō	quā	quō	quibus	quibus	quibus

A.3. b.

He arranged the *feathers* (**pennās**) from the small ones, *which* (**quae**) were on the bottom, to the large ones, *which* (**quās**) he placed on the top, into the shape of a *wing* (**alae**) with *which* (**quā**) he would fly above the waves. His child Icarus saw the *wings* (**alās**) *which* (**quās**) his father was creating and played in the *wax* (**in cerā**) with *which* (**quā**) his father was gluing the feathers, but he did not know his father's plan.

Then Daedalus, *who* (**quī**) had tested the wings himself, prepared his son to fly. Instructing his *son* (**fīlium**), *whom* (**quem**) he had fitted with wings, he said, "Icarus, I warn you to follow the *path* (**viam**) *which* (**quam**) I take, midway between heaven and earth. If you fly too low, the *waves* (**undae**) *which* (**quae**) touch your wings will make them heavy, and if you fly too high, the Sun will burn them. Stick to my course!" He gave kisses to his *son* (**fīliō**), for *whom* (**cui**) he trembled with fear.

B.1.

	Singular M.& F.	N.	Plural M.	F.	N.
Nom.	quī	quid	quī	quae	quae
Gen.	cuius	cuius	quōrum	quārum	quōrum
Dat.	cui	cui	quibus	quibus	quibus
Acc.	quem	quid	quōs	quās	quae
Abl.	quō	quō	quibus	quibus	quibus

B.2.

1. *What* did Daedalus do? (pronoun)
2. *How many* little feathers did Daedalus put in the wings? (adjective),
3. *How large* (were the) feathers Daedalus put in the wings? (adjective)
4. *When* did Daedalus make the wings? (adverb)
5. *Who* made the wings? (pronoun)
6. For *which* child (boy) did he make the wings? (adjective)
7. *From where* did Daedalus and Icarus come? (adverb)
8. *How* did the father make the wings? (adverb)

B.3.

1. What is the remedy for care? (direct question)
2. I will deliberate what the remedy is. (indirect question)
3. Do you know the remedy I seek? (direct question + relative clause)
4. I don't know what remedy you will seek. (indirect question)
5. Who could know such an important remedy? (deliberative question, present action)
6. Who would have known such an important remedy? (deliberative question, past action)
7. Surely no one could find such an important remedy, could he? (deliberative question, present action)
8. Would you like to discover such an important remedy? (deliberative question, present action)
9. I asked who would prefer to lose bad problems/cares. (indirect question)
10. I remember what great cares Aeneas had. (indirect question)

11. In this school you will learn what wisdom is and what vice is. (indirect questions)
12. The child asked what the letters of the alphabet were. (indirect question)
13. There, children used to learn the alphabet by means of a song. (direct statement)
14. The child attendant used to help children when they did not know how much one plus one was. (indirect question)
15. Do you know the story about Arachne? (direct question)
16. I don't know the story, but I would like to hear what you know about Arachne. (indirect question),
17. I don't know what story you are about to tell/declaim. (indirect question)

C. IRREGULAR VERBS: VOLŌ, NŌLŌ, MĀLŌ

		Form	Pres. Indic.	Translation
1.	velim	1st sing.pres.subj.	volō	I am willing
2.	nōlueris	2nd sing. perf. subj	nōn vīs	You are not willing (or fut. perf. indic.)
3.	voluisset	3rd sing.plpf. subj.	vult	he is not willing
4.	māluissēmus	1st pl. plpf. subj.	mālumus	we prefer
5.	māluit	3rd sing. perf. indic.	māvult	he prefers
6.	māluerās	2nd sing. plpf. indic.	māvīs	you prefer
7.	vīs	2nd sing. pres. indic.	vīs	you are willing
8.	mālēmus	1st pl. fut. indic.	mālumus	we prefer
9.	volētis	2nd pl. fut. indic.	vultis	you will be willing
10.	vellēs	2nd sing. imperf. subj.	vīs	you are willing
11.	nōllem	1st sing. imperf. subj.	nōn volō	I am not willing
12.	voluerātis	2nd pl. plpf. indic.	vultis	you are willing

D. DERIVATION

English	Latin source	Latin Meaning	Meaning of English Word
amiss	āmittere	to lose	out of proper order, wrongly
declamation	dēclāmāre	to make a speech	art of declaiming; speech
defamatory	fāma	rumor	slander or libel
delicious	dēliciae	delights	full of delights
describe	scrībere	to write	to give an account of
didactic	discere	to learn	instructive
dignitary	dignus	worthy	one who holds a high rank
disputatious	disputāre	argue	argumentative
dissolution	solvere	loosen, weaken	breaking up into parts or elements
exercise	exerceō	to train, exercise	movement for the purpose of training
fame	fāma	rumor	widespread reputation
formative	formāre	to give shape to	giving form or shape
impurities	pūrus	clean, honest, undefiled	that which makes impure
interrogate	rogāre	ask	ask a series of questions
laboratory	laborare	to work	place where work is done
mutation	mūtāre	to change	a change
non-fiction	fictus	false	literature based on truth
ostentatious	ostendere	to show	intended to attract notice
proposal	prōpōnere	to propose	an offer, a plan proposed
scripture	scrībere	to write	the sacred writings of the Old and New Testament
scholarly	schola	school	befitting a learned person
sedentary	sedēre	to sit	characterized by a seated posture
unnatural	nātūra	nature	not in keeping with nature
vicinity	vicīnus	neighbor	the area or neighborhood
vitiate	vitium	fault	to impair the quality of
volition	velle	to be willing	act of determining by the will

E. NEW TERMINOLOGY

1. *relative pronoun* — subordinates a clause. Its person and number agree with its antecedent, and its case is determined by its position within its own clause (the man *who* did this).
2. *antecedent* — the word to which the relative pronoun refers (the man who did this).
3. *future active participle* — translates "about to (do something)"; it is formed from the stem of the fourth principal part of the verb , to which **ūrus** is added (**doct + ūrus**), and is frequently used in indirect questions when the subordinated question was in the future tense (**Nescīvī quis mē doctūrus esset.** *I didn't know who was going to teach me*).
4. *interrogative pronoun* — introduces a question, has no antecedent (*who* did this?).
5. *relative clause* — always a dependent clause, describing its antecedent (the man *who* did this).
6. *indirect question* — a dependent clause which is a subordinated question (I know *who* did this).
7. *rhetorical question* — a question which does not anticipate a reply (*Who* could do this?).
8. *interrogative adverb* — an adverb which introduces a question (*How* did he do this?).
9. *primary sequence* — present and perfect subjunctive in subordinate clauses when the main verb is in the present or future tense).
10. *secondary sequence* — imperfect and pluperfect subjunctive in subordinate clauses when the main verb is in a past tense).

F. TRANSLATION: ARACHNE AND MINERVA

1. The goddess Minerva heard how Arachne was flourishing. **florēret** (indirect question)
2. Minerva came to see what Arachne was doing. **vidēret** (purpose), **faceret** (indirect question)
3. "You are a good wool-worker," said the aged woman, and she asked who had taught Arachne. **docuisset** (indirect question)
4. The old woman asks whether Minerva taught Arachne. **instituerit** (indirect question)
5. The old woman asked whether Minerva taught Arachne. **instituisset** (indirect question)
6. The old woman will ask where Arachne learned to be a wool worker. **didicerit** (indirect question)
7. No goddess or other teacher taught me how I would make my tapestry. **factūra essem** (indirect question)
8. Let Minerva come to see how beautiful a tapestry I can make! **veniat** (jussive) **videat** (purpose) **possim** (indirect question)
9. When Arachne asked why Minerva was not coming, the Goddess said, "She has come!" **venīret** (indirect question)
10. The others were afraid, but Arachne and Minerva began to compete (to have their contest). (no subjunctive)
11. Who had dyed the threads which both the Goddess and Arachne chose yellow-red and red and golden-colored? (no subjunctive)
12. I don't know who dyed the threads. **imbuerit** (indirect question)
13. Who would not know the stories which Minerva depicted (wrote)? **sciat** (deliberative subjunctive)
14. Arachne did not know, did she, what Minerva was advising with her cruel tales? **monēret**, (indirect question)
15. Arachne depicted on her tapestry how the Gods had made sport of unhappy mortals. **lūsisset**, (indirect question)
16. Arachne's tapestry was too beautiful, too good. (no subjunctive)
17. Envy seized Minerva when she saw the web of a mere woman, and she struck the woman and changed her from a woman into a spider. (no subjunctive)
18. Now the belly has the rest of Arachne, from which (from the belly) she sends out her thread and as a spider works her ancient tapestry.

VII
Pronouns;
Genitive Case;
Indirect Statement

A. Pronouns

A Pronoun, as you have learned, is used in place of a noun. It has the same gender, case, and number as the noun it is replacing. In Chapter VI you learned Latin relative pronouns and interrogative pronouns. In this chapter you will learn the remaining forms of the personal pronouns (I, we, you singular and plural), third person pronouns (**is, ea, id,** *he, she, it,* plural, *they*) and the related adjectives.

Personal Pronouns refer to the first and second person. There is no third person personal pronoun except the reflexive **sē.** Personal pronouns are used in the nominative case only for emphasis. Thus, if the philosopher Descartes had wanted to emphasis his own existence rather than the mere fact that he did exist, he probably would have said, **"Cōgitō, ergo ego sum!"** (*I think, therefore I exist!*) instead of **"Cōgitō, ergo sum."** Compare the effect of using the personal pronoun, nominative case in the following:

> Scīvistī, vīdistī, et tamen id fēcistī!
>
> **Tū** scīvistī, **tū** vīdistī, et **tū** tamen id fēcistī!
>
> **You** *knew it,* **you** *saw it,* and *nevertheless* **you** *did it*!
>
> Sumus quī īnfantiam dēliciīs solvimus.
> > (More Latinate: Infantiam dēliciīs solvimus.)
>
> **Nōs** sumus quī īnfantiam dēliciis solvimus.
>
> **We** *are the ones who weaken infancy with pleasure.*

Third person pronouns are often used to fill the need for a third person personal pronoun. Compare:

> Scīvit, vīdit, et tamen id fēcit!
>
> **Is** scīvit, **is** vīdit, et **is** tamen id fēcit!
>
> **He** *knew it,* **he** *saw it,* and *nevertheless* **he** *did it*!
>
> Sunt quī īnfantiam dēliciīs solvunt.
>
> **Eī** sunt quī īnfantiam dēliciīs solvunt.
> > (More Latinate: Ei īnfantiam deliciis solvunt.)
>
> **They** *are the ones who weaken infancy with pleasure.*

Notice that the shorter version, once the nominative pronoun is omitted, is more characteristic of Latin than the version beginning **sumus quī** or **sunt quī**, both of which would tend to trigger a subjunctive construction which you will encounter in Chapter IX.

These third person pronouns are frequently categorized as *demonstrative* pronouns because they *show* or *demonstrate*, that is, they point something out: *this* man, *that* woman, *these* things.

> **Minerva *eam* monuit, quae nōn audīvit.**
> Minerva warned *her*, who did not listen. (pronoun)

> **Minerva *eam* fēminam monuit, quae nōn audīvit.**
> Minerva warned *that* woman (or *this* woman), who did not listen. (adjective)

Notice that **is, ea, id** can be translated either *this* or *that*; it is not as strong a demonstrative as those you will learn later (these demonstratives in Chapter IX are not at all ambiguous about where they are pointing, as you will see). **is, ea,** and **id** are often midway in demonstrative strength between a very pointed *this here* or *that there*, on the one hand, and, on the other hand, the definite article in English (*the* woman). Latin, as you know, does not have a definite or indefinite (*a* woman) article, but when a need is felt for one, Latin will use this third person demonstrative pronoun for that purpose.

> **Ubi tēlam *eius* vīdit, Minerva invidiam sēnsit.**
> When she saw *her* web, Minerva felt envy.

> **Dea *eam* pulsāvit.**
> The goddess struck *her*.

Notice that, in the first example, **eius** cannot be mistaken as referring to Minerva's web. If the author wanted to refer to the web of the subject of the main clause, it would be necessary to use *a reflexive adjective* instead:

> **Ubi tēlam *suam* vīdit, Minerva invidiam sēnsit.**
> When she saw the (*her own*) web, Minerva felt envy.

A *reflexive pronoun* or a *reflexive adjective* always refers back to the subject of the main verb.

> **Nōs sumus quī *nōs* deliciīs nostrīs solvimus.**
> We are the ones who weaken *ourselves* with our pleasures.

> **Narcissus *sē* vīdit sed nōn vīdit.**
> Narcissus saw *himself* but he did not understand (he did not *see* that he saw himself).

> *Graeca ancilla* animum puerī fābulīs imbuit.
> A *Greek servant* fills the child's mind with stories.(noun)

> *Ea* animum puerī fābulīs imbuit.
> *She* fills the child's mind with stories   (pronoun)

> *Ea ancilla* animum puerī fābulīs imbuit.
> *That servant* fills the child's mind with stories   (demonstrative adjective)

> *Quae ancilla* animum eius fābulīs imbuit?
> *What servant* fills his mind with stories?   (interrogative adjective)

A.1. Write out from memory the following forms:

quī, quae, quod   (Meaning: _____)

	singular			plural		
	M	F	N	M	F	N
Nom.	_____	_____	_____	_____	_____	_____
Gen.	_____	_____	_____	_____	_____	_____
Dat.	_____	_____	_____	_____	_____	_____
Acc.	_____	_____	_____	_____	_____	_____
Abl.	_____	_____	_____	_____	_____	_____

quis, quid   (Meaning: _____)

	singular			plural	
	M. & F.	N		M	F	N

	M. & F.	N		M	F	N
Nom.	_____	_____		_____	_____	_____
Gen.	_____	_____		_____	_____	_____
Dat.	_____	_____		_____	_____	_____
Acc.	_____	_____		_____	_____	_____
Abl.	_____	_____		_____	_____	_____

is, ea, id   (Meaning: _____)

	singular			plural		
	M	F	N	M	F	N
Nom.	_____	_____	_____	_____	_____	_____
Gen.	_____	_____	_____	_____	_____	_____
Dat.	_____	_____	_____	_____	_____	_____
Acc.	_____	_____	_____	_____	_____	_____
Abl.	_____	_____	_____	_____	_____	_____

ego, tū, nōs, vōs   (Meaning: _____)

	singular			plural		
	M	F	N	M	F	N
Nom.	_____	_____	_____	_____	_____	_____
Gen.	_____	_____	_____	_____	_____	_____
Dat.	_____	_____	_____	_____	_____	_____
Acc.	_____	_____	_____	_____	_____	_____
Abl.	_____	_____	_____	_____	_____	_____

sē   (Meaning: _____)

Gen.	_____
Dat.	_____
Acc.	_____
Abl.	_____

A.2. Supply the correct form of the pronouns or adjectives listed to replace or modify each of the following nouns.

Noun	Pronouns	Adjectives
	quī, quis, is.	**quī, medius, novus, ignōtus, suus.**
Example:		
nautam:	quem, quem, eum.	quem; medium; novum; ignōtum; suum.
ingeniī		_____

88

persōnae (*nom*) _____

benevolentiīs _____

lētō (*abl*) _____

ōtia _____

negōtia _____

oculō (*dat*) _____

oculō (*abl*) _____

grammaticīs _____

factīs _____

officiō (*abl*) _____

populō (*dat*) _____

populō (*abl*) _____

glōriae (*gen*) _____

glōriae (*nom*) _____

glōriae (*dat*) _____

A.3. Indicate whether the following are pronouns or adjectives, and identify the case, number and, where possible, the gender:

		Pronoun or Adj.	*Case*	*Number*	*Gender*
1.	vōbīs				
2.	vestrī				
3.	vestrum				
4.	vestra				
5.	vōs				
6.	vestrōs				
7.	meī				
8.	nōs				
9.	nostrum				
10.	nostrōrum				
11.	nostrīs				
12.	nōbīs				
13.	suus				
14.	meīs				
15.	mē				
16.	sibi				
17.	suōs				
18.	suīs				
19.	sē				
20.	suō				

A.4. Translate the following sentences, and then replace the nouns indicated with the correct Latin pronouns:

1. Sic animum **discipulae nostrae** instituāmus.

2. Animus discipulae **impudīca verba** nē discat.

3. Animus eius erret sī **cantica mundī** cognoscat.

4. **Quae cantica** cognoscere dēbet?

5. Fac litterās buxeās et **eīs litterīs** nōmina da.

    (**buxeus, a, um**, *made of box-wood*)

A.5. Translate the following sentences into Latin; the underlined word should be translated as a pronoun or adjective.

1. <u>What</u> did <u>she</u> learn?

2. <u>What</u> letters did <u>she</u> learn?

3. <u>To what</u> school did her father send <u>her</u>?

4. The school <u>to which her</u> father sent her was good.

5. <u>What</u> was the song <u>by means of which we</u> learned the alphabet?

A.6. The Genitive Case. Indicate (a) whether the genitive called for in the underlined words is possessive (pos), objective (obj), partitive (part), or descriptive (desc), (b) whether the underlined word is a noun (n), pronoun (pron), or adjective (adj), and (c) if it is a pronoun, translate it into Latin.

1. Minerva wove a tapestry <u>of great beauty</u>, which showed examples <u>of mortals</u> who failed to acknowledge the <u>gods'</u> superiority.

2. In one corner of <u>Arachne's tapestry</u>, Jupiter was victimizing Europa.

3. In another corner, she showed the victimization <u>of Leda</u>, not yet the mother <u>of Apollo and Diana</u>.

4. Some <u>of the pictures</u> in her web showed Apollo in a <u>hawk's</u> feathers, in a <u>lion's</u> skin, or in a <u>shepherd's</u> outfit.

5. On the outer edge of <u>her tapestry</u>, Arachne wove flowers intertwined with bunches <u>of ivy</u>.

6. Minerva embroidered the edges of <u>her tapestry</u> with olives, the symbol of <u>peace</u>.

7. Minerva sprinkled Arachne with the juice of <u>Hekate's herb</u>.

8. Immediately, at the touch <u>of this herb</u>, the <u>girl's</u> hair dropped off, and <u>her</u> nostrils and <u>her</u> ears fell away, and <u>her</u> head shrank.

9. <u>Her</u> whole body became tiny. <u>Her</u> slender fingers were fastened to <u>her</u> sides, and served as legs, and all the rest <u>of her</u> was belly.

10. From <u>her</u> belly, she now spins <u>her</u> thread, and as a spider is busy with <u>her</u> web as <u>of old</u>.

11. Arachne knew <u>her</u> web was perfect. Minerva felt great jealousy for <u>Arachne's skill</u>, but pity for <u>Arachne</u>.

12. Does any one <u>of you</u> not feel pity <u>for Arachne</u>?

13. It is true she had too much <u>pride</u>.

14. What is the proper limit <u>of pride</u> and of <u>humility</u>?

B. Indirect Statement

Indirect Statement occurs when a direct statement is subordinated to a verb of saying, thinking, believing, etc. The subordinating verb is not necessarily an indicator, however, as to whether the subordinated sentence will be an indirect statement or an indirect question (or an indirect command, which you will learn later). Compare:

1. Direct Statement:

These mortals were wicked.
    Eī hūmānī malī erant.

Indirect Statement:

Minerva's tapestry showed that *these mortals were wicked.*
    Tela Minervae ostendit eos **hūmānōs malōs esse.**

2. Direct Question:

Who was wicked?
    Quī malus erat.

Indirect Question:

Minerva's tapestry showed *who was wicked.*
    Tēla Minervae ostendit quīs **malus esset.**

Notice that the verb *showed* can introduce either an indirect question or an indirect statement. The direct question and the indirect question are both introduced by an interrogative word (*who?*).

The indirect statement is frequently introduced in English by *that*. The core construction of indirect statement is the accusative subject and the infinitive verb. If there is a subordinate clause *within* the subordinated, indirect statement, the verb of the subordinate clause ordinarily will be in the subjunctive mood, even though it was in the indicative mood in the original, direct, statement. Notice also that the rule of sequence of tenses governs the tense of the verb in the subordinated verb within an indirect statement:

Direct Statement:

Mortals *who did not love the gods* were wicked.
    Hūmānī **quī deōs nōn amābant** malī erant.

Indirect Statement:

Minerva's tapestry showed that *mortals who did not love the gods* were wicked.
    Tēla Minervae ostendit **hūmānōs quī deōs nōn amārent** malōs esse.

B.1. Translate the following sentences, and then subordinate them as indicated, so that they become indirect statement.

Special Vocabulary:

Jupiter	**Iuppiter** (*nom. m.sing.*) **Iovis** (*gen.*), **Iovem** (*acc.*),
bull	**taurus, ī,** *m.*
tapestry, web	**tēla, ae,** *f.*
Europa	**Eurōpa, ae,** *f.* (Europa was persuaded to sit on the back of the bull, which was Jupiter in disguise; the bull then ran off with her to Crete).
Minerva	**Minerva, ae,** *f.*

Example:

Iuppiter in taurum sē mutat.

translation: Jupiter is changing himself into a bull.

Tēla hūmānae puellae ostendit: *Iovem in taurum sē mūtāre.*

1. Iuppiter in taurum sē mūtāvit ut Eurōpam captāret.

translation:

Tēla hūmānae puellae ostendit:

2. Ea puella nōn tolerābat cōnsilium quod dederat Minerva.

   translation:

   Audivī:

3. Ea puella nōn tolerābit cōnsilium Minervae.

   translation:

   Crēdō:

4. Ea puella deōs amāre nōn solet.

   translation:

   Crēdō:

5. Minerva eius tēlam nōn probābit, sed suam tēlam probābit.

   translation:

   Sciō:

6. Contemnere Minervam nōn decet.

   translation:

   Arachne didicit:

7. Dea invidiam ingeniī eius puellae sēnsit.

   translation:

   Aliī dīcunt:

8. Et dea et puella pulchrās tēlās fēcīt.

   translation:

   Quis nesciat:

9. Lētum eius puellae nōn erit lētum eius ingeniī.

   translation:

   Puella nescīvit:

C. Latin Derivations

The following words are derivatives of the new vocabulary in Chapter VII. Using a dictionary, indicate from which Latin words the following English words are derived:

English	Latin source	Meaning	Meaning of English Word
1. exclusion			
2. conclusion			
3. clause			
4. deputy			
5. putative			
6. profuse			
7. probative			
8. decorous			
9. glorious			
10. ingenious			
11. lethal			
12. increase			
13. crescent			
14. decrease			

15. intolerable _____ _____ _____

16. contemptible _____ _____ _____

17. inversion _____ _____ _____

18. aversion _____ _____ _____

19. vertical _____ _____ _____

20. verse _____ _____ _____

21. version _____ _____ _____

22. otiose _____ _____ _____

23. negotiate _____ _____ _____

24. official _____ _____ _____

25. office _____ _____ _____

26. popular _____ _____ _____

27. personal _____ _____ _____

28. patriotism _____ _____ _____

29. severe _____ _____ _____

30. contrast _____ _____ _____

31. adversary _____ _____ _____

D. New Terminology

Define and explain the following terms:

1. Descriptive Genitive
2. Partitive Genitive
3. Objective Genitive
4. Reflexive Pronouns
5. Indirect Statement
6. Subject Accusative
7. Future Infinitive
8. Perfect Infinitive
9. Future Active Participle
10. Personal Possessive Adjectives
11. Reflexive Personal Adjectives

E. Translation

THE STORY OF IO

Io was the daughter of the river-god Inachus. Jupiter was attracted to her and pursued her through the forest. Finally the god spread dark clouds over the sky and caught the girl in the dark, but Juno, his jealous wife, saw the cloud and wondered what was causing the cloud. She asked where her husband was, and when she could not find him she suspected he was up to no good, so she went to investigate the cloud. But Jupiter heard her coming, and quickly changed Io into a cow. When Juno saw the cow, she remarked what a beautiful creature it was and asked Jupiter to give it to her as a present. Jupiter did not know any way to avoid granting her request.

Juno took her new gift and gave it to Argus to guard for the goddess. Argus had a hundred eyes, two of which were always sleeping while the others kept guard. Consequently, no matter which way he turned his head, Io was still in front of his eyes. Argus allowed her to graze by day, and at night he shut her up and chained her innocent neck. Instead of a bed she lay on the ground, and she had only muddy rivers to drink. If she wanted to complain, she could make only a lowing sound.

Her unhappy father feared that she had died. Io went to see her father, but he did not recognize her. Still, she followed him and his other daughters, who used to stroke her neck and back. Her aged father gave her grass to eat, and she licked his hand and shed tears, because she could not speak to him and identify herself. Finally, with her hoof she traced the Greek letters of her name, I , in the dusty river bed. In this way Inachus learned what had become of his daughter. "Alas!" he cried, "my poor daughter. There will be no marriage for you. You will have a bull for a husband, and your children will be cattle!"

Then Argus moved her away from her father, up to a high mountain, where he sat down and kept watch in every direction. Finally Jupiter felt pity for her and sent Mercury to kill Argus. Mercury, disguised as a shepherd, went near the place where Argus was sitting and played music on his reed pipe, called a syrinx . Argus liked the sound of the pipe and asked about its history, whereupon Mercury began telling him the long story about Pan and Syrinx, who became the reed-pipe. Soon Argus's head began to nod, and gradually all his eyes closed, and he fell asleep. Quickly Mercury jumped up and cut off his head and Jupiter restored Io to human form. Juno, mourning the loss of her faithful servant, took Argus' eyes and placed them on the feathers of the peacock, her special bird, covering its tail with jewelled stars.

Special Vocabulary

"I" and "Ω"	Greek *iota* and Greek *omega* (= English I + O)
Argus, ī, *m.*	Argus
cessō, -āre, -āvī, -ātus	cease (with infinitive — cease to do something)
colō, colere, coluī, cultūs	cultivate, worship
furtum, -ī, *n.*	trick, theft
harēna, -ae, *f.*	grain of sand
herba, -ae, *f.*	blade of grass
Iō (*nom, dat., acc. or abl.*)	Io
īra, ae *f.*	anger
Iuppiter (*nom.*), Iovem (*accus.*), *m.*	Jupiter
Iūnō (*nom.*), Iūnōnem (*accus.*)	Juno
lacrima, ae, *f.*	tear
lacrimō, lacrimāre, -āvī, -ātus	shed tears
lamberō, -āre, -āvī, -ātus	lick
linigera turba (*nom.*)	the linen-wearing crowd (a reference to the priests of Isis, the Egyptian goddess.)
longus, -a, -um	long
mugiō, -īre, -īvī, -itum	to low, make a lowing sound, to say moo
Nīlus, -ī, *m.*	the river Nile
pater (*nom.*)	father
penna, -ae, *f.*	feather
tandem (*adverb*)	finally
vacca, -ae, *f.*	cow
volucris (*gen.*), *f.*	bird

Translate the following sentences into good English. If a phrase is underlined, indicate whether it is an indirect question or an indirect statement. If the verb is subjunctive, explain why it is subjunctive.

1. Iūnō quaesīvit ubi suus vir <u>esset</u>.

   trans:

   esset

2. Iūnō cognōverat <u>furta</u> suī virī.

   trans:

   furta

3. Iūnō cognōverat <u>suum virum</u> furta facere.

   trans:

   suum virum

4. Iuppiter Iō in vaccam mutāvit quod audīverat Iūnōnem <u>venīre</u>.

   trans:

   venīre

5. Dīcunt Iovem Iō in vaccam mutāvisse quod Iūnō <u>venīret</u>.

   trans:

   venīret

6. Iūnō sē vaccam <u>habere</u> velle dīxit.

   trans:

   habēre

7. Iuppiter crēdidit <u>sē</u> dōnum quod Iūnō <u>petīvisset</u> dare dēbēre.

   trans:

   sē

   petīvisset

8. Iūnō dōnum suum Argō dedit ut id sibi <u>servāret</u>.

   trans:

   servāret

9. Iūnō cognōverat Argum dōnum suum sibi <u>servātūrum esse</u>.

   trans:

   servātūrum esse

10. Oculī Argī Iō vīdēbant. Sī ea mugīret, oculī eām mugīre <u>vidērent</u>. Sī ea lacrimāret, eī oculī vidērent eam lacrimās <u>fundere</u>.

    trans:

    vidērent

    fundere

11. Pater miser eius crēdidit <u>suam fīliam</u> occidisse.

    trans:

    suam fīliam

12. Iō accessit ut patrem <u>vidēret</u>, sed is nescīvit eam <u>esse</u> suam fīliam.

    trans:

    vidēret

    esse

13. Pater vaccae herbās dedit, et vacca eum <u>lamberāvit</u> lacrimāvitque quod eī dīcere nōn potuit.

    trans:

    lamberāvit

14. Tandem in harēnis "I" et "Ω" scrīpsit, ut pater suam fīliam <u>cognosceret</u>.

    trans:

    cognosceret

15. Pater dixit nullās nuptiās suae fīliae <u>futūrās esse</u>, sed <u>eī</u> futūrum esse taurum ut virum vaccāsque ut līberōs.

    trans:

    futūrās esse

    eī

16. Iuppiter autem Mercurium mīsit ut Argum <u>occideret</u>. Mercurius oculōs Argī fābulā longā <u>clausit</u>. Jūnō oculōs suī servī in pennīs volūcris suae servāvit.

    trans:

    occideret

    clausit

17. Dīcunt Iō fūgisse et in multīs terrīs errāvisse quod Iūnō eam multā cum īrā ēgerit, et tandem eam ad Nīlum errāre cessāre, et ibi eam in deam crēvisse, et nunc linigeram turbam eam colere.

    trans:

Key, Chapter VII

A.1.

quī, quae, quod *who, what, which*

	singular			*plural*		
	M.	F.	N.	M.	F.	N.
Nom.	quī	quae	quod	quī	quae	quae
Gen.	cuius	cuius	cuius	quōrum	quārum	quōrum
Dat.	cui	cui	cui	quibus	quibus	quibus
Acc.	quem	quam	quod	quōs	quās	quae
Abl.	quō	quā	quō	quibus	quibus	quibus

quis, quid *who? what?*

	singular			*plural*		
	M. & F.	N.		M.	F.	N.
Nom.	quis	quid		qui	quae	quae
Gen.	cuius	cuius		quōrum	quārum	quōrum
Dat.	cui	cui		quibus	quibus	quibus
Acc.	quem	quid		quōs	quās	quae
Abl.	quō	quō		quibus	quibus	quibus

is, ea, id *he, she, it; this, that*

	singular			*plural*		
	M.	F.	N.	M.	F.	N.
Nom.	is	ea	id	eī, iī	eae	ea
Gen.	eius	eius	eius	eōrum	eārum	eōrum
Dat.	eī	eī	eī	eīs	eīs	eīs
Acc.	eum	eam	id	eōs	eās	ea
Abl.	eō	eā	eō	eīs	eīs	eīs

ego, tū, nōs, vōs *I, you (s.), we, you (pl.)*

	singular			*plural*	
Nom.	ego	tū	nōs		vōs
Gen.	meī	tuī	nostrī/nostrum		vestrī/vestrum
Dat.	mihi	tibī	nōbīs		vōbīs
Acc.	mē	tē	nōs		vōs
Abl.	mē	te	nōbīs		vōbīs

sē *himself, herself, itself*

Nom.	*(none)*
Gen.	suī
Dat.	sibi
Acc.	sē
Abl.	sē

A.2.

ingeniī cuius, cuius, eius,   cuius, mediī, novī, ignōtī, suī.

persōnae quae, quae, eae,   quae, mediae, novae, ignōtae, suae.

benevolentiīs quibus, quibus, eīs,   quibus, mediīs, novīs, ignōtīs, suīs.

lētō quō, quō, eō,   quō, mediō, novō, ignōtō, suō.

ōtia quae, quae, ea,   quae, media, nova, ignōta, sua.

negōtia quae, quae, ea,   quae, media, nova, ignōta, sua.

oculō (*dat*) cui, cui, eī,   cui, mediō, novō, ignōtō, suō.

oculō (*abl*) quō, quō, eō,   quō, mediō, novō, ignōtō, suō.

grammaticīs quibus, quibus, eis,   quibus, mediīs, novīs, ignōtīs, suīs.

factīs quibus, quibus, eīs,   quibus, mediīs, novīs, ignōtīs, suīs.

officiō	quō, quō, eō,	quō, mediō, novō, ignōtō, suō.
populō (*dat*)	cui, cui, eī,	cui, mediō, novō, ignōtō, suō.
populō (*abl*)	quō, quō, eō,	quō, mediō, novō, ignōtō, suō.
glōriae (*gen*)	cuius, cuius, eius,	cuius, mediae, novae, ignōtae, suae.
glōriae (*nom*)	quae, quae, eae,	quae, mediae, novae, ignōtae, suae.
glōriae (*dat*)	cui, cui, ei,	cui, mediō, novō, ignōtō, suae.

A.3.

1. vōbīs — pronoun, dat. or abl. pl.
2. vestrī — pronoun or adj., gen. s., m. or n.
3. vestrum — pronoun, gen. pl. (partitive) or adj. acc. s. m.
4. vestra — adjective, nom. f. s. or neuter pl. nom. or acc.
5. vōs — pronoun, nom. or acc. pl.
6. vestrōs — adjective, acc. m. pl.
7. meī — pronoun, gen. s. or adjective, gen. s., m. or n., or nom. m. pl.
8. nōs — pronoun, nom. or acc. pl.
9. nostrum — pronoun, gen. pl. (partitive) or adj. acc. s. m.
10. nostrōrum — adj., gen. pl. masc. or neut.
11. nostrīs — adj., dat. or abl. pl.
12. nōbīs — pronoun, dat. or abl. pl.
13. suus — adj., nom. masc. sing.
14. meīs — adj., abl. or dat.. sing (all genders)
15. mē — pronoun, acc. or abl. s.
16. sibi — pronoun, dat. s. or pl.
17. suōs — adj., acc. masc. pl.
18. suīs — adj., dat. or abl. pl. all genders
19. sē — pronoun, acc. or abl. s. or plural
20. suō — adj., m. or n., dat. or abl. s.

A.4.

1. Let us teach the mind of our student in the following way, **eius.**
2. Do not let the student's mind learn shameful songs, **ea.**
3. If she should learn those songs, her mind would go astray, **ea.**
4. What songs should she learn? **quae.**
5. Make letters of box-wood and give names to those letters. **quibus.**

A.5.

1. Quid ea didicit?
2. Quās litterās ea didicit?
3. In quem lūdum (in quam scholam) pater eius eam mīsit?
4. Schola in quam (lūdus in quem…erat bonus) pater eius eam mīsit erat bona.
5. Quid erat canticum quō nōs litterās (elementa) didicimus?

A.6.

1. of great beauty (*desc adj + n*)
   examples of mortals (*obj n*)
   the gods' superiority. (*pos n*)
2. corner of tapestry (*part n*)
   Arachne's (*pos n*)
3. the victimization of Leda (*obj n*)
   the mother of Apollo and Diana. (*pos n*)
4. Some of the pictures (*part n*)
   in a hawk's feathers (*pos n*)
   in a lion's skin (*pos n*)
   in a shepherd's outfit. (*pos n*)

5. edge of <u>her</u> (*pos pron*), **eius**
   <u>tapestry</u> (*part n*)
   bunches <u>of ivy</u>. (*part n*)

6. <u>her</u> (*pos pron*), **eius**
   of <u>tapestry</u> (*pos n*), **tēlae**
   the symbol <u>of peace</u>. (*pos n*)

7. with the juice of <u>herb</u>. (*pos n*)
   <u>Hekate's</u> (*pos n*)

8. at the touch <u>of this herb</u>, (*obj adj + n*), **eius herbae**
   the <u>girl's</u> hair (*pos n*), **eius** (**capellae** [nom.] **eius** [gen])
   <u>her</u> nostrils (*pos pron*), **eius**
   <u>her</u> ears (*pos pron*), **eius**
   <u>her</u> head (*pos pron*), **eius**

9. <u>Her</u> whole body (*pos pron*), **eius**
   <u>Her</u> slender fingers (*pos pron*), **eius**
   to <u>her</u> sides (*pos pron*), **eius**
   all the rest <u>of her</u> (*part pron*), **eius**

10. From <u>her</u> belly (*pos pron*), **eius** (**ex eius ventrō**)
    <u>her</u> thread (*pos pron*), **eius**
    <u>her</u> web (*pos pron*), **eius**
    as <u>of old</u>. (*not genitive - this is an adverbial expression, meaning "in the past"*)

11. <u>her</u> web (*poss adj*), **suam tēlam**
    jealousy for <u>skill</u> (*obj n*)
    <u>Arachne's</u> (*pos n*)
    pity <u>for Arachne</u> (*obj n*)

12. anyone <u>of you</u> (*part pron*), **vestrum** (**ūllus vestrum**)
    pity <u>for Arachne</u> (*obj n*)

13. too much <u>pride</u>. (*part n*)

14. limit <u>of pride</u> and of <u>humility</u> (*obj n*)

B.1.

1. Jupiter changed himself into a bull in order to capture Europa.
   Tēla hūmānae puellae ostendit Iovem in taurum sē mūtāvisse ut Eurōpam captāret.
   The girl's tapestry showed that Jupiter changed himself into a bull in order to capture/seize Europa.

2. That girl did not tolerate (was not tolerating) the advice which Minerva had given.
   Audīvī eam puellam nōn toleravisse cōnsilium quod dedisset Minerva.
   I have heard that that girl did not tolerate (was not tolerating) the advice which Minerva had given.

3. That girl will not tolerate Minerva's advice.
   Crēdō eam puellam nōn tolerātūram esse cōnsilium Minervae.
   I believe that that girl will not tolerate Minerva's advice.

4. That girl is not accustomed to loving the gods.
   Crēdō eam puellam deōs amāre nōn solēre.
   I believe that that girl is not accustomed to loving the gods.

5. Minerva will not approve of her (Arachne's) tapestry, but she will approve of her own.
   Sciō Minervam eius tēlam nōn probātūram esse, sed suam tēlam probātūram esse.
   I know that Minerva will not approve of her tapestry.

6. It is not fitting (it is not proper) to scorn the goddess Minerva.
   Arachne didicit contemnere deam Minervam nōn decēre.
   Arachne learned that it is not fitting to scorn the goddess Minerva.

7. The goddess felt envy for that girl's talent.
   Aliī dīcunt deam invidiam ingeniī eius puellae sēnsisse.
   Other people say that the goddess felt envy for that girl's talent.

8. Both the goddess and the girl made beautiful webs.
   Quis nesciat et deam et puellam pulchrās tēlās fēcisse.
   Who would not know that the goddess and the girl made beautiful webs.

9.　The death of that girl will not be the death of her talent.
　　Puella nescīvit suum lētum nōn futūrum esse lētum suī ingeniī.
　　The girl did not know that her own death would not be the death of her talent.

C. Latin Derivations

		Latin Source	Meaning	Meaning of English Word
1.	exclusion:	**ex, claudere**	*close out*	omission.
2.	conclusion:	**cum, claudere**	*close with*	the final settlement; the end.
3.	clause:	**claudere**	*to close*	a group of words containing a subject and a predicate; part of a written composition containing a complete sense in itself.
4.	deputy:	**dē, pūtare**	*about, from, to think*	a person appointed to act for another or others.
5.	putative:	**pūtare**	*to think*	commonly regarded as such; reputed, supposed.
6.	profuse:	**prō, fundere**	*in front of, to pour*	abundant; extravagant.
7.	probative:	**probāre**	*to approve*	designed for testing or trial; providing proof or evidence.
8.	decorous:	**decōrus**	*fitting, proper*	proper, decent, conventional; characterized by proper conduct, dress, or behavior.
9.	glorious:	**glōria**	*glory*	admirable, delightful; conferring glory.
10.	ingenious:	**ingenium**	*talent, genius*	clever, inventive.
11.	lethal:	**lētum**	*death*	deadly.
12.	increase:	**in, crescere**	*into, to grow*	to grow larger.
13.	crescent:	**crescere**	*to grow*	growing.
14.	decrease:	**dē, crescere**	*down, to grow*	to grow smaller.
15.	intolerable:	**in, tolerāre**	*not, to endure*	unbearable.
16.	contemptible:	**contemnere**	*to scorn*	worthy of scorn; despicable
17.	inversion:	**in, vertere**	*in, to turn*	act of reversing position, direction, or tendence; or, turned upside down.
18.	aversion:	**ab, vertere**	*from, to turn*	turning away.
19.	vertical:	**vertere**	*to turn*	perpendicular to the horizon; upright
20.	verse:	**vertere**	*to turn*	a succession of metrical feet written or orally composed as one line; one of the lines of a poem.
21.	version:	**vertere**	*to turn*	a translation; a particular account or form of something, as compared with other accounts of it.
22.	otiose:	**ōtium**	*leisure*	at leisure; inactive; lazy.
23.	negotiate:	**negōtium**	*business, lack of leisure*	to deal with others in the preparation of a treaty, or of a business deal, to arrange for an agreement by discussion of terms.
24.	official:	**officium**	*duty, obligation*	(noun): a person who holds an office; (adj.): related to an office or duty.
25.	office:	**officium**	*duty, obligation*	a room or place for the transaction of business; a position of authority.
26.	popular:	**populus**	*the people, the nation*	regarded with favor by the general public.

27.	personal:	**persōna**	*a character, an individual*	having to do with a particular person; private; individual.
28.	patriotism:	**patria**	*native land*	devotion to one's country
29.	severe:	**sevērus**	*strict, stern; harsh*	serious; rigidly restrained in taste or style; plain; hard to do or endure
30.	contrast:	**contrā**	*against*	to set in opposition in order to show differences.
31.	adversary:	**ad, vertere**	*towards, to turn*	an unfriendly opponent.

D. New Terminology

1. **Descriptive Genitive:** describes a quality in another noun; must be modified by an adjective (a person *of good taste*; a thing *of great beauty*).
2. Partitive Genitive: indicates that one noun or pronoun is part of another (one *of the books*; no part *of the building*).
3. **Objective Genitive:** indicates that one noun or pronoun is the object of the verbal root of another noun or adjective (fear *of the night*; mindful *of your words*).
4. **Reflexive Pronouns:** pronouns that refer back to the subject of the sentence. All personal pronouns, if they agree with the subject, can be reflexive. The third person singular or plural has a special reflexive pronoun, **sē**, which has no nominative form.
5. **Indirect Statement:** a statement subordinated by verbs of saying, thinking, knowing, feeling, believing, and similar expressions; the subject of the indirect statement is in the accusative case, and the main verb is an infinitive. (I know *that you want to do this*. **Sciō tē hoc facere velle.**)
6. **Subject Accusative:** the subject of an indirect statement.
7. **Future Active Infinitive:** "to be about to do something"; consists of the future active participle and the infinitive **esse**.
8. **Perfect Active Infinitive:** "to have done something"; consists of the perfect stem plus **-isse** (**fēcisse**).
9. **Future Active Participle:** "about to do something"; a verbal adjective, consisting of the stem of the fourth principle part of the verb (**fact-**) plus **-ūrus, -a, -um: factūrus, -a, -um.**
10. **Personal Possessive Adjectives: meus, tuus, noster, vester.**
11. **Reflexive Personal Adjectives: suus, -a, -um** (3rd person singular or plural), or, if they agree with the subject, any of the personal possessive adjectives: *I will read my* (**meās**) letter; *you* will read *your* (**tuās**) letter, etc.

E. Translation - The Story of Io

1. Juno asked where her husband was.
   esset — verb in indirect question, secondary sequence
2. Juno knew the deceptions of her husband.
   furta — accusative, direct object
3. Juno knew that her husband practiced deceptions.
   suum virum — subject accusative in indirect statement
4. Jupiter changed Io into a cow because he had heard that Juno was coming.
   venīre — verb in indirect statement
5. They say that Jupiter changed Io into a cow because Juno was coming.
   venīret — imperfect subjunctive, verb in subordinate clause in indirect statement.
6. Juno said that she wanted to have the cow.
   habēre — complementary infinitive (**velle** is the verb of indirect statement)
7. Jupiter believed that he was obligated to give the gift which Juno had asked for.
   sē — subject of indirect discourse, referring to Jupiter
   petīvisset — verb in subordinate clause in indirect statement.
8. Juno gave her gift to Argus so that he would guard it for her.
   servāret — imperfect subjunctive in purpose clause.
9. Juno knew that Argus would protect her gift for her.
   servātūrum esse — future infinitive verb in indirect statement
10. Argus' eyes were watching Io. If she were lowing, his eyes would be watching her low. If she were crying, his eyes would be watching her shed tears.
    vidērent — imperfect subjunctive in present contrary to fact condition
    fundere — infinitive verb of indirect statement

11. Her unhappy father believed that his daughter had died.
    suam fīliam — (her) father - accusative subject of infinitive verb
12. Io approached to see him, but he did not know that she was his daughter.
    vidēret — imperfect subjunctive in purpose clause
    esse — infinitive verb of indirect statement
13. The father gave grass to the cow, and the cow licked him and wept because she could not speak to him.
    lamberāvit — indicative verb
14. Finally she wrote in the sand, "I" and " ", so that her father would r ecognize her..
    cognosceret — imperfect subjunctive in purpose clause.
15. The father said that his daughter (dative of possession) would have no marriage, but that she would have a bull as a husband and cattle as children.
    futūrās esse — future infinitive verb of indirect statement
    eī — dative of possession
16. Jupiter however sent Mercury to kill Argus. Mercury closed Argus' eyes with a long tale. Juno saved the eyes of her servant in the feathers of her bird. (a peacock).
    occideret — imperfect subjunctive in purpose clause.
    clausit — perfect indicative
17. People (They) say that Io fled and wandered in many lands because Juno drove her with much anger, and that finally she ceased wandering at the river Nile, and that there she grew into a goddess, and that now the linen-garbed crowd worship her.

VIII
Third Declension (1), _eō, īre_ and Compounds; Constructions of Time and Place

A. The Third Declension

Nouns of the first declension are known as _a-stem_ nouns because of the characteristic -a- in all but the Dative and Ablative plural endings. Nouns of the second declension are also known as vowel-stem nouns. With the exception of third declension _i-stem_ nouns (which you will encounter in Chapter XI), nouns of the third declension are _consonant-stem_ nouns.

A.1. Decline the following nouns, and compare the endings in each case to see if you can identify similar patterns in these declensions. Translate the nominative singular.

	1st Declension	2nd Declension		3rd Declension			
Sing.		_masc._	_neuter_	_mute stems_		_liquid stems_	
Nom.	hōra	annus	vulgus	dux	lēx	cōnsul	corpus
Gen.	hōrae	annī	vulgī	ducis	lēgis	cōnsulis	corporis
Dat.							
Acc.							
Abl.							
Plural							
Nom.							
Gen.							
Dat.							
Acc.							
Abl.							
(Nom. Sing) Trans.							

Third declension nouns whose stem ends with a *mute consonant* —*p, t, d, c, g*— will tend to add *-s* to form the nominative singular:

Stem	Stem. + s	Final form of Nom. Sing.	(Gen. Sing.)
duc-	duc-**s**	dux	ducis
lēg-	lēg-**s**	lēx	lēgis
lībertāt-	lībertāt-**s**	lībertās	lībertātis
virtūt-	virtūt-**s**	virtūs	virtūtis
brevitāt-	brevitāt-**s**	brevitās	brevitātis
probābilitāt-	probābilitāt-**s**	probābilitās	probābilitātis
vēritāt-	vēritāt-**s**	vēritās	vēritātis

Notice that when **-s** is added to **-c** or **-g**, the combination of consonants becomes **-x**, and when **-s** is added to **-t**, the **-t** is dropped, leaving the single consonant **-s** for the nominative singular form. Another group of regular third declension nouns have *liquid and nasal stems* (ending in *l, n,* or *r*).

A.2. Rearrange the following nouns according to the final consonant in their stems: (l-stem, n-stem, or r-stem), identify the stem and genitive, and give the meaning in English:

arbor	homō	opīniō
audītor	iūs	orātiō
corpus	mōs	ōrātor
cōnsul	multitūdō	pater
dēfensiō	narrātiō	rūs
genus	nōmen	tempus

	Nom. sing.	Stem	Genitive	English Meaning
l-stem				
n-stem				
r-stem				

104

A.3. Identify the case of the following nouns, change them to the plural in the same case, and translate the new plural form:

	Case	Plural equivalent	Translation
patrī			
vēritātem			
annum			
virtūtis			
ōrātōrī			
ōrātiōnī			
opīniōne			
tempus			
virtūs			
cōnsule			
iūrī			
iniūriae			
legī			
factī			
hominī			
annī			
nōmine			
mōrem			
genus			
arboris			
temporis			
lēgis			

B. Eō, Īre, and Compounds

B.1. Change the following indicative verbs to the singular and translate the new form:

	Singular Equivalent	Translation
adībāmus		
inībāmus		
redībimus		
abībāmus		
perīmus		
periimus		
perībimus		
praeterīmus		
praeterierimus		
praeteriimus		

praetereunt _____ _____

praeterierunt _____ _____

prōdīmus _____ _____

prōdītis _____ _____

prōdībunt _____ _____

redeunt _____ _____

abeunt _____ _____

adeunt _____ _____

ambīstis _____ _____

ambībātis _____ _____

ambībitis _____ _____

redīstis _____ _____

redībātis _____ _____

B.2. Change the following subjunctive verbs to the indicative, identify the tense, and translate the new form:

	Indicative Equivalent	Tense	Translation
adeam			
inīrēs			
redīret			
abīrēmus			
pereāmus			
perierīmus			
perīerint			
praetereāmus			
praeterierīmus			
praetereānt			
praetereās			
praeterīssent			
prōdīssēs			
prōdīssēmus			
prōdierim			
redeant			
abeās			
adeātis			
ambīsset			
ambīrent			
ambierint			
redierītis			
redīrēmus			

C. Constructions of Place and Time

C.1. Translate the following into good Latin, and indicate whether the underlined phrases show *place where, place to which, or place from which.*

a. Place Constructions:

1. Let's go <u>to the city</u>. (**urbs, urbem,** *f.*, city)
2. We live <u>in the city.</u>
3. We departed <u>from the city.</u>
4. Let's go <u>to Rome.</u>
5. We live <u>in Rome.</u>
6. We departed <u>from Rome.</u>
7. Let's go <u>to Italy.</u>
8. We live <u>in Italy.</u>
9. We departed <u>from Italy.</u>
10. Let's go <u>to Europe</u>. (**Eurōpa, ae,** *f.* , Europe)
11. We live <u>in Europe.</u>
12. We departed <u>from Europe.</u>
13. Let's go <u>to the countryside.</u>
14. We live <u>in the countryside.</u>
15. We departed <u>from the countryside.</u>
16. Let's go <u>home.</u>
17. We live <u>at home.</u>
18. We departed <u>from home.</u>

b. Constructions of Time. Indicate whether the underlined phrase shows a) *time when or within which,* or b) *duration of time*, and whether it would translate into the ablative or accusative case:

1. <u>For a long time</u> Narcissus gazed at the beautiful boy in the water.
2. <u>One day</u> Echo saw him and fell in love with him.
3. <u>Every day</u> she followed him everywhere, but he ignored her.
4. Icarus played with his father's tools <u>all day long</u>, unaware that the yellow wax would be his undoing.
5. <u>For the first hours</u> of their flight, Icarus followed his father's instructions.
6. <u>At high noon</u>, when the sun is at its highest point, Icarus had a sudden longing to fly higher.
7. He was safe <u>throughout that part of the flight</u> in which he followed his father's instructions.
8. <u>During his early years</u>, Phaethon had never met his father.
9. <u>On his fifteenth birthday</u>, he asked the Sun to prove that he was Phaethon's father.
10. <u>Within a few hours</u>, the Sun would regret that he had agreed to his son's request.

D. Terminology Review

1. What consonants are found at the end of a *liquid stem*? What consonants are found at the end of a *mute stem*?
2. When is the locative case used?
3. What is the usual gender of third declension nouns ending in the nominative singular in **-tor, -tōris**?

4. What is the usual gender of third declension nouns ending in the nominative singular in **-tās, -tātis**?

5. What is the gender of third declension nouns ending in the nominative singular in **-tūs, -tūtis**?

6. What is the gender of third declension nouns ending in the nominative singular in **-us**?

E. Translation

ERYSICHTHON AND CERES

Erysichthon was a man who scorned the gods and never made offerings of incense on their altars. One day he cut down a tree in a grove that was sacred to Ceres, the goddess of grain. Under this huge, aged oak tree the Dryads, nymphs of the forest, used to hold their dances, often joining hands in a circle and embracing its trunk, which measured fifteen cubits. Its height too was much greater than that of the other trees, but this did not deter Erysichthon from ordering his men to cut it down. When his men hesitated to cut it down, Erysichthon grabbed the axe and shouted, "Even if this tree should be a goddess, and not just a tree the goddess loves, still I would bring its top down to the earth!" As he said these words he held his axe, ready to strike the trunk. The oak tree of Ceres trembled and groaned, and the leaves and acorns began to turn white and the long branches lost their color. Then, when he struck a gash in its side, blood flowed out where the bark was slit open. Everyone stood still in horrified amazement. One man tried to prevent the sacrilege, but Erysichthon angrily swung his axe at him and cut off his head.

Then a voice from the tree said, "I who dwell within this tree am a nymph whom Ceres dearly loves. I warn you with my dying breath, that punishment for your wickedness is at hand." But Erysichthon persisted. The nymphs appealed to Ceres to punish him, and Ceres decided to do so with deadly Hunger. Since fate does not allow Ceres and Hunger to meet, she sent a mountain spirit, an Oread, to convey Ceres' instructions, that Hunger should bury herself in the wicked stomach of this impious man, and let no amount of food defeat her.

Erysichthon was sleeping peacefully, but he dreamed that he was feasting, and chewed uselessly at nothing, grinding his teeth together, and cheating himself by swallowing a mere pretence of food. When he awoke he was furiously hungry. Immediately he ordered that all the food on earth be brought to him. So great a quantity of food, which would have satisfied whole countries, was not enough for him. The more he ate, the more he desired. All his fortune soon dwindled away, but still his dreadful hunger remained. Finally when he had eaten all his wealth, and nothing remained but his daughter, he sold her, but she escaped, running to the nearby waters. She appealed to Neptune to save her, and the god did not scorn her prayer. The god changed her into a fisherman. When her father finally learned she could change her shape, he sold her often to different masters, and she escaped in the form of a horse, or a bird, or an ox or a stag, and thus obtained food for her gluttonous father. Finally, however, he began to bite and gnaw at his own limbs, and fed his body by eating it away.

Special vocabulary:

adnuō, ere, adnuī, —	nod assent
alimentum, ī, *n.*	nourishment
āēr, āēris, *n.*	air (the area between earth and sky)
caedō, -ere, cecīdī, caesus	to cut, cut down, kill
Cerēs, Cereris, *f.*	Ceres, the goddess of grain
coīre	(**cum** + **īre**) to come together
dēns, dentis, *m.*	tooth
dormiō, -īre, -īvī, -ītus	to sleep
Erysichthon, -onis, *m.*	Erysichthon

108

ēdūcō, -āre, -āvī, -ātus	to bring up, rear, educate
Fātum, -ī, *n.*	Fate (*usually plural*: The Fates)
Famēs, Famis, *f.*	Hunger (*personified*); hunger
mōra, -ae, *f.*	delay
ōs, ōris, *n.*	mouth
poena, -ae, *f.*	penalty, punishment
pontus, -i, *m.*	sea
poscō, ere, poposci, —	urgently request
praecordia, -ōrum, *n.* (*pl.*)	internal organs
sacrilegus, -a, -um	impious, godless, wicked
sinō, -ere, sīvī, situs	permit, allow (*plus complementary infinitive*)
solacia, -ae, *f.*	solace
vānus, -a, -um	empty
vendō, -ere, -didī, -ditus	sell

Translate the following sentences and explain the syntax of the underlined words.

1. Erysichthonis fīlia <u>sua</u> iūra āmisit quod famēs magna patrem <u>suum</u> cēpit.

2. Nam dīcunt <u>Erysichthonem</u> deōs saepe contempsisse, sed <u>ūnō tempore eum</u> et arborem Cereris cecīdisse.

3. Quandō Erysichthon arborem caedere incipiēbat, ex mediō <u>arbore</u> sonum audīvit:

   "Nympha sum quae in hāc Cereris <u>arbore</u> vīvō. Magnās poenās tibi ā Cerere petō, solāciam <u>meī lētī</u>."

4. Nymphae aliae ad <u>Cererem</u> adeunt poenamque Erysichthonis petunt, et Cerēs adnuit.

5. Fāta <u>Cererem Famemque</u> coīre nōn sinunt. Cerēs <u>nympham</u> ergō mīsit ut Famem iubēret, "Famēs <u>sē</u> in <u>praecordia</u> virī sacrilegī spīrat nē <u>satis cibī</u> habeat. Quid satis sit populō, nōn satis sit <u>ūnī</u>."

6. Nympha verba Cereris <u>Famī</u> dixit fūgitque, nē famem <u>sentīret</u>. Famēs verba Cereris audīvit et ad <u>virum</u> sacrilegum adiīt. Sē in <u>virum</u> spīrāvit <u>domumque</u> fūgit.

7. Erysichthon dormiēbat. Crēdidit <u>sē</u> cibum mordēre. Ōra vāna ad cibum movēbat <u>dentemque</u> in <u>dente</u> claudēbat.

8. Tum quid <u>terra</u>, <u>quid</u> pontus, quid āēr ēdūcāre possit sibi iubet.

9. Sic cibum Erysichthonis <u>ōra</u> accipiunt petuntque. Cibus in eō <u>cibī</u> causā est.

10. Tandem fīlia sōla, quae <u>digna eō patre</u> nōn est, manet. Neptūnus formam <u>eius</u> mūtāvit, sed pater <u>fīliam corpora</u> trānsformāre posse sēnsit et <u>dominīs</u> multīs saepe vendidit. Sic <u>ea</u> nōn iusta alimenta patrī dabat.

Key, Chapter VIII

A.1.

	1st Declension	2nd Declension		3rd Declension			
Sing.		*masc.*	*neuter*	*mute stems*		*liquid stems*	
Nom.	hōra	annus	vulgus	dux	lex	cōnsul	corpus
Gen.	hōrae	annī	vulgī	ducis	lēgis	cōnsulis	corporis
Dat.	hōrae	annō	vulgo	ducī	lēgī	cōnsulī	corporī
Acc.	hōram	annum	vulgus	ducem	lēgem	cōnsulem	corpus
Abl.	hōrā	annō	vulgō	duce	lēge	cōnsule	corpore
Plural							
Nom.	hōrae	annī	vulga	ducēs	lēgēs	cōnsulēs	corpora
Gen.	hōrārum	annōrum	vulgōrum	ducum	lēgum	cōnsulum	corporum
Dat.	hōrīs	annīs	vulgīs	ducibus	legibus	cōnsulibus	corporibus
Acc.	hōrās	annōs	vulga	ducēs	lēgēs	cōnsulēs	corpora
Abl.	hōrīs	annīs	vulgīs	ducibus	legibus	cōnsulibus	corporibus
(Nom. Sing.)							
Trans.	*hour*	*year*	*the multitude*	*leader*	*law*	*consul*	*body*

A.2.

Nom. sing.	Stem	Genitive	Meaning
l-stem			
cōnsul	cōnsul-	cōnsulis	consul (highest Roman magistrate)
n-stem			
dēfensiō	dēfensiōn-	dēfensiōnis	defense
homō	homin-	hominis	human being
multitūdō	multitudin-	multitūdinis	multitude
narrātiō	narrātiōn-	narrātiōnis	narrative
nōmen	nōmin-	nōminis	name
opīniō	opīniōn-	opīniōnis	opinion
ōrātiō	ōrātiōn-	ōrātiōnis	speech
r-stem			
arbor	arbor-	arboris	tree
audītor	audītor-	audītoris	listener
corpus	corpor-	corporis	body
genus	gener-	generis	race, species, gender
iūs	iūr-	iūris	right, law, justice
mōs	mōr-	mōris	custom
ōrātōr	ōrātōr-	ōrātōris	speaker
pater	patr-	patris	father
rūs	rūr-	rūris	countryside
tempus	tempor-	temporis	time

A.3.

	Case	Plural equivalent	Translation
patrī	dat.	patribus	to fathers
vēritātem	accus.	vēritātēs	truths
annum	accus.	annōs	years
virtūtis	gen.	virtūtum	of virtues
ōrātōrī	dat.	ōrātōribus	to the speakers
ōrātiōnī	dat.	ōrātiōnibus	for the speeches
opīniōne	abl.	opīniōnibus	with opinions

tempus	nom. or accus.	tempora	times
virtūs	nom.	virtūtēs	virtues
cōnsule	abl.	cōnsulibus	(with, by) consuls
iūrī	dat.	iūribus	rights
iniūriae	dat.	iniūriīs	for injuries
lēgī	dat.	lēgibus	to laws
factī	gen.	factōrum	of deeds
hominī	dat.	hominibus	for human beings
annī	gen.	annōrum	of years
nōmine	abl.	nōminibus	by means of names
mōrem	accus.	mōrēs	character, customs
genus	nom. or accus.	genera	races, genders, sorts
arboris	gen.	arborum	of trees
temporis	gen.	temporum	of times
lēgis	gen.	lēgum	of laws

B.1.

	Singular Equivalent	*Translation*
adībāmus	adībām	I used to approach (was approaching)
inibāmus	inībām	I used to enter
redībimus	redībō	I shall return
abībāmus	abībām	I used to go away
perīmus	pereō	I am perishing
periimus	periī	I have perished
perībimus	perībō	I shall perish
praeterīmus	praetereō	I am omitting
praeterierimus	praeterierō	I shall have omitted
praeteriimus	praeteriī	I have omitted
praetereunt	praeterit	(s)he is omitting
praeteriērunt	praeteriit	(s)he has omitted
prōdīmus	prōdeō	I am going forth
prōdītis	prōdīs	you go forth
prōdībunt	prōdībit	(s)he will go forth
redeunt	redit	(s)he is returning
abeunt	abit	(s)he is going away
adeunt	adit	(s)he is approaching
ambīstis	ambīstī	you have solicited
ambībātis	ambībās	you used to solicit
ambībitis	ambībis	you shall solicit
redīstis	redīstī	you have returned
redībātis	redībās	you used to return

B.2.

	Indicative Equivalent	*Tense*	*Translation*
adeam	adeō	pres.	I am approaching
inīrēs	inībās	imperf.	you were entering (used to enter)
redīret	redībat	imperf.	he was returning
abīrēmus	abībāmus	imperf.	we were departing
pereāmus	perīmus	pres.	we are perishing
perierīmus	periimus	perf.	we have perished
perīerint	periērunt	perf.	they have perished
prabtereāmus	praeterimus	pres.	we are omitting
praeterierīmus	praeteriimus	perf.	we have omitted
prabtereānt	praetereunt	pres.	they are omitting
praetereās	praeterīs	pres.	you are omitting
praeterīssent	praeterierant	pluperf.	they had omitted
prōdissēs	prōdīerās	pluperf.	you had gone forth

prōdīssēmus	prōdierāmus	pluperf.	we had gone forth
prōdierim	prōdiī	perf.	I have gone forth
redeant	redeunt	pres.	they are returning
abeās	abīs	pres.	you (s.) are departing
adeātis	adītis	pres.	you (pl.) are departing
ambīsset	ambierat	pluperf.	(s)he had solicited
ambīrent	ambībant	imperf.	they used to solicit
ambierint	ambiērunt	perf.	they have solicited
redierītis	redīstis	perf.	you (pl.) have returned
redīrēmus	redībāmus	imperf.	we used to return (were returning)

C.1.

a. Place Constructions:

1.	Ad urbem adeāmus.	place to which.
2.	In urbe vīvimus.	place where.
3.	Ab urbe abiimus.	place from which
4.	Rōmam adeāmus.	place to which.
5.	Romae vīvimus.	place where (locative)
6.	Rōmā abiimus.	place from which.
7.	Ad Italiam adeāmus.	place to which.
8.	In Italiā vīvimus.	place where
9.	Ab Italiā abiimus.	place from which.
10.	Ad Eurōpam adeāmus.	place to which.
11.	In Eurōpā vīvimus.	place where
12.	Ab Eurōpā abiimus.	place from which.
13.	Rūs adeāmus.	place to which.
14.	Rūrī vīvimus	place where (locative)
15.	Rūre abiimus.	place from which.
16.	Domum adeāmus.	place to which.
17.	Domī vīvimus	place where (locative)
18.	Domō abiimus.	place from which.

b. Constructions of Time.

1. For a long time, b) duration of time, accusative case.
2. One day a) time when, ablative case.
3. Every day a) time within which, ablative case.
4. All day long, b) duration of time, accusative case.
5. For the first hours b) duration of time, accusative case.
6. At high noon, a) time when, ablative case.
7. Throughout that part b) duration of time, accusative case
8. During his early years, b) duration of time, accusative case
9. On his fifteenth birthday, a) time when, ablative case.
10. Within a few hours, a) time within which, ablative case.

D. TERMINOLOGY REVIEW

1. liquid stem ends in *l, r, n*, mute stem ends in *p, t, d, c, g*.
2. with the names of cities, towns, small islands, **domus,** and **rūs**.
3. 3rd decl. nouns ending in **-tor, -tōris:** masculine.
4. 3rd decl. nouns ending in **-tās, -tātis:** feminine.
5. 3rd decl. nouns ending in **-tūs, -tūtis:** feminine
6. 3rd decl. nouns ending in **-us:** neuter

E. TRANSLATION. ERYSICHTHON AND CERES

1. *The daughter of Erysichthon lost her rights because a great hunger seized her father.*
   (**sua** (*accus. n. s.*) modifies **iūra**, direct object of **āmīsit**; **suum** (*accus. m. s.*) modifies **patrem**, direct object of **cēpit**.)

2. *For they say that Erysichthon often scorned the gods, but at one time (on one occasion) he even cut down the tree of Ceres.* (**Erysichthonem** and **eum** are both subject accusative in indirect statement; **ūnō tempore** is ablative of time when.)

3. *When Erysichthon was beginning to cut down the tree, from the middle of (from within) the tree he heard a sound: "I am a nymph who lives in this tree of Ceres. I seek from Ceres great punishment for you, a solace for my death."* (**arbore**, ablative governed by **in; meī lētī**, objective genitive governed by **solāciam**.)

4. *Other nymphs go to Ceres and ask for Erysichthon's punishment, and Ceres nods assent* (approves). **Cererem**, accusative governed by **ad**, showing motion towards.

5. *The Fates do not permit Ceres and Hunger to come together. Therefore Ceres sent a nymph to command Hunger: "Let Hunger breathe herself into the inner organs of the impious man so that he will never have enough food. Let what is enough for an entire people not be enough for one man."*
   Cererem Famemque, subjects accusative of **coīre; nympham**, direct object of **mīsit; sē**, reflexive pronoun, direct object of **spīrat; in**, meaning *into*, governs **praecordia**, which is accusative plural. **satis**, accusative object, governs **cibī**, partitive genitive. **ūnī**, dative of reference, governed by **satis**.

6. *The nymph spoke Ceres' words to Hunger and fled so that she would not feel hunger. Hunger heard Ceres' words and went to the impious man. She breathed herself into the man and fled home (to her home).* (**Famī**, dative, governed by **dixit; sentīret**, imperfect subjunctive in negative purpose clause. **ad** (*toward*) governs the accusative **virum. in** plus the accusative, meaning *into*, governs **virum; domum** is accusative *place to which*, with verbs of motion.)

7. *Erysichthon was sleeping. He believed he was biting food. He was moving his empty mouth toward the food and was closing tooth upon tooth.*
   (**sē**, a reflexive pronoun and subject accusative with infinitive verb in indirect statement. **dentem**, accusative, direct object; **dente**, ablative governed by preposition **in**, *"on, onto."*)

8. *Then, what the earth, what the sea, what the air is able to produce, he orders for himself.*
   (**terra**, nominative, one of three possible subjects of **possit; quid**, accusative, interrogative pronoun introducing indirect question, *"what thing?"*)

9. *Thus the mouth of Erysichthon receives and seeks food. The food inside him is a reason for food.* (**ōra** nominative, subject [note that the plural of this word is often used instead of the singular]; **cibī**, objective genitive, governed by **causa**.)

10. *Finally his daughter alone, who did not deserve this father, remains. Neptune changed her form, but the father perceived that his daughter was able to transform her body and often sold her to many masters. Thus she gave her father unjust nourishment.*
    The adjective **digna** governs the ablative, **eō patre:** *"worthy of (+ ablative)"*; **eius**, possessive genitive pronoun, *"of her."* **fīliam**, subject accusative with infinitive verb in indirect statement; **corpora**, direct object in indirect statement; **dominīs**, dative, indirect object ("sold to *masters*"). **ea**, feminine singular nominative pronoun.

IX
Demonstrative and Intensive Pronouns and Adjectives, Result Clauses, Relative Clauses of Characteristic, Diagramming Latin Sentences

A. Demonstrative and Intensive Pronouns and Adjectives

In Chapter VI you learned that the third person pronoun, **is, ea, id,** can also function as a mild demonstrative pronoun or adjective. In this chapter you are learning the more strongly deictic or demonstrative pronouns and their related adjectives. **hic, haec, hoc,** points to something here with respect to the speaker. It is sometimes helpful to associate the English word "here" with **hic, haec, hoc,** since both begin with an h-, *this (here)* (as opposed to *that (there)*, which in Latin would be **ille, illa, illud**).

The mere sound of **ipse, ipsa, ipsum,** with the abruptly sounding **p** followed by **s,** is consistent with the intensifying force of this pronoun. Say it aloud:

Ego **ipse** dixit:	I ***myself*** *have spoken.*
Iovī **ipsō** dixit:	*She spoke to Jupiter **himself**.*
Ipsa adnuit:	*She **herself** nodded approval.*

Similarly the sound of **iste, ista, istud** inherently implies disapproval, for the **t** following **is-** seems to make almost a hissing sound:

Iste haec fēcit.	***That one*** or ***This one*** *(of yours) did these things.*
Echo **istum Narcissum** amāvit.	*Echo loved **that Narcissus** (of yours).*

The suffix **-dem** appears in a number of other Latin words as well as **Īdem, eadem, idem** (*the same*), which is a stronger version of **is, ea, id** (*this, that*)—consequently **is** and **idem** never are used together.

A.1. Learn the pronoun paradigms by reciting them aloud, e.g., "hic, haec, hoc; huius, huius, huius," etc.

a. Decline the following in the *feminine singular* only:

	hic	**ille**	**ipse**	**iste**	**īdem**
Nom.					
Gen.					
Dat.					
Acc.					
Abl.					

b. Now decline them in the *neuter plural* only:

	hoc	**illud**	**ipsum**	**istud**	**idem**
Nom.					
Gen.					
Dat.					
Acc.					
Abl.					

c. Provide the correct Latin pronoun for each of the following in the case indicated:

Nominative:

this man _____

that woman _____

those girls _____

the girl herself _____

the same things _____

the thing itself _____

those things (of yours) _____

Accusative:

this woman _____

that woman _____

the same woman _____

the same women _____

the woman herself _____

this thing _____

that thing _____

those things _____

the thing itself _____

Dative:

to these women _____

for that girl _____

to the same girl _____

to the girls themselves _____

for that woman (of yours) _____

for the same men _____

for the man himself _____

that man _____

the very man _____

the same man _____

the man himself _____

those men (of yours) _____

these boys _____

this boy _____

the very things _____

this very thing _____

d. These pronouns, like the relative pronoun and the demonstrative pronoun **is, ea, id,** also function as adjectives, which is their function in the following phrases. Identify the case and number of these phrases, and then translate them into English. Your translation should reflect the case. For example, **huius feminae** should *not* be translated "this woman," but "of this woman."

	Case and Number:	*Translation:*
1. eius generis		
2. illīus generis		
3. eā lēge ipsā		
4. eādem lēge solā		
5. illō eōdem tempore		
6. hōc ipsō tempore		
7. istō mōre novō		
8. huius nōminis tōtīus		
9. illud nōmen sōlum		
10. illā eādem virtūte		
11. istī eīdem virtūtī		
12. in eius fronte ipsā		
13. Iovī ipsī		
14. istam deam		
15. eōdem dolōre		
16. istīus saevae amōris		
17. illā vōce pulchrā		
18. vestīgiīs eīsdem		
19. sanguinis ipsīus		
20. hanc spēluncam		

A.2. Compare the effect of these pronouns in the following versions of the story of Echo and Narcissus, and translate them accordingly:

a. Ūnō tempore Ēchō pulchrum adulescentem vīdit. Nōmen **eius** adulescentis erat Narcissus. Ēchō tum magnum amōrem Narcissī sēnsit sed **eī** dīcere nōn potuit. Ubi autem **īs** errat, ibi **ea** errat, sed **is eam** nōn videt. Ūnō autem tempore, dum **īs** sōlus sedēbat, Narcissus sonum audīvit et magnā vōce vocāvit, "Quis ibi est?" Ēchō parvā vōce reddidit, "Est?" **Īs** dixit, "Venī!" et **ea id verbum** reddidit. Quoniam nēmō vēnit, Narcissus vocāvit, "Nōnne veniēs ad mē?" Ēchō extrēmum* verbum reddidit et magnō cum amōre ad **eum** cucurrit. **Īs** autem puer **eam** nōn amāvit. "Tē nōn amō," dixit, et fūgit dum **ea** misera reddidit, "amō." **Ea** tum ibi mānsit et Deī corpus eius in rūpem mūtāvērunt. Nunc vox **eius** sōla manet. Sī **eam** vocēs, tibi tuum verbum extrēmum* reddat. [*extrēmus, -a, -um, last, final]

b. Ūnō tempore Ēchō pulchrum adulescentem vīdit. Nōmen **illīus** adulescentis erat Narcissus. Ēchō tum magnum amōrem Narcissī sēnsit sed **illī** dīcere nōn potuit. Ubi autem **ille** errat, ibi **haec** errat, sed **ille hanc** nōn videt. Ūnō autem tempore, dum **ille** sōlus sedēbat, Narcissus sonum audīvit et magnā vōce vocāvit, "Quis ibi est?" Ēchō parvā vōce reddidit, "Est?" **Ille** dixit, "Venī!" et **haec** idem reddidit. Quoniam nēmō vēnit, Narcissus vocāvit, "Nōnne veniēs ad mē?" Ēchō extrēmum verbum reddidit et magnō cum amōre ad **illum** cucurrit. **Ille** autem puer **hanc** nōn amāvit. "Tē nōn amō," dixit, et fūgit dum **haec** misera reddidit, "amō." **Haec** tum ibi mānsit et deī corpus eius in rūpem mūtāvērunt. Nunc vox **huius** sōla manet. Sī **hanc** vocēs, tibi tuum verbum extrēmum reddat.

c. Ūnō tempore Ēchō pulchrum adulescentem vīdit. Nōmen **huius** adulescentis erat Narcissus. Ēchō tum magnum amōrem Narcissī sēnsit sed **huic** dīcere nōn potuit. Ubi autem **hic** errat, ibi **illa** errat, sed **hic illam** nōn videt. Ūnō autem tempore, dum **hic** sōlus sedēbat, Narcissus sonum audīvit et magnā vōce vocāvit, "Quis ibi est?" Ēchō parvā vōce reddidit, "Est?" **Hic** dixit, "Venī!" et **illa** idem reddidit. Quoniam nēmō vēnit, Narcissus vocāvit, "Nōnne veniēs ad mē?" Ēchō extrēmum verbum reddidit et magnō cum amōre ad **hunc** cucurrit. **Hic** autem puer **illam** nōn amāvit. "Tē nōn amō," dixit, et fūgit dum **illa** misera reddidit, "amō." **Illa** tum ibi mānsit et deī corpus eius in rūpem mūtāvērunt. Nunc vox **illīus** sōla manet. Sī **illam** vocēs, tibi tuum verbum extrēmum reddat.

d. Ūnō tempore Ēchō pulchrum adulescentem vīdit. Nōmen **illīus** adulescentis erat Narcissus. Ēchō tum magnum amōrem Narcissī sēnsit sed **illī** dīcere nōn potuit. Ubi autem **ille** errat, ibi **haec** errat, sed **is eam** nōn videt. Ūnō autem tempore, dum **ille** sōlus sedēbat, Narcissus sonum audīvit et magnā vōce vocāvit, "Quis ibi est?" Ēchō parvā vōce reddidit, "Est?" **Ille** dixit, "Venī!" et **ea idem** reddidit. Quoniam nēmō vēnit, Narcissus vocāvit, "Nōnne veniēs ad mē?" Ēchō extrēmum verbum reddidit et magnō cum amōre ad **eum** cucurrit. **Ille** autem puer **eam** nōn amāvit. "Tē nōn amō," dixit, et fūgit dum **haec** misera reddidit, "amō." **Haec** tum ibi mānsit et Deī corpus eius in rūpem mūtāvērunt. Nunc vox **eius** sōla manet. Sī **eam** vocēs, tibi tuum verbum extrēmum reddat.

e. Ūnō tempore Ēchō pulchrum adulescentem vīdit. Nōmen **illīus** adulescentis erat Narcissus. Ēchō tum magnum amōrem Narcissī sēnsit sed **illī** dīcere nōn potuit. Ubi autem **ille** errat, ibi **haec** errat, sed **is eam** nōn videt. Ūnō autem tempore, dum **ille** sōlus sedēbat, Narcissus sonum audīvit et magnā vōce vocāvit, "Quis ibi est?" Ēchō parvā vōce reddidit, "Est?" **Ille** dixit, "Venī!" et **ea idem** reddidit. Quōniam nēmō vēnit, Narcissus vocāvit, "Nōnne veniēs ad mē?" Ēchō extrēmum verbum reddidit et magnō cum amōre ad **eum** cucurrit. **Iste** autem puer **hanc** nōn amāvit. "Tē nōn amō," dixit, et fūgit dum **ea** misera reddidit, "amō." **Ea ipsa** tum ibi mānsit et Deī corpus eius in rūpem mūtāvērunt. Nunc vox **eius** sōla manet. Sī **eam** vocēs, tibi tuum verbum extrēmum reddat.

f. Ūnō tempore Ēchō pulchrum adulescentem vīdit. Nōmen **illīus** adulescentis erat Narcissus. Ēchō tum magnum amōrem Narcissī sēnsit sed **illī ipsī** dīcere nōn potuit. Ubi autem **ille** errat, ibi **ista** errat, sed **is eam** nōn videt. Ūnō autem tempore, dum **ille** sōlus sedēbat, Narcissus sonum audīvit et magnā vōce vocāvit, "Quis ibi est?" Ēchō parva vōce reddidit, "Est?" **Ille** dixit, "Venī!" et **ista idem** reddidit. Quōniam nēmō vēnit, Narcissus vocāvit, "Nōnne veniēs ad mē?" Ēchō extrēmum verbum reddidit et magnō cum amōre ad **eum** cucurrit. **Ipse** autem puer **istam** nōn amāvit. "Tē nōn amō," dixit, et fūgit dum **ea** misera reddidit, "amō." **Ea** tum ibi mānsit et Deī corpus eius in rūpem mūtāvērunt. Nunc vox **istīus** sōla manet. Sī **istam** vocēs, tibi tuum verbum extrēmum reddat.

Observe that in passage a), the speaker objectively refers to Narcissus as **īs** and to Echo as **ea**, (*he* and *she*).

In passage b), the speaker refers consistently to Narcissus as **ille** and to Echo as **haec**, *that man* and *this woman*. The effect of the speaker's use of these pronouns is relatively neutral, although **haec** suggests that the speaker feels somewhat closer, physically if not emotionally, to Echo.

In passage c), the reverse is true: now Narcissus is **hic**, *this one*, and Echo is **illa**, *that one*. Note how the perspective, if not the tone, of the speaker thus changes.

In passage d), the tone becomes less rigid, as other demonstratives, especially **is** and **ea**, are used alternatively with the **ille** and **haec**.

In passages e) and f), notice how the speaker begins to take sides, first with Echo in e) by referring to Narcissus, as his cruelty to Echo emerges in the story, as **iste**, and then with Narcissus, by referring to Echo as **ista**.

It is not always easy to make these innuendoes evident in written translation. English can add *of yours* to imply the hostility of **iste**, or it can convey hostility with the tone of the spoken voice. So, too, **ipse**, which requires some kind of emphasis, and which is often expressed in English by the suffix *self*, "*he himself, you, yourself, kings themselves,*" etc. Demonstrative pronouns greatly enrich the tone and variation of what is being said, and they can also trim the language down so that it does not have to keep repeating the same nouns in the narrative flow.

B. Result Clauses and Relative Clauses of Characteristic

B.1.

a. The following words or phrases in an English sentence frequently indicate that either a *clause of result* or a *clause of purpose* will follow, in English as well as in Latin. Indicate which terms anticipate a clause of purpose, and which ones anticipate a clause of result.

Type of Clause

to, as in "We did it *to* help you." _____

in order to, as in, "We spoke up *in order to* be heard." _____

so _____ *that*, e.g.:

  so small that, as in "It is *so small that* we can barely see it." _____

  so big that, as in "The elephant was *so big that* it terrified the Romans." _____

  so far away that, as in "Your home is *so far away that* we rarely go there." _____

so that, as in "We set out early *so that* we would reach Rome by nightfall." _____

lest, as in "They ran away *lest* they be injured." _____

b. Indicate whether the underlined phrases show *purpose* or *result*:

1. Doctors sometimes rim the cup of medicine with honey <u>to make children drink the bitter contents</u>.
2. They sweeten the container in such a way <u>that children unthinkingly drink its contents</u>.
3. My book has so little honey and so much absinth <u>that it will not be sweet</u>.
4. My book will be so good for you <u>that it will not need sweetening</u>.
5. My book is intended to be good for you <u>so that it will not need sweetening</u>.

c. Translate the following sentences and indicate whether the underlined verb shows purpose or result. If it is a result clause, identify the adverb that anticipates result.

1. Iste est malus.
2. Iste est tam malus ut multī eum <u>timeant</u>.
3. Ūnus ōrātōrum illōrum in eius scholā iniit ut bene dīcere <u>disceret</u>.
4. Tam bene studuit ut bene dīcere <u>didicerit</u>.
5. Librum scrīpsit ut discipulīs auxilium <u>daret</u>.

6. Librum ita scrīpsit ut discipulīs auxilium <u>dederit</u>.

7. Erysichthon deōs tam contempsit ut arborem Cereris ipsīus
  <u>ceciderit</u>. (caedō, caedere, cedidī, caesus, *cut down*)

8. Tam saevē arborem cecidit ut Cerēs istī dūram poenam <u>mīserit</u>.

B.2. Clauses of Characteristic

The verb of a relative clause that is anticipated by a generalizing statement, as opposed to a specific statement, will be in the subjunctive mood and will be translated in English by a phrase such as the *sort of*, *of such a sort*, etc. Compare the following:

Erysichthon erat vir qui fīliam vendidit.   (indicative)

Erysichthon was the man who sold his daughter

Erysichthon erat qui fīliam venderet.   (subjunctive)

Erysichthon was the kind of man who would sell his daughter.

B.2. a. Translate the following sentences and indicate whether the subordinate clause is descriptive (*indicative*), or characteristic.

1. Sunt quī hoc facerent.

2. Est vir quī hoc facit.

3. Nēmō est quī mē servābit.

4. Nēmō est quī mē servet.

5. Quis est poēta quī hunc librum scrīpsit?

6. Quis est quī librum huius generis scrībat?

7. Cerēs est dea quī cibum hominibus dat.

8. Cerēs est dea quī cibum hominibus det.

C. Diagramming Latin Sentences

At this point it may be helpful to try diagramming some of the Latin passages in *Traditio*, which will make translation of periodic sentences less daunting than they might at first appear to be.

The first thing to do on encountering a periodic sentence is to identify the main clause of the periodic sentence. The traditional approach to this problem is to try first to find the main verb and its subject, a goal not always as easy as it sounds. You have learned that the main verb tends to be at the end of the sentence. Sometimes, however, the main verb may be placed earlier in the sentence.

C.1. Consider, for example, the passage on p. 162-3, passage 2, where Ovid manipulates word order to depict the complexity of the situation:

Herculēs vōta Iovī parābat

  ubi <u>Fāma</u>.........praecessit ad Dēianīrae aurēs.

    <u>quae</u> vērīs addere falsa semper amat

      et (<u>quae</u>) ē minimō sua per mendācia crescit.

This sentence begins with the main clause, including both subject (Hercules) and verb (was preparing). The first subordinate clause is temporal, indicating when this happened: "when Rumor went to Deianira's ears." The next two clauses are descriptive, both of them giving us some information about Rumor (**Fama**): 1) she "always loves to add false things to true things" and 2) she "increases (in size) from a very small thing through her own lies." Ovid's creative use of word order captures the confusion of gossip as it makes its way to Deianira; for example he separates **vērīs** and **falsa** with the complementary infinitive, **addere**.

Ē minimō sua per mendācia traces the growth of this little piece of gossip into information which will ultimately render Deianira distraught and willing to try desperate measures to change it. Finally, the placement of **praecessit** at the beginning of its clause, and its object at the end, captures its deliberate, steady movement toward her ears—a dreadful goal, under the circumstances, because of the reaction its arrival will trigger.

The next sentence is less complicated, with the main clause introducing an indirect statement. Note that the subject, **Fāma**, is placed at the end of the main clause:

> Huic dixit Fāma
>> Herculem, virum eius, fēminae alterīus amōrem sentīre.

> "Rumor told this woman [Deianira]
>> that Hercules, her husband, loved another woman."

The **quae** introducing the third sentence serves as a connective to what we have learned in the previous sentences about Rumor. English would say, "And this news," since it refers back to the rumor just described, as well as being the subject of **terruit**:

> Quae fāma adeō illam terruit
>> ut multās lacrimās fūderit.

> "And this news so [**adeō**] terrified that woman
>> that [result clause] she shed many tears."

The second paragraph begins by showing the uncertainty in her mind about what she should do. Note how Ovid buries **animus** between **partēs** and **variās** to portray physically what is going on in her mind, as it goes this way and that, "in various directions": **In partes animus varias abiit.**

Only the punctuation connects this independent clause with the next (**constituit ...vestem mittere**) She finally decides to do something: **constituit** governs a complementary infinitive with its own direct object: "to send the garment," which a relative clause describes; and finally; a purpose clause (**ut redderet**) explains why she decided to do this.

> constituit tandem vestem...quam centaurus saevus ōlim suō sanguine
>> imbuerat, mittere
>>> ut (vestis) vīrēs redderet amōrī...

> "Finally she decided to send the garment...
>> which the cruel centaur had dipped in his own blood, so that it
>>> would restore strength (**vīrēs**) to love."

The complications in the next sentence are due to Ovid's attempt to convey the lack of awareness not only of the sender of the cloak, but also of the messenger carrying it. Hence his use of **nescius** to describe both persons—the sender and the person carrying it. (And he also applies it to the person receiving it, in the simple sentence that follows.) Grammatically, it is a compound sentence with an indirect question in one of the independent clauses. Literally, in Ovid's word order, it reads,

> "To the servant, she herself, unaware, hands over her own sorrow,
>> unaware what she was handing over,
>>> and orders the servant to give the gifts to her husband."

If we put the Latin into English word order it would read:

> ipsa nescia trādit dolorem suum servō ignāro ['unaware']
>> quid trādit [indirect question]
>>> et iubet servum dare dōna virō.

The word order at the beginning of the third paragraph puts the subject at the end, thereby emphasizing whose body is set on fire by the poisonous cloak, and this person,

Hercules, remains as the subject of the rest of the paragraph. The second sentence of the paragraph is another compound sentence. The first independent clause has a temporal clause (**dum potuit**), and the second has two result clauses (**ut nōn...potuerit**, and **[ut] Oetam implēverit**.):

"He repressed (his) moan [as long as he could]
but the pain was <u>so great</u>
<u>that he couldn't</u> endure the pain
and <u>(that) he filled</u> Mt. Oeta [with his cries]"

[Hercules] repressit gemitum [suā virtūte (ablative of means)]
dum potuit [reprimere gemitum] sed dolor erat <u>tantus</u>
<u>ut</u> [result] <u>nōn potuerit</u> tolerāre [dolōrem]
<u>implēveritque</u> Oetam [suīs vocibus].

C. 2. Now consider passage 4 , page 163-164 in the text.

Boccaccio's prose is relatively conventional. Observe, however, that placing the number of the labor at the beginning of the first two sentences emphasizes each of these labors. (Words placed at the beginning and at the end of a sentence are in the most emphatic positions.).

In the seventeenth labor (it was) the thief Cacus (that) Hercules killed.
The thirty-first labor [accusative] he was not able to overcome.

In the next sentence, the second clause (a temporal clause) is in the reverse order of the first clause which is the main clause), emphasizing that the same thing was done to Hercules that Hercules did to the monsters:

Postquam [ille, implied subject] **superāvit mōnstra**
For after he killed the other monsters,
illum superāvit amor.
love [subject] overcame that man.
Deianira however remembered the *offerings* (**mūnera**) [main clause]
which (**quae**) she had once received from the centaur Nessus;
she herself (**ipsa**) believed *that thing* (**id**)....was true. [main clause]
which (**quod**) the *centaur*.....had said
when about to *die.* (**moritūrus**)
In order to recall the love of Hercules (**Ut...revocāret**)   [purpose clause]
she secretly sent to him (**illī**) the centaur's *cloak* (**vestem**), [main clause]
which (**quam**) Hercules put on.

The next sentence begins by anticipating a result clause with the adverb **sic**:
(His) sweat *released* the poisoned blood [main clause]
in such a way (**sic**)
through the pores...
which (**quōs**) the heat had enlarged
that (**ut**) the blood flowed into his internal organs;

In the final portion of the sentence, the subject of **incendit** is the poisoned blood which aroused *such* (**adeō**) intolerable pain *that* [result] he decided to die (**mōrī** is a complementary infinitive.)

The second paragraph begins with two compound sentences: He constructed a pyre on Mt. Oeta, and he gave his arrows and their container (a quiver) to Philoctetes. Then he climbed onto the pyre and ordered Philoctetes to set fire to it (**eam**, the pyre); and in this was (**sic**) he exhaled his weary soul (**anima**, feminine, means the breath of life, or life itself). Note that here **sic** does not anticipate a subordinate, result clause.

The accusative **Hunc** at the beginning of the next sentence links the train of thought to the preceding sentences, and also emphasizes the object rather than the author, **Seneca...dīcit**, *Seneca says*, is followed by an indirect statement:

> Seneca...*says* [main clause]
> (in his tragedy, *Hercules Oetaeus*)
> *that* Jupiter (**Iovem**, subject accus.) welcomed him [**hunc**] into heaven.

Another compound sentence follows; the second half of the compound contains a description of Hebe which is set in apposition to her:

> Then Jupiter reconciled him (**eum**) and Juno [main clause]
> and betrothed *Hebe*...to him [main clause]
> the *goddess* of youth and *the daughter* of Juno. [apposition]

The last two sentences quote Homer. Thus the two phrases, **Homērus dīcit** and **Dīcit** both introduce indirect statement:

> Homer however says (in the *Odyssey*) [main clause]
> *that* Ulysses (subject accusative) saw him (in the Underworld).

> He (Homer) nevertheless says [main clause]
> *that* <u>he</u> (**eum**) (subject accusative)...is not the true Hercules
> <u>whom</u> (**quem**) Ulysses saw
> but [that he is] his image.

D. Vocabulary Review: Verb Roots

The following list contains some of the more basic verbs you have learned in the first nine chapters of *Traditio*, some of which you have encountered in their basic forms, others in compound verbs. This is a good time to review all the principal parts of these verbs, including the fourth principal part, since you will need to know it not only in order to form or recognize future active participles, but to work in the passive voice, which will be introduced in Chapter X. If you have not already begun compiling verb lists on your computer or in flash cards, do so now, using this list as a beginning.

agō	cēdō	dūcō	fugiō	incendō	mōnstrō	scindō	sum	videō
ardeō	claudō	eō	fundō	legō	noscō	scrībō	teneō	vīvō
audiō	discō	faciō	gerō	līberō	nōlō	sentiō	trahō	volō
cadō	dīcō	fleō	habeō	mandō	pōnō	servō	veniō	
capiō	doceō	fluō	iaciō	mālō	premō	stō	vertō	

a. Begin reviewing these verbs by rearranging them according to conjugation; then supply the remaining principal parts and meanings, and indicate whether they are transitive (trans.) or intransitive (intrans.).

Example: *Principal Parts and Meaning*   *Transitive or Intransitive*
dō   **dō, dare, dedī, datus** , give   Transitive
(conjugation: irregular)
(Note: In compounds becomes 3rd conj., **-dō, -dere, -didī, -ditus**)

Principal Parts   *Meaning*   *Transitive/Intransitive*

1st conjugation: _____ _____ _____

_____ _____ _____

_____ _____ _____

_____ _____ _____

122

2nd conjugation: _____   _____   _____
_____   _____   _____
_____   _____   _____
_____   _____   _____
_____   _____   _____

3rd conjugation: _____   _____   _____
_____   _____   _____
_____   _____   _____
_____   _____   _____
_____   _____   _____
_____   _____   _____
_____   _____   _____
_____   _____   _____
_____   _____   _____
_____   _____   _____
_____   _____   _____
_____   _____   _____
_____   _____   _____
_____   _____   _____
_____   _____   _____
_____   _____   _____
_____   _____   _____

3rd iō: _____   _____   _____
_____   _____   _____
_____   _____   _____
_____   _____   _____

4th conjugation: _____   _____   _____
_____   _____   _____
_____   _____   _____

Irregular: _____   _____   _____
_____   _____   _____
_____   _____   _____
_____   _____   _____

E. Derivations: Latin Phrases in Current Use

Identify the correct definition for the following terms, common today in English.

Latin abbreviations and phrases

A.D. (Annō Dominī) _____

alter ego _____

deus ex machinā _____

etc. (et cetera) _____

ex parte _____

fl. (floruit) _____

i.e. (id est) _____

ibid. (ibidem) _____

in principiō _____

in tōtō _____

inter alia _____

inter aliōs _____

ipse dixit _____

ipsō factō _____

magnum opus _____

mea culpa _____

n.b. (notā bene) _____

nōlī mē tangere _____

per sē _____

persōnae drāmatis _____

persōna nōn grāta _____

prō tempore _____

q.e.d. (quod erat dēmōnstrātum) _____

q.v. (quod vidē) _____

quid nunc _____

quid prō quō _____

sic _____

sine quā nōn _____

tempus fugit _____

terra firma _____

vox populī _____

Meaning

a. note this well

b. another I

c. he himself said

d. in itself

e. for the time being

f. refer back to this ("and see this [for more detail]")

g. my mistake

h. the masks of a drama

i. the voice of the people

j. solid land

k. he (or she) was in his (her) prime

l. in the year of our Lord

m. in the same place

n. time flies

o. what in exchange for what

p. without which not (something essential)

q. what now? (a gossip)

r. an unwelcome person

s. masterpiece

t. thus

u. the god out of the machine (an unlikely solution)

v. by the deed itself

w. in the beginning

x. among other people

y. in its entirely

z. that is, in other words

aa. among other things

bb. on one side only

cc. don't touch me

dd. and so forth (and the rest)

ee. the thing which had been proven

Key, Chapter IX

A.1.

a. *fem. sing.*

haec	illa	ipsa	ista	eadem
huius	illīus	ipsīus	istīus	eiusdem
huic	illī	ipsī	istī	eīdem
hanc	illam	ipsam	istam	eandem
hāc	illā	ipsā	istā	eādem

b. *neuter pl.*

haec	illa	ipsa	ista	eadem
hōrum	illōrum	ipsōrum	istorum	eōrundem
hīs	illīs	ipsīs	istīs	eīsdem
haec	illa	ipsa	ista	eadem
hīs	illīs	ipsīs	istīs	eīsdem

c. *Nominative:*

		Dative:	
this man	**hic**	to these women	**eīs**
that woman	**illa**	for that girl	**eī**
those girls	**illae**	to the same girl	**eīdem**
the girl herself	**ipsa**	to the girls themselves	**eīsdem**
the same things	**eadem**	for that woman (of yours)	**istī**
the thing itself	**ipsum**	for the same men	**eīsdem**
those things (of yours)	**ista**	for the man himself	**eīdem**

Accusative

this woman	**hanc**	that man	**illum**
that woman	**illam**	the very man	**eundem**
the same woman	**eandem**	the same man	**eundem**
the same women	**eāsdem**	the man himself	**ipsum**
the woman herself	**ipsam**	those men (of yours)	**istōs**
this thing	**hoc**	these boys	**hōs**
that thing	**illud**	this boy	**hunc**
those things	**illa**	the very things	**eadem**
the thing itself	**ipsum**	this very thing	**hoc idem**

d.

		Case and Number	*Translation*
1.	eius generis	gen. sing	of this kind
2.	illīus generis	gen. sing.	of that kind
3.	eā lēge ipsā	abl. sing	by this law itself
4.	eādem lēge solā	abl. sing	by the same law alone (only by the same law)
5.	illō eōdem tempore	abl. sing.	at that same time
6.	hōc ipsō tempore	abl. sing.	at this very time
7.	istō mōre novō	abl. sing.	by that new custom of yours
8.	huius nōminis tōtīus	gen. sing.	of this entire name
9.	illud nōmen sōlum	nom. or accus. sing.	that name alone
10.	illā eādem virtūte	abl. sing.	by that same virtue
11.	istī eīdem virtūtī	dat. sing.	to or for that same virtue of yours
12.	in eius fronte ipsā	in + abl. sing.	on his very forehead
13.	Iovī īpsī	dat. sing.	to Jupiter himself
14.	istam deam	accus. sing.	that goddess of yours
15.	eōdem dolōre	abl. sing.	by that same sorrow
16.	istīus saevae amōris	gen. sing.	of that savage love of yours
17.	illā vōce pulchrā	abl. sing.	with that beautiful voice
18.	vestīgiīs eīsdem	abl. or dat. pl.	for or by means of the same tracks
19.	sanguinis ipsīus	gen. sing.	of blood itself
20.	hanc spēluncam	accus. sing.	this cave

A.2.

a. At one time Echo saw a beautiful young man. The name of **this** young man was Narcissus. Echo then felt a great love for Narcissus but she was not able to speak **to him**. Where **he** wanders, however, there **she** wanders, but **he** does not see **her**. Once (at one time), however, while **he** was sitting alone, Narcissus heard a sound and called loudly, "Who is there?" Echo with a little voice (softly) replied "There?" **He** said "Come!" and **she** repeated **this word**. Since no one came, Narcissus called, "You will come to me, won't you?" Echo repeated the last word and with great love ran toward **him**. But **this** boy did not love **her**. "It is not you I love," he said and ran away while **she**, unhappy repeated, "I love." Then **she** remained there and the Gods changed her body into a cliff. Now **her** voice alone remains. If you should call **her**, she will repeat to you your last word.

b. At one time Echo saw a beautiful young man. The name of **that** young man was Narcissus. Echo then felt a great love for Narcissus but she was not able to speak **to him** (**that man**). Where **that man** wanders, however, there **this woman** wanders, but **that man** does not see **this woman**. Once (at one time), however, while **that man** was sitting alone, Narcissus heard a sound and called loudly, "Who is there?" Echo with a little voice (softly) replied "There?". **That man** said "Come!" and **this woman** repeated the same thing. Since no one came, Narcissus called, "You will come to me, won't you?" Echo repeated the last word and with great love ran toward **that man**. But **that man** did not love **this woman**. "It is not you I love," he said and ran away while **this woman**, unhappy, repeated, "I love." Then **this woman** remained there and the Gods changed her body into a cliff. Now the voice alone of **this woman** remains. If you should call **this woman**, she will repeat to you your last word.

c. At one time Echo saw a beautiful young man. The name of **this** young man was Narcissus. Echo then felt a great love for Narcissus but she was not able to speak to **this man**. Where **this man** wanders, however, there **that woman** wanders, but **this man** does not see **that woman**. Once (at one time), however, while **this man** was sitting alone, Narcissus heard a sound and called loudly, "Who is there?" Echo with a little voice (softly) replied "There?". **This man** said "Come!" and **that woman** repeated the same thing. Since no one came, Narcissus called, "You will come to me, won't you?" Echo repeated the last word and with great love ran toward **this man**. But **this man** did not love **that woman**. "It is not you I love," he said and ran away while **that woman**, unhappy, repeated, "I love." Then **that woman** remained there and the Gods changed her body into a cliff. Now the voice alone of **this woman** remains. If you should call **that woman**, she will repeat to you your last word.

d. At one time Echo saw a beautiful young man. The name of **that** young man was Narcissus. Echo then felt a great love for Narcissus but she was not able to speak to **that man**. Where **that man** wanders, however, there **this woman** wanders, but **he** does not see **her**. Once (at one time), however, while **that man** was sitting alone, Narcissus heard a sound and called loudly, "Who is there?" Echo with a little voice (softly) replied "There?". **That man** said "Come!" and **she** repeated **the same thing**. Since no one came, Narcissus called, "You will come to me, won't you?" Echo repeated the last word and with great love ran toward **him**. But **that** man (**of yours** [pejorative]) did not love **her**. "It is not you I love," he said and ran away while **this woman**, unhappy, repeated, "I love." Then this woman remained there and the Gods changed her body into a cliff. Now **her** voice alone remains. If you should call **her**, she will repeat to you your last word.

e. At one time Echo saw a beautiful young man. The name of **that young man** was Narcissus. Echo then felt a great love for Narcissus but she was not able to speak to **that man**. Where **that man** wanders, however, there **this woman** wanders, but **he** does not see **her**. Once (at one time), however, while **that man** was sitting alone, Narcissus heard a sound and called loudly, "Who is there?" Echo with a little voice (softly) replied "There?". **That man** said "Come!" and **she** repeated **the same thing**. Since no one came, Narcissus called, "You will come to me, won't you?" Echo repeated the last word and with great love ran toward **him**. But **that** man (**of yours**) did not love **this woman**. "It is not you I love," he said and ran away while she, unhappy, repeated, "I love." Then **she herself** remained there and the Gods changed her body into a cliff. Now **her** voice alone remains. If you should call **her**, she will repeat to you your last word.

f. At one time Echo saw a beautiful young man. The name of **that young man** was Narcissus. Echo then felt a great love for Narcissus but she was not able to speak to **that man himself**. Where **that man** wanders, however, there **this woman (of yours)** wanders, but **he** does not see **her**. Once (at one time), however, while **that man** was sitting alone, Narcissus heard a sound and called loudly, "Who is there?" Echo with a little voice (softly) replied "There?". **That man** said "Come!" and **that woman of yours** repeated **the same thing**. Since no one came, Narcissus called, "You will come to me, won't you?" Echo repeated the last word and with great love ran toward **him**. But the man **himself** did not love **that woman of yours**. "It is not you I love," he said and ran away while **she**, unhappy, repeated, "I love." Then **she** remained there and the Gods changed her body into a cliff. Now the voice alone **of that woman** remains. If you should call **that woman (of yours)**, she will repeat to you your last word.

B.1.

a.

	Type of Clause
to, as in "We did it to help you."	purpose
in order to, as in, "We spoke up in order to be heard."	purpose
so _____ that, e.g.:	
so small that, as in "It is *so small that* we can barely see it."	result
so big that, as in "The elephant was *so big that* it terrified the Romans."	result
so far away that, as in "Your home is *so far away that* we rarely go there."	result
so that, as in "We set out early *so that* we would reach Rome by nightfall."	purpose
lest, as in "They ran away *lest* they be injured."	purpose

b.

1. purpose
2. result
3. result
4. result
5. purpose

c.

1. This man of yours is evil.
2. This man of yours is so evil that many people fear him. (result - **tam**)
3. One of those speakers entered his school in order to learn to speak well. (purpose)
4. He studied so well that he learned to speak well. (result - **tam**)
5. He wrote a book to give help to his students. (purpose)
6. He wrote the book in such a way that he gave help to his students. (result - **ita**)
7. Erysichthon so despised the gods that he cut down the tree of Ceres herself. (result - **tam**)
8. He cut down the tree so cruelly that Ceres sent him a harsh punishment. (result - **tam**)

B.2. a.

1. characteristic; There are people who would do this.
2. descriptive; He is the man who is doing this.
3. descriptive; No one exists who will save me.
4. characteristic; There is no one who would save me.
5. descriptive; Who is the poet who wrote this book?
6. characteristic; Who is there who would write a book of this sort?
7. descriptive; Ceres is the goddess who give human beings food.
8. characteristic; Ceres is the kind of goddess who would give human beings food.

D. Vocabulary Review

(For Meanings and additional Compounds, check vocabulary listings and earlier chapters)

	Principal parts	*Meanings*	*Transitive/Intransitive*
1st conjugation:			
līberō	-āre, -āvī, -ātus	set free	Transitive
mandō	-āre, -āvī, -ātus	entrust	Transitive
monstrō	-āre, -āvī, -ātus	show	Transitive
servō	-āre, -āvī, -ātus	save	Transitive
2nd conjugation:			
ardeō	-ēre, arsī, arsus	be on fire	Intransitive
doceō	-ēre, -uī, -itus	teach	Transitive
fleō	-ēre, flēvī, flētus	weep	Intransitive
habeō	-ēre, -uī, -itus	have	Transitive
teneō	-ēre, -uī, tentus	hold	Transitive
videō	-ēre, vīdī, vīsus	see	Transitive
3rd conjugation:			
agō	-ere, ēgī, actus	do	Transitive
cadō	-ere, cecidī, cāsus	fall	Intransitive
cēdō	-ere, cessī, cessus	go	Intransitive
claudō	-ere, clausī, clausus	close	Transitive
discō	-ere, didicī, —	learn	Transitive
dīcō	-ere, dīxī, dictus	say	Transitive
dūcō	-ere, dūxī, ductus	lead	Transitive
fluō	-ere, fluxī, fluctus	flow	Intransitive
fundō	-ere, fūdī, fūsus	pour	Transitive
gerō	-ere, gessī, gestus	do accomplish	Transitive
incendō	-ere, incendī, incēnsus	set fire to	Transitive
legō	-ere, lēgī, lectus	choose; read	Transitive
noscō	-ere, nōvī, nōtus	learn	Transitive
pōnō	-ere, pōsuī, positus	place, put	Transitive
premō	-ere, pressī, pressus	press	Transitive
scindō	-ere, scīdī, scissus	cut, tear	Transitive
scrībō	-ere, scrīpsi, scrīptus	write	Transitive
trahō	-ere, traxī, tractus	drag, draw	Transitive
vertō	-ere, vertī, versus	turn	Transitive
vīvō	-ere, vīxī, vīctus	live	Intransitive
3rd -iō:			
capiō	-ere, cēpī, captus	seize, capture	Transitive
faciō	-ere, fēcī, factus	make, do	Transitive
fugiō	-ere, fūgi, fugitum	flee, avoid	Intransitive
iaciō	-ere, iēcī, iactus	throw, hurl	Transitive
4th conjugation:			
audiō	-īre, audīvī, audītus	hear, listen to	Transitive
sentiō	-īre, sēnsī, sēnsus	feel, perceive	Transitive
veniō	-īre, vēnī, ventus	come	Intransitive
Irregular:			
eō	īre, īvī, ītum	go	Intransitive
mālō	mālle, māluī, —	prefer	Intransitive
nōlō	nōlle, nōluī, —	be unwilling	Intransitive
stō	stāre, stetī, status	stand	Intransitive
sūm	esse, fuī, futūrus	be	Intransitive
volō	velle, voluī, —	be willing, want	Intransitive

128

E. TERMINOLOGY-DERIVATIONS: LATIN PHRASES IN CURRENT USE

Latin abbreviations and phrases	*Meaning*
A.D. (Annō Dominī)	l. in the year…
alter ego	b. another I
deus ex machinā	u. the god out of the machine
etc. (et cetera)	dd. and so forth
ex parte	bb. on one side only
fl. (floruit)	k. he (she) was in his (her) prime
i.e. (id est)	z. that is, in other words
ibid. (ibidem)	m. in the same place
in principiō	w. in the beginning
in tōtō	y. in its entirety
inter alia	aa. among other things
inter aliōs	x. among other people
ipse dixit	c. he himself said
ipsō factō	v. by the deed itself
magnum opus	s. masterpiece
mea culpa	g. my mistake
n.b. (notā bene)	a. note this well
nōlī mē tangere	cc. don't touch me
per sē	d. in itself
persōnae drāmatis	h. the masks of drama
persōna nōn grāta	r. an unwelcome person
prō tempore	e. for the time being
q.e.d. (quod erat dēmōnstrātum)	ee. the thing which had been proven
q.v. (quod vidē)	f. refer back to this
quid nunc	q. what now?
quid prō quō	o. what in exchange for what?
sic	t. thus
sine quā nōn	p. without which, not
tempus fugit	n. time flies
terra firma	j. solid land
vox populī	i. the voice of the people

<h1>X
The Passive Voice</h1>

Until now, every verb you have read and written in Latin has been in the *active voice*. This means that the subject of the verb has been the *agent*, the person or thing that causes the action to take place or, in the case of an intransitive verb, is simply its subject:

Fēmina **mihi dixit.**	*The woman* spoke to me.
Magister **est fēmina.**	*The teacher* is a woman.
Herculēs **Cācum in spēluncā conclūsit.**	*Hercules* enclosed Cacus in a cave.

The passive voice of a verb, in English as well as in Latin, indicates that the subject of the verb is the recipient of the action of the verb. Thus the direct object of an active verb becomes the subject of a passive verb. To convey the agent—the person or thing causing the action to take place—with a passive verb, English and Latin indicate *by whom or by what* the action is carried out. Latin uses the ablative case for this purpose: the ablative of means or instrument (without a preposition) is used if a *thing* is the agent. If the agent is a person, or a thing that has been personified (such as Hunger, or Rumor), the ablative of agent must be used with the passive voice. The ablative of agent is always introduced by the preposition **ā** or **ab** (before a vowel).

> We are being summoned *by the woman* .
> **Ā** *fēminā* **vocāmur.**
>
> Cacus was enclosed in a cave *by Hercules.*
> **Cācus in spēluncā** *ab Hercule* **conclūsus est.**

It is necessary to learn the passive forms of verbs before proceeding further with examples.

A. The Present Stem

Learning the passive voice is not as overwhelming a task as it might first appear: the rules are the same for verbs formed on the present stem (present, imperfect, future, both indicative and subjunctive).

What is new are the personal endings:

	Singular endings, passive voice	(Compare active voice endings)
1st	**-or**	(-ō, -m)
2nd	**-ris**	(-s)
3rd	**-tur**	(-t)
	Plural endings, passive voice	
1st	**-mur**	(-mus)
2nd	**-minī**	(-tis)
3rd	**-ntur**	(-nt)

The Passive voice in the present, imperfect, and future tenses are formed as follows:

Present tense:	These endings are added directly to the present stem.
Imperfect tense, indicative mood:	These endings are added directly to the present stem + **-bā-**
Imperfect tense, subjunctive mood:	These endings are added directly to the present active infinitive.
Future tense, indicative mood:	These endings are added directly to the present stem + **-bi-** (1st and 2nd conjugations) or **-ē-** (3rd and 4th conjugations).
Present Infinitive:	For the first, second and fourth conjugations, the final **-e** of the infinitive is replaced by final **-ī**. For the third conjugation, the entire infinitive ending, **-ere**, is replaced by final **-ī**.

A.1.

a) Conjugate the following verbs in the passive voice in the tenses and moods indicated, and translate.

i. **mōnstrāre**   PRESENT TENSE, INDICATIVE MOOD

	Singular	Translation	Plural	Translation
1st	_____	_____	_____	_____
2nd	_____	_____	_____	_____
3rd	_____	_____	_____	_____

PRESENT TENSE, SUBJUNCTIVE MOOD

	Singular	Plural
1st	_____	_____
2nd	_____	_____
3rd	_____	_____

ii. **removēre**   IMPERFECT TENSE, INDICATIVE MOOD

	Singular	Translation	Plural	Translation
1st	_____	_____	_____	_____
2nd	_____	_____	_____	_____
3rd	_____	_____	_____	_____

IMPERFECT TENSE, SUBJUNCTIVE MOOD

	Singular	Plural
1st	_____	_____
2nd	_____	_____
3rd	_____	_____

iii.　　**iaciō**　　　FUTURE TENSE, INDICATIVE MOOD

	Singular	Translation	Plural	Translation
1st	_____	_____	_____	_____
2nd	_____	_____	_____	_____
3rd	_____	_____	_____	_____

b) Write a synopsis of each of the following in the passive voice, as indicated:

1.　　**dare,** 1st person plural

	Indicative	Translation	Subjunctive
Pres.	_____	_____	_____
Imperf.	_____	_____	_____
Future	_____	_____	_____

2.　　**tollere,** 3rd person plural

	Indicative	Translation	Subjunctive
Pres.	_____	_____	_____
Imperf.	_____	_____	_____
Future	_____	_____	_____

3.　　**colere,** 2nd person plural

	Indicative	Translation	Subjunctive
Pres.	_____	_____	_____
Imperf.	_____	_____	_____
Future	_____	_____	_____

4.　　**rapere,** 2nd person singular

	Indicative	Translation	Subjunctive
Pres.	_____	_____	_____
Imperf.	_____	_____	_____
Future	_____	_____	_____

5.　　**petere,** 3rd person singular

	Indicative	Translation	Subjunctive
Pres.	_____	_____	_____
Imperf.	_____	_____	_____
Future	_____	_____	_____

6.   **vidēre,** 1st person singular

	Indicative	Translation	Subjunctive
Pres.	_____	_____	_____
Imperf.	_____	_____	_____
Future	_____	_____	_____

c) Change the following to the passive voice and translate:

	Active	Passive	Translation
1.	vidēbimus	_____	_____
2.	vidētis	_____	_____
3.	vidēbant	_____	_____
4.	videās	_____	_____
5.	videāmus	_____	_____
6.	vidēre	_____	_____
7.	capiam	_____	_____
8.	capiēs	_____	_____
9.	capiat	_____	_____
10.	capimus	_____	_____
11.	relinquō	_____	_____
12.	relinquat	_____	_____
13.	relinquēmus	_____	_____
14.	vincimus	_____	_____
15.	vincāmus	_____	_____

d) Change the following infinitives to the passive voice and translate:

	Active	Passive	Translation
1.	capere	_____	_____
2.	dūcere	_____	_____
3.	tenēre	_____	_____
4.	locāre	_____	_____
5.	cōgere	_____	_____
6.	sentīre	_____	_____
7.	interficere	_____	_____
8.	dare	_____	_____
9.	regere	_____	_____
10.	instituere	_____	_____

e) Translate the following sentences into English:

1. Dīcunt Erysichthonem deōs contemnisse. (**Erysichthon, -onis,** m , "Erysichthon")

2. Nympha poenam Erysichthonis petēbat.

3. Erysichthon magnam famem sentiēt.

4. Multī hominēs deōrum beneficia pervertunt.

5. Saturnum deum esse fingis.

6. Iovem "patrem deōrum hominumque" dīcimus.

7. Bovēs trāns flūmen Herculēs dūcēbat.

f) Translate the following sentences into Latin:

1. Erysichthon is said to have scorned the gods.

2. Punishment of Erysichthon was requested (**petere**) by the nymph.

3. The kindnesses (**beneficium,** ī, *n*) of the gods are subverted (**pervertere**) by many people.

4. Saturnus is believed by you to be a god.

5. Jupiter is called by us, "father of gods and of men."

6. A great hunger will be felt by Erysichthon.

7. The cattle were being led across the river by Hercules.

B. The Perfect Stem

The tenses based on the perfect stem—perfect, pluperfect and future perfect—consist of the fourth principal part of the verb, which is the perfect passive participle, plus forms of the verb **esse:**

The *Perfect Passive* consists of the perfect passive participle plus the present forms of **esse: sum, es, est,** etc. for the indicative, and **sim, sīs, sit,** etc. for the subjunctive.

The *Pluperfect Passive* consists of the perfect passive participle plus the imperfect forms of **esse: eram, erās, erat,** etc. for the indicative, and **essem, essēs, esset,** etc. for the subjunctive.

The *Future Perfect Passive* consists of the perfect passive participle plus the future forms of **esse: erō, eris, erit,** etc. for the indicative.

The Perfect Passive Infinitive consists of the perfect passive participle plus the present infinitive, **esse.**

B.1

a) Conjugate the following in the passive voice in the tenses and moods indicated, and translate.

i. **mōnstrāre**   PRESENT TENSE, INDICATIVE MOOD

	Singular	Translation	Plural	Translation
1st				
2nd				
3rd				

PRESENT TENSE, SUBJUNCTIVE MOOD

	Singular	Plural
1st	_____	_____
2nd	_____	_____
3rd	_____	_____

ii. **removēre** PLUPERFECT TENSE, INDICATIVE MOOD

	Singular	Translation	Plural	Translation
1st	_____	_____	_____	_____
2nd	_____	_____	_____	_____
3rd	_____	_____	_____	_____

PLUPERFECT TENSE, SUBJUNCTIVE MOOD

	Singular	Plural
1st	_____	_____
2nd	_____	_____
3rd	_____	_____

iii. **iaciō** FUTURE PERFECT TENSE, INDICATIVE MOOD

	Singular	Translation	Plural	Translation
1st	_____	_____	_____	_____
2nd	_____	_____	_____	_____
3rd	_____	_____	_____	_____

b) Write a synopsis of each of the following in the passive voice, as indicated:

i. **dare,** 1st person plural

	Indicative	Translation	Subjunctive
Pres.	_____	_____	_____
Imperf.	_____	_____	_____
Future	_____	_____	_____

ii. **tollere,** 3rd person plural

	Indicative	Translation	Subjunctive
Pres.	_____	_____	_____
Imperf.	_____	_____	_____
Future	_____	_____	_____

iii.   **colere,** 2nd person plural

	Indicative	Translation	Subjunctive
Pres.	_____	_____	_____
Imperf.	_____	_____	_____
Future	_____	_____	_____

iv.   **rapere,** 2nd person singular

	Indicative	Translation	Subjunctive
Pres.	_____	_____	_____
Imperf.	_____	_____	_____
Future	_____	_____	_____

v.   **petere,** 3rd person singular

	Indicative	Translation	Subjunctive
Pres.	_____	_____	_____
Imperf.	_____	_____	_____
Future	_____	_____	_____

vi.   **vidēre,** 1st person singular

	Indicative	Translation	Subjunctive
Pres.	_____	_____	_____
Imperf.	_____	_____	_____
Future	_____	_____	_____

c) Change the following to the passive voice and translate:

	Active	Passive	Translation
1.	vīderimus	_____	_____
2.	vīdistis	_____	_____
3.	vīdērunt	_____	_____
4.	vīderās	_____	_____
5.	vīdissēmus	_____	_____
6.	vīdisse	_____	_____
7.	cēpī	_____	_____
8.	cēperis	_____	_____
9.	cēperāmus	_____	_____
10.	cēpissēmus	_____	_____
11.	relīquī	_____	_____
12.	relīquit	_____	_____
13.	relīquerāmus	_____	_____
14.	vīcimus	_____	_____
15.	vīcerimus	_____	_____

d) Change the following infinitives to the passive voice and translate:

	Active	Passive	Translation
1.	cēpisse	_____	_____
2.	duxisse	_____	_____
3.	tenuisse	_____	_____
4.	locāvisse	_____	_____
5.	coēgisse	_____	_____
6.	sēnsisse	_____	_____
7.	interfēcisse	_____	_____
8.	dedisse	_____	_____
9.	rexisse	_____	_____
10.	ēgisse	_____	_____

e) Translate the following sentences into English.

1. Dixērunt Erysichthon deōs contemnisse.

2. Nympha poenam Erysichthonis petīvit.

3. Erysichthon magnam famem sēnserit.

4. Multī hominēs deōrum beneficia pervertērunt.

5. Saturnum deum esse finxistī.

6. Iovem "patrem deōrum hominumque" diximus.

7. Bovēs trāns flūmen Herculēs duxerat.

f) Translate the following sentences into Latin:

1. It has been said by many people that Erysichthon scorned the gods.

2. The gods have been said to have been scorned by Erysichthon.

3. The punishment of Erysichthon has been requested by that nymph.

4. Great hunger (**famēs, -is**, *f.*) will have been felt by Erysichthon.

5. The kindnesses of the gods have been subverted by many men.

6. Saturnus has been imagined by you (pl.) to be a god.

7. Saturnus used to be thought to have been a god.

8. Jupiter has been called "the father of gods and men" by us.

9. The cattle had been led across the river by Hercules.

10. Hercules' cattle had been led across the river by him (himself).

B.2. You may find it helpful at this point to review the fourth principal parts of all the verbs you have learned in chapters I-X. In the earlier chapters of this Workbook, you were asked to categorize the verbs you have learned by conjugation. Now you will find it helpful to further break down those categories according to the form of the fourth principal part.

a) List all verbs under the appropriate category with their principal parts.

b) Try to list at least one English derivative which is formed from the perfect passive participle of each verb.

   i.   First Conjugation, participles ending in **-ātus**. This will include the majority of first conjugation verbs.

   ii.   Irregular verbs whose infinitives end in **-are**.

   iii. Second Conjugation verbs ending in

         -ētus

         -itus

         -sus

         -tus

   iv.   Third Conjugation verbs ending in

         -itus

         -tus

         -sus

   v.   Fourth Conjugation verbs ending in

         -ītus

         -sus

         -tus

C. Terminology Review

Explain what is meant by the following terms:

1. passive voice

2. active voice

3. ablative of personal agent

4. ablative of means or instrument

5. perfect passive participle

D. Translation:

THE BIRTH OF HERCULES

When Hercules and his younger brother, Iphikles, were still infants, Juno sent two huge serpents to destroy them in their crib. Hercules, who was about ten months old, amazed his parents and servants and onlookers by grabbing the serpents and choking them to death. The amazed parents consulted the seer Tiresias, who then foretold that Hercules would slay great beasts on land and on the sea, and would even help Jupiter defeat the Giants when they tried to overcome the ruler of gods and men. The depictions of this popular episode are found in numerous paintings that survive from antiquity.

Special Vocabulary

anguis, is, *m or f.*	serpent, snake	**nox, noctis,** *f.*	night, darkness
consistō, ere	to come to a halt, stop	**ōs, ōris,** *n.*	the mouth, lips
cubiculum, ī, *n.*	bedroom	**parēns, parentis,** *m. or f.*	parent
diū *(adverb)*	for a long time	**pēs, pedis,** *m.*	foot

138

duo (*nom. pl. m.*)	two	**rīdeō, ēre, rīsī, rīsus**	to laugh, smile
guttur, gutturis, *n.*	throat, gullet	**serpō, ere, serpsī, —**	to creep, crawl, slither
lambō, ere	to lick	**sībilus, a, um**	hissing
ligō, āre, āvī, ātus	to tie, bind	**taeda, ae,** *f.*	torch
manibus	with his hands	**terreō, ēre, uī, itus**	to terrify
māter, mātris, *f.*	mother	**ursa, ae,** *f.*	bear
		(**Ursa Magna,** the Big Dipper)	

D.1. Translate the following sentences.

1. Quandō Herculēs erat parvus puer, duo anguēs ā Iūnōne missī sunt ut puerum interficerent.

2. Nox erat et Ursa Magna in mediō caelō consistere vīsa est.

3. Istī magnī anguēs domum Herculis advēnērunt perque ianuās serpsērunt.

4. Oculī istōrum sanguine et flammīs imbūtī ardēbant, sībilaque ōra linguīs lambēbant.

5. Sed ubi ad parva corpora puerōrum serpserant, subitō Iuppiter lūcem fēcit. Lux ā Iove facta est.

6. Iuppiter illam lūcem fēcit ut puerōs monēret.

7. Puerī oculīs suīs istōs anguēs, qui ut sibi nocēret advēnissent, vīdērunt.

8. Parvus Iphiklēs magnā vōce flēre incipiēbat, sed parvus Herculēs ipse istōs anguēs manibus parvīs rapuit.

9. Istī anguēs suīs gutturibus ab Hercule tenēbantur. Eōrum guttura manibus ligāre vīsus est Herculēs.

10. Circum medium parvum Herculem ligāre incipiēbant sed puer nōn diū ligārī potuit. Parvus Herculēs istīs anguibus ligārī incipiēbat.

11. Istī anguēs perībunt. Istī perītūrī sunt. Vincantur enim ab illō puerō dūrō. Ā puerō dūrō tollantur. Nunc interfectī sunt. Nunc anguēs ē terrā sublātī pereunt. Anguēs, ē terrā sublāti interfectīque ā puerō dūrō, periērunt.

12. Iphiklēs ā mātre patreque puerōrum flēre audiēbatur. Iphiklēs magnā cum vōce flēre vidēbatur. Māter paterque vēniēbantque ut discerent cūr puer flēret.

13. Pater arma sua cēpit ut puerōs ā perīculō servāret. Armīs patris puerī ā perīculō servābuntur. Pater puerōs servātūrus erat.

14. Servī taedās fēcērunt incendēruntque. Servī taedās tollunt. Taedae ā servīs tollēbantur. Taedae ā servīs factae incēnsaeque sublātae sunt.

15. Pater māterque servīque sīc advēnērunt et Herculem in cubiculō cum anguibus interfectīs invēnērunt.

16. Parentēs territī sunt, sed puer rīsit et anguēs saevōs ad eōrum pedēs pōsuit. Anguēs interfectī ad pedēs positī sunt.

Key, Chapter X

A.1.

a)   i. **mōnstrāre**   Present Tense, Indicative Mood

	Singular	*Translation*	*Plural*	*Translation*
1st	**mōnstror**	I am being shown	**mōnstrāmur**	we are being shown
2nd	**mōnstrāris**	you are being shown	**mōnstrāminī**	you are being shown
3rd	**mōnstrātur**	he is being shown	**mōnstrantur**	they are being shown

Present Tense, Subjunctive Mood

Singular	*Plural*
mōnstrer	**mōnstrēmur**
mōnstrēris	**mōnstrēminī**
mōnstrētur	**mōnstrentur**

     ii. **removēre**   Imperfect Tense, Indicative Mood

	Singular	*Translation*	*Plural*	*Translation*
1st	**removēbar**	I was being removed	**removēbāmur**	we were being removed
2nd	**removēbāris**	you were being removed	**removēbāminī**	you were being removed
3rd	**removēbātur**	he was being removed	**removēbantur**	they were being removed

Imperfect Tense, Subjunctive Mood

Singular	*Plural*
removērer	**removērēmur**
removērēris	**removērēminī**
removērētur	**removērentur**

     iii. **iaciō**   Future Tense, Indicative Mood

	Singular	*Translation*	*Plural*	*Translation*
1st	**iaciar**	I will be thrown	**iaciēmur**	we will be thrown
2nd	**iaciēris**	you will be thrown	**iaciēminī**	you will be thrown
3rd	**iaciētur**	he will be thrown	**iacient**	they will be thrown

b) Synopses

1. **dare,** 1st person plural

	Indicative	*Translation*	*Subjunctive*
Pres.	damur	we are being given	dēmur
Imperf.	dabāmur	we were being given	darēmur
Future	dabimur	we will be given	——

2. **tollere,** 3rd person plural

	Indicative	*Translation*	*Subjunctive*
Pres.	tolluntur	they are being elevated or destroyed	tollantur
Imperf.	tollēbantur	they were being elevated or destroyed	tollerentur
Future	tollentur	they will be elevated or destroyed	——

3. **colere,** 2nd person plural

	Indicative	*Translation*	*Subjunctive*
Pres.	coliminī	you are being worshipped	colāminī
Imperf.	colēbāminī	you were being worshipped	colerēminī
Future	colēminī	you will be worshipped	——

4. **rapere,** 2nd person singular

	Indicative	Translation	Subjunctive
Pres.	raperis	you are being snatched away	rapiāris
Imperf.	rapiēbāris	you were being snatched away	raperēris
Future	rapiēris	you will be snatched away	——

5. **petere,** 3rd person singular

	Indicative	Translation	Subjunctive
Pres.	petitur	he is being sought or asked (for)	petātur
Imperf.	petēbātur	he was being sought or asked (for)	peterētur
Future	petētur	he will be being sought or asked (for)	——

6. **vidēre,** 1st person singular

	Indicative	Translation	Subjunctive
Pres.	videor	I am seen or I seem	videar
Imperf.	vidēbar	I used to be seen or I seemed	vidērer
Future	vidēbor	I will be seen or I will seem	——

c)

	Active	Passive	Translation
1.	vidēbimus	vidēbimur	We will seem or be seen
2.	vidētis	vidēminī	You (pl) seem or are seen
3.	vidēbant	vidēbantur	They seem or are seen
4.	videās	videāris	You (s) would seem or be seen
5.	videāmus	videāmur	We would seem or be seen
6.	vidēre	vidērī	to seem or to be seen
7.	capiam	capiar	I will be seized (or subjunctive, let me be seized)
8.	capiēs	capiēris	You (s) will be seized
9.	capiat	capiātur	Let him be seized
10.	capimus	capimur	We are being seized
11.	relinquō	relinquor	I am left, abandoned
12.	relinquat	relinquātur	Let him be left, abandoned
13.	relinquēmus	relinquēmur	We will be left, abandoned
14.	vincimus	vincimur	We are being conquered
15.	vincāmus	vincāmur	Let us be conquered

d)

	Active	Passive	Translation
1.	capere	capī	to be seized
2.	dūcere	dūcī	to be led
3.	tenēre	tenērī	to be held
4.	locāre	locārī	to be placed
5.	cōgere	cōgī	to be compelled
6.	sentīre	sentīrī	to be perceived
7.	interficere	interficī	to be killed
8.	dare	darī	to be given
9.	regere	regī	to be ruled, directed
10.	instituere	instituī	to be established

e)
1. They say that Erysichthon scorned the gods.
2. The nymph was requesting punishment of Erysichthon.
3. Erysichthon will feel a great hunger.
4. Many people corrupt the benefits of the gods.
5. You imagine that Saturn is a god.
6. We call Jupiter "the father of gods and of men."
7. Hercules was leading the cattle across the river.

f)

1. Erysichthon deōs contemnisse dīcitur.
2. Poena Erysichthonis ā nympha petēbātur.
3. Beneficia deōrum ā multīs hominibus pervertuntur.
4. Saturnus deus esse ā tē fingitur/crēditur.
5. Juppiter "pater deōrum hominumque" ā nōbīs dīcitur.
6. Magna famēs ab Erysichthone sentiētur.
7. Bovēs trāns fluvium ab Hercule dūcēbantur.

B.1.

a)   i. **mōnstrāre**   Perfect Tense, Indicative Mood

	Singular	*Translation*	*Plural*	*Translation*
1st	**mōnstrātus sum**	I have been shown	**mōnstrātī sumus**	we have been shown
2nd	**mōnstrātus es**	you have been shown	**mōnstrātī estis**	you have been shown
3rd	**mōnstrātus est**	he has been shown	**mōnstrātī sunt**	they have been shown

Perfect Tense, Subjunctive Mood

Singular	*Plural*
mōnstrātus sim	**mōnstrātī sīmus**
mōnstrātus sīs	**mōnstrātī sītis**
mōnstrātus sit	**mōnstrātī sint**

   ii. **removēre**   Pluperfect Tense, Indicative Mood

	Singular	*Translation*	*Plural*	*Translation*
1st	**remōtus eram**	I had been removed	**remōtī erāmus**	we had been removed
2nd	**remōtus erās**	you had been removed	**remōtī erātis**	you had been removed
3rd	**remōtus erat**	he had been removed	**remōtī erant**	they had been removed

Pluperfect Tense, Subjunctive Mood

Singular	*Plural*
remōtus essem	**remōtī essēmus**
remōtus essēs	**remōtī essētis**
remōtus esset	**remōtī essent**

   iii. **iaciō**   Future Perfect Tense, Indicative Mood

	Singular	*Translation*	*Plural*	*Translation*
1st	**iactus erō**	I shall have been thrown	**iactī erimus**	we shall have been thrown
2nd	**iactus eris**	you will have been thrown	**iactī eritis**	you will have been thrown
3rd	**iactus erit**	he will have been thrown	**iactī erint**	they will have been thrown

b)

i. **dare,** 1st person plural

	Indicative	*Translation*	*Subjunctive*
Pres.	datī sumus	we have been given	datī erīmus
Imperf.	datī erāmus	we had been given	datī essēmus
Future	datī erimus	we shall have been given	——

ii. **tollere,** 3rd person plural

	Indicative	*Translation*	*Subjunctive*
Pres.	sublātī sunt	they have been elevated or destroyed	sublātī erint
Imperf.	sublātī erant	they had been elevated or destroyed	sublātī essent
Future	sublātī erunt	they will have been elevated or destroyed	——

iii. **colere,** 2nd person plural

	Indicative	Translation	Subjunctive
Pres.	cultī estis	you have been worshipped	cultī erītis
Imperf.	cultī erātis	you had been worshipped	cultī essētis
Future	cultī eritis	you will have been worshipped	——

iv. **rapere,** 2nd person singular

	Indicative	Translation	Subjunctive
Pres.	raptus es	you have been snatched away	raptus sīs
Imperf.	raptus erās	you had been snatched away	raptus essēs
Future	raptus eris	you will have been snatched away	——

v. **petere,** 3rd person singular

	Indicative	Translation	Subjunctive
Pres.	petītus est	he has been asked	petītus sit
Imperf.	petītus erat	he had been asked	petītus esset
Future	petītus erit	he will have been asked	——

vi. **vidēre,** 1st person singular

	Indicative	Translation	Subjunctive
Pres.	vīsus sum	I seemed or was seen	vīsus sim
Imperf.	vīsus eram	I had seemed or had been seen	vīsus essem
Future	vīsus erō	I will have seemed or will have been seen	——

c)

	Active	Passive	Translation
1.	vīderimus	vīsī erimus	we shall have been seen (or we shall have seemed)
2.	vīdistis	vīsī estis	you (pl) have been seen
3.	vīdērunt	vīsī sunt	they have been seen
4.	vīderās	vīsus erās	you had been seen
5.	vīdissēmus	vīsī essēmus	(plpf. subjunctive)
6.	vīdisse	vīsī esse	to have been seen
7.	cēpī	captus sum	I have been captured
8.	cēperis	captus eris	you will have been captured
9.	cēperāmus	captī erāmus	we had been captured
10.	cēpissēmus	captī essēmus	(plpf. subjunctive)
11.	relīquī	relictus sum	I have been abandoned
12.	relīquit	relictus est	he has been abandoned
13.	relīquerāmus	relictī erāmus	we had been abandoned
14.	vīcimus	victī sumus	we have been conquered
15.	vīcerimus	victī erimus	we shall have been conquered

d)

	Active	Passive	Translation
1.	cēpisse	captus esse	to have been captured
2.	duxisse	ductus esse	to have been led
3.	tenuisse	tentus esse	to have been held
4.	locāvisse	locātus esse	to have been placed
5.	coēgisse	coāctus esse	to have been compelled
6.	sēnsisse	sēnsus esse	to have been perceived
7.	interfēcisse	interfectus esse	to have been killed
8.	dedisse	datus esse	to have been given
9.	rexisse	rectus esse	to have been led or guided
10.	ēgisse	actus esse	to have been done, led, spent, driven

e)
1. They said that Erysichthon had scorned the gods.
2. A nymph sought punishment for Erysichthon.
3. Erysichthon will have felt a great hunger.
4. Many people have corrupted the benefits of the gods.
5. You imagined that Saturn is a god.
6. We have called Jupiter "the father of gods and of men."
7. Hercules had led the cattle across the river.

f)
1. Erysichthonem deōs contemnisse ā multīs dictus est.
2. Dī ab Erysichthone contemnātī esse dictī sunt.
3. Poena Erysichthonis ab illā nymphā petīta est.
4. Magna famēs ab Erysichthone sēnsa erit.
5. Deōrum beneficia ā multīs hominibus perversa sunt.
6. Saturnus deus esse ā vōbīs fictus est.
7. Saturnus deus fuisse ā nōbīs fingēbātur.
8. Juppiter pater deōrum hominumque ā nōbīs dictus est.
9. Bovēs trāns fluvium ab Hercule ductae erant.
10. Bovēs Herculis trāns fluvium ab eō ipsō ductae erant.

B.2.

CHAPTERS I-X PERFECT PASSIVE PARTICIPLES OF ALL VERBS

i. First Conjugation:
-ātus

	Derivatives from perfect passive participle (obs. = *obsolete*)
agitō, -āre, -āvī, -ātus	agitate
ambulō, -āre, -āvī, ambulātus	ambulatory, perambulation
amō, -āre, -āvī, amātus	amatory
appellō, -āre, -āvī, appellātus	appellation
cantō, -āre, -āvī, cantātus	incantation
captō, -āre, -āvī, captātus	captation (obs., *the act of snatching at*)
cēlō, -āre, -āvī, cēlātus	celation (obs., *concealment*)
cōgitō, -āre, -āvī, cōgitātus	cogitate, cogitation
commendō, -āre, -āvī, -ātus	recommendation
cūrō, -āre, -āvī, -ātus	curative
dēclāmō, -āre, -āvī, -ātus	declamation
dēlīberō, -āre, āvī, -ātus	deliberate
disputō, -āre, āvī, -ātus	disputation
errō, -āre, -āvī, -errātus	erratic
formō, -āre, -āvī, formātus	formative
labōrō, -āre, -āvī, labōrātus	elaborate
laudō, -āre, -āvī, laudātus	laudatory
līberō, -āre, -āvī, līberātus	liberate
locō, -āre, -āvī, locātus	location
mōnstrō, -āre, -āvī, mōnstrātus	monstrate (obs., *to show*)
dēmōnstrō, -āre, -āvī, -ātus	demonstrate
mūtō, -āre, -āvī, mūtātus	mutation
optō, -āre, -āvī, optātus	optative
parō, -āre, -āvī, parātus	preparation
plantō, -āre, -āvī, plantātus	plantation
probō, -āre, -āvī, probātus	probation
pugnō, -āre, -āvī, pugnātus	pugnacious
putō, -āre, -āvī, putātus	putative
pulsō, -āre, -āvī, pulsātus	pulsate
rogō, -āre, -āvī, rogātus	interrogative, interrogate
servō, -āre, -āvī, servātus	conservation
sperō, -āre, -āvī, spērātus	desperate

spīrō, -āre, -āvī, spīrātus — inspiration
superō, -āre, -āvī, superātus — superation (obs., *conquest*)
tolerō, -āre, -āvī, tolerātus — tolerate
vītō, -āre, -āvī, vītātus — inevitable
vocō, -āre, -āvī, vocātus — vocative, invocation

ii. irregular -are
dō, dare, dedī, datus — dative, data [*for dō compounds, see 3rd conj.* -itus]

sonō, -āre, sonuī, sonitus — sonorous
stō, stāre, stetī, status — static, statue

iii. Second Conjugation:
-ētus
fleō, -ēre, -ēvī, flētus
impleō, -ēre, implēvī, implētus — implete (*to fill*)

-itus
exerceō, -ēre, exercuī, exercitus — exercise
debeō, -ēre, debuī, debitus — debit
habeō, -ēre, habuī, habitus — habit
moneō, -ēre, monuī, monitus — admonition; monitory
noceō, -ēre, nocuī, nocitus — nocive; nociferous (obs., *harmful*)
valeō, -ēre, valuī, valitus (-ūrus) — evaluate

-tus 2nd
doceō, -ēre, docuī, doctus — doctor
moveō, -ēre, mōvi, mōtus — motion; motor
   removēre, remōtus — remote
teneō, -ēre, tenuī, tentus — tentacle

-sus
ardeō, -ēre, arsī, arsus — arson
censeō, -ēre, censī, cēnsus — census
iubeō, -ēre, iussī, iussus — jussive
maneō, -ēre, mānsī, mānsus — mansion
   remaneō, remānsus — remansion (obs., *act of remaining*)
mordeō, -ēre, momordī, morsus — morsel
respondeō, -ēre, respondī, respōnsus — response
sedeō, -ēre, sēdī, sessus — session
videō, -ēre, vīdī, vīsus — vision

iv. Third Conjugation:
-itus
-dō compounds:
   addō, -ere, addidī, additus — addition
   reddō, -ere, reddidī, redditus — reddition (obs., *restoration of something*)
   subdō, -ere, subdidī, subditus — subdition (obs., *fraudently substituted*)
   trādō, -ere, trādidī, trāditus — tradition
crēdō, -ere, crēdidī, crēditus — credit
fugiō, -ere, fūgī, fūgitus (-itūrus) — fugitive
gignō, -ere, genuī, genitus — congenital
(noscō, -ere, nōvī, nōtus) — noted
   cognoscō, -ere, cognōvī, cognitus — cognition
pōnō, -ere, posuī, positus — position
   prōpōnō, prōpositus — proposition
petō, -ere, petīvī, petītus — petition

quaerō, -ere, quaesīvī, quaesītus	inquisition

-tus

agō, -ere, -ēgī, actus	act, active
cōgō, coēgī, coactus	coagulates; coaction (= *force, compulsion*)
cōnstituō, -ere, cōnstituī, cōnstitūtus	constitution
contemnō, -ere, contempsī, contemptus	contempt
crescō, -ere, crēvī, crētus	concrete
dīcō, -ere, dixī, dictus	diction, dictionary
dūcō, -ere, duxī, ductus	duct; aqueduct; product
dēdūcō, dēductus	deduct
fingō, -ere, finxī, fictus	fiction
fluō, -ere, fluxī, fluctus	fluctuate
imbuō, -ere, imbuī, imbūtus	imbute (obs., *soak*)
instituō, -ere, instituī, institūtus	institute
legō, -ere, lēgī, lectus	select
ostentō, -ere, ostendī, ostentus (or ostēnsus)	ostentive (obs., *ostensive*)
rapiō, -ere, rapuī, raptus	rapture
regō, -ere, rexī, rectus	correct, direct, erect
relinquō, -ere, relīquī, relictus	derelict
scrībō, -ere, scrīpsī, scrīptus	manuscript
solvō, -ere, solvī, solūtus	solution
tollō, -ere, sustulī, sublātus	sublated (*exalted*) or sublation (*removal*)
trahō, -ere, traxī, tractus	tractor
distrahō, distractus	distract
extrahō, extractus	extract
vincō, -ere, vīcī, victus	victuals
vīvō, -ere, vixī, vīctus	victor, victim

3rd -iō verbs

capiō, -ere, cēpī captus	captive
accipiō, acceptus	accept
incipiō, inceptus	inception
faciō, -ere, fēcī, factus	fact
interficiō, interfectus	
perficiō, perfectus	perfect
prōficiō, prōfectus	profection (*projection, advancement*)
iaciō, -ere, iēcī, iactus	trajectory

-sus

cadō, -ere, cecidī, cāsus	casual
occidō, -ere, occidī, occāsus	occasion
cēdō, -ere, cessī, cessus	cession (*a yielding*)
excēdō, excessus	excess
praecedō, praecessus	precession
claudō, -ere, clausī, clausus	clause
conclūdō, -ere, conclūsī, conclūsus	conclusion
exclūdō, -ere, exclūsī, exclūsus	exclusive
comedō, -ere, comedī, comesus	esurient (*hungry*) (cum + edō, edere)
fundō, -ere, fūdī, fūsus	fuse
prōfundō, prōfūsus	profuse
incendō, -ere, incendī, incēnsus	incense
lūdō, -ere, lūsī, lūsus	lusory; delusion
mittō, -ere, mīsī, missus	missile
āmittō, āmissus	amiss
pellō, -ere, pepulī, pulsus	pulse

expellō, expulī, expulsus	expulsion
premō, -ere pressī, pressus	press
opprimō, oppressus	oppress
reprimō, repressus	repress
scindō, -ere, scīdī, scissus	scission (*a fissure, a split*)
vertō, -ere, vertī, versus	verse
avertō, aversus	aversion
convertō, conversus	conversion
pervertō, perversus	perverse

v. Fourth Conjugation:

-itus

audiō, -īre, -īvī, -ītus	auditory
scio, -īre, scīvi, scītus	
nesciō, nescītus	

-sus

sentiō, sentīre, sēnsī, sēnsus	sense, sensate

-tus

veniō, -īre, vēnī, ventus	
adveniō, adventus	advent
inveniō, inventus	invent
prōveniō, prōventus	provent (obs., *profit, revenue*)
(-tum — irregular, compounds of eō, īre)	
eō, ere, īvi, itum	
abeō, abitum	
adeō, aditum	
ambiō, ambitus	ambition
ineō, initum	initial, initiate
pereō, peritum	
praetereō, praeteritum	preterite (obs., *past, gone by*)
prōdeō, prōditum	
redeō, reditum	redition (obs., *return*)

C. TERMINOLOGY REVIEW

1. When the verb is in the *passive voice,* the subject of the verb is the recipient of the action: *he is called; he is struck; he is thought about.*
2. When the verb is in the *active voice,* the subject of the verb is the agent of a transitive verb, the person or thing *doing* the action; in an intransitive verb the subject is the person or thing described by the verb: *he exists; he is happy.*
3. The *ablative of personal agent* is the person responsible for the action of a verb in the passive voice. It is always introduced by the preposition **ā** (before a consonant) or **ab** (before a vowel), and is only used with persons or things that have been personfied. It is translated *by.*
4. The *ablative of means or instrument* tells what *thing* is responsible for the action of a passive or active verb. It is never introduced by a preposition; it is usually translated *by, with,* or *by means of.*
5. The *perfect passive participle* is the fourth principle part of the verb. It can be used as a verbal adjective (**liber *scrīptus,*** the written book, **vir *laudātus,*** the praised man).

D.   TRANSLATION

1. When Hercules was a small child, two serpents were sent by Juno to kill the child.
2. It was Night, and Ursa Magna (the Big Dipper) seemed to stand still in the middle of the sky.
3. Those huge serpents came to Hercules' home and slithered through the doors.
4. Their eyes, stained with blood and flames, were blazing and they were licking their hissing lips with their tongues.
5. But when they had approached the children's little bodies, suddenly Jupiter made a bright light . Light was made by Jupiter.

6. Jupiter made that light to warn the children.
7. The children with their own eyes saw the serpents who had come to harm them.
8. Little Iphikles loudly (with a loud voice) began to cry, but little Hercules himself seized those serpents with his little hands.
9. Those serpents were held by their throats (abl. means) by Hercules (abl. of agent). Hercules seemed to bind their throats with his hands.
10. They began to bind little Hercules around the middle (of his body) but the boy could not be bound for a long time. Little Hercules began to be bound by those serpents.
11. Those serpents will perish. Those serpents are about to perish (destined to perish). Let them be defeated by that tough child. Let them be destroyed by the tough child. Now they have been killed. Now the serpents, raised from the ground, are perishing. The serpents, raised from the ground and killed by the tough child, have perished.
12. Iphikles was heard weeping by the mother and father of the children. Iphikles seemed to weep loudly. The mother and father came to learn why the child was weeping.
13. The father seized his weapons to save the children from danger. The children will be saved from danger by the father's weapons. The father was about to save the children.
14. The servants made torches and set them aflame. The slaves are raising up the torches. The torches were being raised up by the slaves. The torches made and set aflame were raised up by the servants.
15. The father and mother and servants thus approached and found Hercules in the bedroom with the dead serpents.
16. The parents were terrified, but the child laughed and placed the savage serpents at (their) feet. The dead serpents were placed at their feet.

XI
Third Declension I-Stem Nouns and Adjectives; Present Participles; Ablative Absolute; Passive Periphrastic

A. Distinguishing Third Declension I-Stem Nouns From Regular Third Declension Nouns

All nouns of the Third Declension are identified by the genitive singular ending **-is**. Additionally, nouns which satisfy one of the following categories will be *Third Declension i-stem Nouns*, which means that

    i. Their genitive plural endings will be **-ium** instead of **-um**,

    ii. The accusative plural of masculine and feminine nouns will sometimes be **-īs** instead of **-ēs**.

    iii. The accusative plural of neuter i-stem nouns is **-ia**, and the ablative singular of these neuter nouns is **-ī**.

Below are the categories which distinguish i-stem nouns from regular third declension nouns. Note that the noun must satisfy *all* the stipulations under one of these categories to qualify as a third-declension i-stem noun.

    1. A noun is an *i-stem noun* if:

        (a)   it is *parisyllabic*, (i.e., has an equal number of syllables in *both* the nominative and the genitive singular;

        (b)   it is masculine or feminine gender;

        (c)   it ends in **-is** or **-ēs** (nom.) and **-is** (gen.).

Examples:

i-stem nouns			not i-stem nouns		
cīvis, cīvis, *m. or f.*		*citizen*	**pater, patris,** *m.*		*father*
nūbēs, nūbis, *f.*		*cloud*	**mīles, mīlitis,** *m.*		*soldier*

(**pater** satisfies rules *a* and *b*, but not *c*; **mīles** satisfies rules *b* and *c*, but not *a*).

2. A noun is an *i-stem noun* if:

    (a)   it is masculine or feminine

    (b)   its nominative singular ends in **-s** or **-x**

    (c)   its stem ends in two consonants.

Note that Third Declension Adjectives fit into this category, even though they can be neuter as well as masculine or feminine.

Examples:

i-stem nouns		not i-stem nouns	
sors, sortis, *f.*	*chance*	**princeps, principis,** *m.*	*head person*
nox, noctis, *f.*	*night*	**dux, ducis,** *m.*	*leader*

(**princeps** and **dux** satisfy *a* and *b*, but not *c*).

3. A noun is an *i-stem noun* if:

    (a)   it is neuter

    (b)   it ends in **-al**, **-ar**, or **-e**.

Examples:

i-stem nouns		not i-stem nouns	
capital, capitālis, *n.*	*capital crime*	**genus, generis,** *n.*	*race, type*
pulvīnar, pulvīnāris, *n.*	*cushioned seat*	**Caesar, Caesāris,** *m .*	*Caesar*
navāle, navālis, *n.*	*harbor*		

(**genus** does not satisfy *b*; **Caesar** does not satisfy *a* . Note that the stem of neuter forms ending in **-al** or **-ar** in the nominative is the same as the nominative case).

A.1. Indicate whether the following third-declension nouns are i-stems, and explain which of the above sets of rules they satisfy (some of these nouns will be new to you).

Category 1. parasyllabic

           2. nominative ends in **-s** or **-x**; 2-consonants in stem

           3. neuter ends in **-al, -ar, -e**.

		i-stem?	*which category?*
aequor, aequoris, *n.*	the sea	_____	_____
corpus, corporis, *n.*	body	_____	_____
nōmen, nōminis, *n.*	name	_____	_____
fīnis, fīnis, *f.*	boundary	_____	_____
senex, senis, *m.*	old man	_____	_____
pēs, pedis, *m.*	foot	_____	_____
cōnsul, cōnsulis, *m.*	consul	_____	_____
poēma, poēmatis, *n.*	poem	_____	_____
mors, mortis, *f.*	death	_____	_____
orbs, orbis, *m.*	sphere	_____	_____

urbs, urbis, *f.*	city	_____	_____
aedēs aedis, *f.*	temple	_____	_____
dēns, dentis, *m.*	tooth	_____	_____
mēnsis, mēnsis, *m.*	month	_____	_____
mēns, mentis, *f.*	mind	_____	_____
laus, laudis, *f.*	praise	_____	_____
puteal, puteālis, *n.*	well enclosure	_____	_____
caput, capitis, *n.*	head	_____	_____

A.2. Translate and decline in Latin the following phrases.

a. **laus magna**   translation _____

	Singular	*Plural*
Nom.	_____	_____
Gen.	_____	_____
Dat.	_____	_____
Acc.	_____	_____
Abl.	_____	_____

b. **caput illud**   translation _____

	Singular	*Plural*
Nom.	_____	_____
Gen.	_____	_____
Dat.	_____	_____
Acc.	_____	_____
Abl.	_____	_____

c. **princeps noster**   translation _____

	Singular	*Plural*
Nom.	_____	_____
Gen.	_____	_____
Dat.	_____	_____
Acc.	_____	_____
Abl.	_____	_____

d. **mēnsis longus**   translation _____

	Singular	*Plural*
Nom.	_____	_____
Gen.	_____	_____
Dat.	_____	_____
Acc.	_____	_____
Abl.	_____	_____

152

e. **mēns tua** translation _____

	Singular	*Plural*
Nom.	_____	_____
Gen.	_____	_____
Dat.	_____	_____
Acc.	_____	_____
Abl.	_____	_____

f. **animal dūrum** translation _____

	Singular	*Plural*
Nom.	_____	_____
Gen.	_____	_____
Dat.	_____	_____
Acc.	_____	_____
Abl.	_____	_____

g. **gēns fortis** translation _____

	Singular	*Plural*
Nom.	_____	_____
Gen.	_____	_____
Dat.	_____	_____
Acc.	_____	_____
Abl.	_____	_____

h. **senex potēns** translation _____

	Singular	*Plural*
Nom.	_____	_____
Gen.	_____	_____
Dat.	_____	_____
Acc.	_____	_____
Abl.	_____	_____

i. **imāgō brevis** translation _____

	Singular	*Plural*
Nom.	_____	_____
Gen.	_____	_____
Dat.	_____	_____
Acc.	_____	_____
Abl.	_____	_____

j. **mors impendēns**   translation _____

	Singular	*Plural*
Nom.	_____	_____
Gen.	_____	_____
Dat.	_____	_____
Acc.	_____	_____
Abl.	_____	_____

k. **nūbēs obscūra** translation _____

	Singular	*Plural*
Nom.	_____	_____
Gen.	_____	_____
Dat.	_____	_____
Acc.	_____	_____
Abl.	_____	_____

l. **quāle mare**   translation _____

	Singular	*Plural*
Nom.	_____	_____
Gen.	_____	_____
Dat.	_____	_____
Acc.	_____	_____
Abl.	_____	_____

A.3. Third Declension Adjectives and Adverbs formed from Third Declension Adjectives

a) Adjectives belong *either* to the first and second declensions, *or* to the third declension.

b) *All present active participles* are third declension adjective.

c) All third declension adjectives are *i-stems*. This means that third-declension adjectives end in **-ium** (instead of **-um**) in the genitive plural, **-ia** in neuter nominative and accusative endings, and, like neuter i-stem nouns, end in **-ī** (instead of **-e**) in the ablative singular. Additionally, they often end in **-īs** (instead of **-ēs**) in the accusative plural masculine and feminine.

d) Adverbs are formed from adjectives of the first and second declension by adding **-ē** to the stem. Adverbs formed from third declension adjectives add **-iter** to the stem, unless the stem ends in **-nt** (as it does for all present active participles) in that case, only **-er** is added to form an adverb.

e) You will note that there are also a number of adverbs which you have learned that are not formed according to these rules.

A.3. a. Change the following adjectives into adverbs and translate the adverbs:

	Adverb	Translation
acer		
aequus		
aeternus		
augustus		
brevis		
celer		
cīvīlis		
commūnis		
decōrus		
dignus		
dulcis		
ēlegāns		
fēlix		
fortis		
honestus		
immortālis		
impius		
impudīcus		
iustus		
obscūrus		
potēns		
prosperus		
rectus		
sevērus		
superbus		
varius		
vērus		

A.3.b. Translate the following adverbs. Check your work, not in the Chapter Key, but by looking these adverbs up in the cumulative vocabulary at the back of *Traditio*.

	Translation
adeō	
bene	
certē	
circum	
citō	
contrā	

cūr _____

deinde _____

diū _____

ergō _____

hīc _____

hōdiē _____

iam _____

ibi _____

idcircō _____

inde _____

ita _____

item _____

lībenter _____

male _____

mox _____

nōn _____

nōnne _____

num _____

numquam _____

nunc _____

ōlim _____

parum _____

procul _____

prope _____

quam _____

quandō _____

quidem _____

quoque _____

saepe _____

satis _____

scīlicet _____

simul _____

sīc _____

sīcut _____

sōlum _____

tam _____

tum _____

ubi _____

umquam _____

B. Present Active Participles

Present active participles are verbal adjectives of the third declension. This means that they decline like third declension **i**-stem adjectives (except in ablative absolute, when they agree with third declension **i**-stem nouns, ending in an **-e** instead of in an **-i**). They are *active* in meaning.

B.1. a. Identify the verbs on which the present active participles in the following sentences are based, and then translate each sentence.

1. Ūnus puer flēns, alter monstra interficiēns, sonum sonuit.

2. Puer ista mōnstra vidēns guttura eōrum sūmpsit. (**guttur, gutturis,** *n* neck)

3. Pater haec nōn intellegēns auxilium petīvit.

4. Mater puerum flēre dēsinentem continuit.

5. Omnēs Herculem puerum clārum esse merentem laudāvērunt.

6. Omnēs haec videntēs Herculem laudābunt.

7. Ille sapiēns patrī nōn intelligentī auxilum dabit.

8. Mōnstra ad pedēs patris iactāns, puer rīsit. (**rideō, -ēre, rīsī, rīsus,** to laugh, smile)

9. Juppiter Herculem post mortem in caelum tollēns divīnum fēcit.

10. Nēmō mihī praesentī nocēbit.

B.1. b. Translate the following phrases and then change them to the plural, retaining the case of the original.

1. nubēs discēdēns
2. princeps pacāns
3. ille merēns
4. cīvis dēlīberantis
5. patrem intellegentem
6. animālī fugientī
7. rege subicientī
8. rēgī subicientī
9. rēge subiciente
10. nūbem augentem
11. mare turbāns
12. senī memorantī
13. senis accipientis
14. principī praesēntī
15. capite cadente
16. noctem nocentem
17. istā vī

C. Ablative Absolute and Passive Periphrastic:

The *Ablative Absolute* consists of an *ablative subject* with an *ablative participle*. Note that there can be no grammatical connection between the ablative absolute and subject of the main clause. If there is, then an ablative absolute construction cannot be used.:

When *I* was *ruling* the empire, *I made* peace:

(cannot be ablative absolute, since both clauses share the same subject)

Ego imperium *regēns* **pācem** *fēcī*.

Instead of a participle, a noun or a non-verbal adjective is sometimes used.

participle: **Augustō *dūcente*,** nihil timēmus.

When Augustus is leading, we fear nothing.

Because Augustus is leading, we fear nothing.

Although Augustus is leading, we fear nothing.

If Augustus is leading, we fear nothing.

noun: **Augustō *duce*,** nihil timēmus.

When Augustus is the leader, we fear nothing.

Because Augustus is the leader, we fear nothing.

Although Augustus is the leader, we fear nothing.

If Augustus is the leader, we fear nothing.

adjective: **Augustō *forte*,** nihil timēmus.

When Augustus is strong, we fear nothing

Because Augustus is strong, we fear nothing

If Augustus is strong, we fear nothing.

Although Augustus is strong, we fear nothing

The participle can be in the *active or passive voice*, and in the *present, past or future tense*:

a)   Augustō vincente, nihil timēmus. (*present active participle*)

When Augustus is winning, we fear nothing.

b)   Augustō victō, omnia timēmus. (*perfect passive participle*)

Because Augustus has been defeated, we fear everything.

c)   Augustō victūrō, omnēs fēlīcēs sunt. (*future active participle*)

Because Augustus is about to win, all the people are happy.

d)   Augustō vincendō, nēmō felix est. (*future passive participle*)

Because Augustus must be defeated, no one is happy.

In all the above examples, the tense of the verb in the main clause is *present*. The tense of the participle, like the verbs in dependent subjunctive clauses, must always be translated in relation to the tense of the main verb. Thus, if we put the main verbs in the *past*, then the translations would be as follows:

a)   Augustō vincente, nihil timuimus. (*present active participle*)

When Augustus *was* winning, we *feared* nothing.

b)   Augustō victō, omnia timuimus. (*perfect passive participle*)

Because Augustus *had been* defeated, we *feared* everything.

c)   Augustō victūrō, omnēs fēlīcēs erant. (*future active participle*)

Because Augustus *was* about to win, all the people *were* happy.

d)   Augustō vincendō, nēmō fēlix erat. (*future passive participle*)

Because Augustus *had to be* defeated, no one *was* happy.

158

Similarly, if the main verb is in the future tense, the translations would be as follows.

a)   Augustō vincente, nihil timēbimus. *(present active participle)*
       When Augustus *is* winning, we *shall* fear nothing.

b)   Augustō victō, omnia timēbimus. *(perfect passive participle)*
       If Augustus *has been* defeated, we *shall fear* everything.

c)   Augustō victūrō, omnēs fēlīcēs erunt. *(future active participle)*
       If Augustus *is about* to win, all the people *will be* happy.

d)   Augustō vincendō, nēmō fēlix erit. *(future passive participle)*
       Because Augustus *must be* defeated (in the future), no one *will be* happy.

C.1. a. Translate the following sentences. Then turn to the Key, check your translations, and try to translate the English translations back into Latin. (Based on Ch. IX, X and XI vocabulary.)

1. Poētā canente, omnēs fēlīcēs sunt.

2. Lībertāte auctā, omnēs pācem petent.

3. Tuīs verbīs rectē intellectīs, omnia nōbīs timenda sunt.

4. Omnibus gentibus pacātīs, Rōmam rediī.

5. Illā gente pacandā, bellum gessī.

6. Illīs verbīs memorātīs, bella cīvīlia fūgit.

7. Bellō āversō, omnēs gentēs principem laudāvit.

8. Ille vir, deae ob īram, terrā marīque iactātus est. Illō virō terrā marīque iactātō, Iūnō pacāta est.

9. Iunōne nōn pacātā, ille vir ad Italiam vēnit.

10. Mortālibus membrīs perītīs, stēlla Herculis florēre incēpit.

11. Nōmine audītō, Herculēs ab omnibus accepta est.

12. Ab illō nova dīcente Herculēs nōmen quaesīvit.

13. Illī nova dīcentī Herculēs urbem ostendit.

14. Graecē dīcēns, Herculēs nōmen quaesīvit.

15. Graecē respondentī Herculēs sapiēns esse vīsus est.

16. Claudiō deō factō, nōn alius princeps in caelum advēnit.

17. Causīs bellī memorātīs, omnēs flēbant.

18. Mē puerō, pater erat paedagōgus.

19. Fābulīs docentibus, puerī sapientēs nōn factī sunt.

20. Crustulīs datīs, discipulī fēlīciter labōrant. (**crustula, -ōrum,** *n. pl.* cookies)

21. Bovēs, actae trāns fluvium ab Hercule, in spēluncam tractae sunt.

22. Herculēs, sentiēns multās bovēs āmissās esse, ab illō locō excēdere incēpit.

23. Aliae bovēs mugientēs Herculem excedentem convertērunt.

24. Bōbus trāns fluvium actīs, Herculēs fessus erat.

25. Multīs bōbus āmissīs, Herculēs ab illō locō excēdere incēpit.

26. Hercule excessūrō, bovēs mugīvērunt.

27. Bōbus audītīs, Herculēs in spēluncam inīvit.

28. Spēluncā inventā, Herculēs bovēs līberāvit.

29. Cācō inventō interfectōque, omnēs cīvēs eius locī vēnērunt ut spēluncam vidērent.

30. Fāmā audītā, Dēianīra territa est.

31. Fāmā audītā, Dēianīra vestem ad Herculem mīsit.

32. Veste acceptā, Herculēs periit.

33. Herculem, florentem sine membrīs hūmānīs, deus in caelō posuit.

34. Membrīs hūmānīs āmissīs, deus Herculem in caelum mōvit.

C.1. b. Translate the underlined passages into Latin as ablative absolute:

1. <u>When the monsters had been killed</u>, the infant Hercules smiled.

2. <u>Although many cattle were missing</u>, Hercules began to leave without them.

3. <u>After waging wars successfully</u>, I returned to Rome.

4. <u>After establishing freedom</u>, Brutus became one of the first two consuls.

5. Some people felt that there should be a funeral procession with <u>Victory going first</u> and with <u>children singing a dirge</u>. (**praecēdere**, to go first, precede; **nēnia, -ae,** *f,* a dirge)

C.2. Passive Periphrastic

In a passive periphrastic construction, the verb consists of the *future passive participle* plus the appropriate form of the verb, *to be.* The agent of the action is expressed not by the ablative of agent, but by the *dative of agent* (remember that the dative is never governed by a preposition).

Translate the following, explaining the construction of the words and phrases underlined.

   a. Bovēs <u>Herculī</u> trāns fluvium <u>agendae</u> <u>sunt</u>.

   b. <u>Bovēs</u> ex illō locō dūcendae erant.

   c. Herculēs <u>bōbus</u> vocandus erat.

   d. Bovēs <u>excedentēs</u> audiendae erunt.

   e. <u>Spēlunca</u> ineunda erat.

   f. Bovēs <u>ā Cācō</u> līberandae sunt.

   g. Bovēs ā Cācō <u>Herculī</u> liberandae erant.

h. Cācus inveniendus erat ut omnēs <u>cīvēs</u> līberārentur.

i. Spēlunca omnibus <u>cīvibus</u> videnda erat.

j. Spēlunca ab omnibus <u>cīvibus</u> vīsa erat.

k. Fāma <u>Dēianīrae</u> audienda crēdendaque erit.

l. Vestis <u>servō</u> ad Herculem ferenda erat.

m. Vestis <u>Herculī</u> nōn accipienda est.

n. Vestis Dēianīrae nōn est mittenda nē Herculēs <u>tollātur</u>.

o. Eius amor <u>mei</u> reddendus est. Amor <u>mihi</u> recipiendus est.

p. <u>Membra</u> hūmāna tollenda erant ut deus Herculem in <u>caelum</u> tollere posset.

q. <u>Membra</u> hūmāna tollenda erant ut deus Herculem in <u>caelō</u> pōnere posset.

r. Haec mihi <u>fābula</u> scrībenda est.

s. Haec verba <u>omnibus discipulīs</u> legenda et discenda sunt.

t. Illa eadem verba ab <u>omnibus sapientibus</u> memorāta sunt.

D. Diagramming Sentences

Diagram *Legenda 6a and 6b* on pages 210-211 of *Traditio,* and explain the grammatical construction of each clause (e.g., is it a relative clause? an indirect question? ablative absolute? etc.)

E. Derivations

Match the following words or expressions, which are regularly found in English, with their English meaning.

aliās	a. They all depart
alibi	b. replacing a parent
antebellum	c. a musical piece appropriate to the evening
cui bonō	d. nothing new under the sun
cuius bonō	e. calm
deō volente	f. the place where one departs
dēsiderātum	g. an assumed name (noun)
et al. (et aliī)	h. in the place cited
exeunt omnēs	i. prewar
exit	j. a refusal to plead guilty but acceptance of the punishment
ex post factō	k. outside the city
in locō parentis	l. whom does it benefit?
in loc. cit. (in locō citātō)	m. for each person
nihil sub sōle novum	n. and others
nocturne	o. orally
nōlō contendere	p. elsewhere

pacific	q. something wanted or needed
per capita	r. of its own kind
q.e.d. (quod erat demōnstrātum)	s. retrospectively, subsequently
suburban	t. whose benefit?
suī generis	u. which has already been proven
vīvā vōce	v. if god is willing

Key, Chapter XI

A.1.

aequor, aequoris, *n.*	no
corpus, corporis, *n.*	no
nōmen, nōminis, *n.*	no
fīnis, fīnis, *f.*	1 (parasyllabic)
senex, senis, *m.*	no
pēs, pedis, *m.*	no
cōnsul, cōnsulis, *m.*	no
poēma, poēmatis, *n.*	no
mors, mortis, *f.*	2 (**-s** or **-x**; 2-consonants in stem)
orbs, orbis, *m.*	2 (**-s** or **-x**; 2-consonants in stem)
urbs, urbis, *f.*	2 (**-s** or **-x**; 2-consonants in stem)
aedēs, aedis, *f.*	1 parasyllabic
dēns, dentis, *m.*	2 (**-s** or **-x**; 2-consonants in stem)
mēnsis, mēnsis, *m.*	1 (parasyllabic)
mēns, mentis, *f.*	2 (**-s** or **-x**; 2-consonants in stem)
laus, laudis, *f.*	no
puteal, puteālis, *n.*	3 (neuter ends in **al, ar,** or **e**)
caput, capitis, *n.*	no

A.2

a. laus magna, *great praise*

	Singular	Plural
Nom.	laus magna	laudēs magnae
Gen.	laudis magnae	laudum magnārum
Dat.	laudī magnae	laudibus magnīs
Acc.	laudem magnam	laudēs magnās
Abl.	laude magnā	laudibus magnīs

b. caput illud, *that head or person*

	Singular	Plural
Nom.	caput illud	capita illa
Gen.	capitis illius	capitum illōrum
Dat.	capitī illī	capitibus illīs
Acc.	caput illud	capita illa
Abl.	capite illō	capitibus illīs

c. princeps noster, *our chief*

	Singular	Plural
Nom.	princeps nostrum	principēs nostrī
Gen.	principis nostrī	principum nostrōrum
Dat.	principī nostrō	principibus nostrīs
Acc.	principem nostrum	principēs nostrōs
Abl.	principe nostrō	principibus nostrīs

d. mēnsis longus, *a long month*

	Singular	Plural
Nom.	mēnsis longus	mensēs longī
Gen.	mensis longī	mensium longōrum
Dat.	mensī longō	mensibus longīs
Acc.	mensem longum	mensēs longōs
Abl.	mense longō	mensibus longīs

e. mēns tua, *your mind*

	Singular	Plural
Nom.	mēns tua	mentēs tuae
Gen.	mentis tuae	mentium tuārum
Dat.	mentī tuae	mentibus tuīs
Acc.	mentem tuam	mentēs tuās
Abl.	mente tuā	mentibus tuīs

f. animal dūrum, *hard (tough) animal*

	Singular	Plural
Nom.	animal dūrum	animālia dūra
Gen.	animālis durī	animālium dūrōrum
Dat.	animālī dūrō	animālibus dūrīs
Acc.	animal dūrum	animālia dūra
Abl.	animālī dūrō	animālibus dūrīs

g. gēns fortis, *brave race or people*

	Singular	Plural
Nom.	gēns fortis	gentēs fortēs
Gen.	gentis fortis	gentium fortium
Dat.	gentī fortī	gentibus fortibus
Acc.	gentem fortem	gentēs fortēs (or -īs)
Abl.	gente fortī	gentibus fortibus

h. senex potēns, *powerful old man*

	Singular	Plural
Nom.	senex potēns	senēs potentēs
Gen.	senis potentis	senum potentium
Dat.	senī potentī	senibus potentibus
Acc.	senem potentem	senēs potentēs
Abl.	sene potentī	senibus potentibus

i. **imāgō brevis,** *brief likeness*

	Singular	Plural
Nom.	imāgō brevis	imāginēs brevēs
Gen.	imāginis brevis	imāginum brevium
Dat.	imāginī brevī	imāginibus brevibus
Acc.	imāginem brevem	imāginēs brevēs (-īs)
Abl.	imāgine brevī	imāginibus brevibus

j. **mors impendēns,** *imminent death*

	Singular	Plural
Nom.	mors impendēns	mortēs impendentēs
Gen.	mortis impendentis	mortium impendentium
Dat.	mortī impendentī	mortibus impendentibus
Acc.	mortem impendentem	mortēs impendentēs (-īs)
Abl.	morte impendentī	mortibus impendentibus

k. **nūbēs obscūra,** *dark cloud*

	Singular	Plural
Nom.	nūbēs obscūra	nūbēs obscūrae
Gen.	nūbis obscūrae	nūbium obscūrārum
Dat.	nūbī obscūrae	nūbibus obscūrīs
Acc.	nūbem obscūram	nūbēs obscūrās
Abl.	nūbe obscūrā	nūbibus obscūrīs

l. **quāle mare,** *what kind of sea*

	Singular	Plural
Nom.	quāle mare	quālia maria
Gen.	quālis maris	quālium marium
Dat.	quālī marī	quālibus maribus
Acc.	quāle mare	quālia maria
Abl.	quālī marī	quālibus maribus

A.3. a.

	Adverb	Translation
acer	acriter	keenly
aequus	aequē	equally, justly
aeternus	aeternē	eternally
augustus	augustē	majestically
brevis	breviter	briefly
celer	celeriter	quickly
cīvīlis	cīvīliter	civilly, in a civil manner
commūnis	commūniter	commonly
decōrus	decōrē	properly
dignus	dignē	worthily
dulcis	dulciter	sweetly
ēlegāns	ēleganter	luxuriously
fēlix	fēlīciter	happily
fortis	fortiter	bravely, strongly
honestus	honestē	honorably
immortālis	immortāliter	immortally
impius	impiē	with irreverence
impudīcus	impudīcē	immodestly
iustus	iustē	justly
obscūrus	obscūrē	in darkness, darkly
potēns	potenter	powerfully
prosperus	prosperē	prosperously
rectus	rectē	correctly
sevērus	sevērē	sternly
superbus	superbē	proudly
varius	variē	in various ways
vērus	vērē	truly

A.3. b.

The adverbs in A.3.b are listed in chapters I-XI and in the cumulative vocabulary, pages 366 ff.

B.1. a.

1. **flēns, interficiēns,** from **flēre** and **interficere**
   One *weeping* child, and one *who was killing* monsters, made a noise.
2. **vidēns,** present active participle of **vidēre**
   The child, *seeing* those monsters, took hold of their necks.
3. **intellegēns,** from **intellegere**
   The father, *not understanding* these things, sought assistance.

4. **dēsinentem,** from **dēsinere**
   The mother held the child *who was ceasing* to cry.
5. **merentem,** from **mereō**
   Everyone praised the child Hercules, *who deserved* to be famous.
6. **videntēs,** from **vidēre**
   Everyone, *seeing* these things, will praise Hercules.
7. **intelligentī,** from **intellegere**
   That wise man will give assistance to the father *who does not understand.*
8. **iactāns,** from **iactāre**
   Throwing the monsters at the feet of the father, the child smiled.
9. **tollēns,** from **tollere**
   Jupiter, *elevating* Hercules after his death into the sky, made him divine.
10. **praesentī,** from **praesum**
    No one will harm me *while I am present (while I am before them,* hence, *in their presence).*

B.1. b.

1. the departing cloud, **nūbēs discēdēntēs**
2. the pacifying leader, **principēs pacāntes**
3. that deserving *(person)*, **illī merentēs**
4. of the thinking *(deliberating)* citizen, **cīvium dēlīberantium**
5. the understanding father, **patrēs intellegentēs**
6. for *or* with the fleeing animal, **animālibus fugientibus** *(dat. or abl.)*
7. *(by, with)* the *(subordinating)* subjecting king, **rēgibus subicientibus**
8. *(to, for)* the *(subordinating)* subjecting king, **rēgibus subicientibus**
9. with the king subjecting *(ablative absolute)*, **rēgibus subicientibus**
10. the growing cloud, **nūbēs augentēs**
11. the surging *(disrupting)* sea, **maria turbantia**
12. to the old man who *(is, was)* remembering, **senibus memorantibus**
13. of the welcoming old man, **senum accipientium**
14. to the emperor in his presence, **principibus praesēntibus**
15. with the head falling, **capitibus cadentibus** *(abl. absolute)*
16. the night which *(is, was)* inflicting harm, **noctēs nocentēs**
17. with that violence of yours, **istīs vīribus**

C.1. a.

1. When/because/if/although the poet is singing, all the people are (everyone is) happy.
2. When/because/although/if freedom has been increased, all the people will seek peace.
3. If your words are correctly understood, everything must be feared by us. [If I understand your words correctly, we must fear everything.]
4. When all the peoples had been pacified, I returned to Rome.
5. Since that nation had to be pacified, I waged war.
6. Because those words had been remembered [i.e., because/when/although he remembered those words], he avoided civil wars.
7. Because/when war had been turned away/averted, all the peoples praised the chief.
8. That man was tossed about on land and on the sea because of the anger of the goddess. When that man had been tossed on land and on the sea, Juno was [finally] pacified/placated.
9. When/although Juno had not been placated, that man came to Italy.
10. When [his] mortal limbs had perished, the constellation of Hercules began to flourish.
11. When [his] name had been heard, Hercules was welcomed by all. [When they heard his name, everyone welcomed Hercules.]
12. Hercules asked that man who was saying strange things his name. [i.e., H. asked that saying-strange-things man what his name was.]
13. Hercules showed the city to that person who was saying strange things.
14. Hercules, speaking in Greek, asked [his] name.
15. Hercules seemed, to the person answering in Greek, to be wise.
16. After Claudius had been made a god, no other ruler came into the sky [heavens].
17. When they remembered the reasons for the war, everyone wept/began to weep/was weeping.

18. When I was a boy, [my] father was [my] child-attendant.
19. Because fairy-tales were doing the teaching, the children did not become [were not made] wise.
20. When cookies have been given [when they have been given cookies], students work happily.
21. The cattle, (which had been) driven across the river by Hercules, have been dragged into the cave.
22. Hercules, perceiving that many cattle had been lost, began to depart from that place.
23. The other cattle, which were lowing, turned Hercules around as he was departing.
24. When the cattle had been driven across the river, Hercules was exhausted.
25. Because many cattle had been lost, Hercules began to depart from that place.
26. When Hercules was about to depart, the cattle lowed.
27. When he had heard the cattle, Hercules entered the cave.
28. When he had discovered the cave, Hercules liberated the cattle.
29. When Cacus had been found and killed, all the citizens of that place came to see the cave.
30. When she had heard the rumor, Deianira was terrified.
31. When she had heard the rumor, Deianira sent the cloak to Hercules.
32. Because he had accepted the cloak, Hercules perished.
33. A god placed Hercules, who was flourishing without human limbs, in the sky.
34. When (his) human limbs had been lost, a god moved Hercules into the sky.

C.1. b.

1. Monstrīs interfectīs
2. Multīs bōbus absentibus
3. Bellīs prosperē gestīs
4. Lībertāte institūtā
5. Victōriā praecēdente; līberīs nēniam canentibus.

C.2. PASSIVE PERIPHRASTIC

a. The cattle <u>must be led</u> across the river <u>by Hercules</u>. (dative of agent, fut. passive periphrastic)
b. <u>The cattle</u> had to be led from that place. (nominative, subject)
c. Hercules had to be called <u>by the cattle</u>. (dative of agent)
d. The <u>departing</u> cattle will have to be heard. (pres. act. participle, nom. pl.)
e. <u>The cave</u> had to be entered. (nominative, subject)
f. The cattle must be freed <u>from Cacus</u>. (ablative of separation)
g. The cattle had to be freed <u>by Hercules</u> (dative of agent) from Cacus. (ablative of separation)
h. Cacus had to be found so that all <u>citizens</u> would be freed. (nominative, subject of purpose clause)
i. The cave had to be seen by all the <u>citizens</u>. (dative of agent)
j. The cave had been seen by all the <u>citizens</u>. (ablative of agent)
k. The rumor will have to be heard and believed <u>by Deianira</u>. (dative of agent)
l. The cloak had to be handed over <u>by the slave</u> to Hercules. (dative of agent)
m. The cloak must not be received/accepted <u>by Hercules</u>. (dative of agent)
n. The cloak must not be sent by Deianira so that Hercules will not be <u>destroyed</u>. (subjunctive, purpose)
o. His love <u>for me</u> must be restored. (objective gen.) Love must be restored <u>by me</u>. (dative of agent)
p. (His) human <u>limbs</u> had to be destroyed so that the god could raise Hercules into the <u>sky</u>. (subject.; *in* + accus.)
q. (His) human <u>limbs</u> had to be destroyed so that the god would be able to place Hercule in the <u>sky</u>. (*in* + abl.)
r. I must write this <u>story</u>. (nominative, subject)
s. These words must be read and learned by <u>all students</u>. (dative of agent)
t. Those same words have been remembered <u>by all wise people</u>. (abl. of agent)

D. DIAGRAMMING SENTENCES.

Legenda 6a. The passage contains a series of announcements introduced by *Nuntiātur Iovī*, it is announced to Jupiter, followed by a series of subordinated statements, which are therefore in indirect statement (subject accusative (underlined) + an infinitive verb).

Nuntiātur Iovī	*It is announced to Jupiter that*
a) <u>hominem</u> vēnisse	a) *a man has come*
b) <u>minantem</u> nescioquid;	b) *(he is) threatening something*
c) <u>eum</u> assidue movēre caput et	c) *he continuously moves his head and*
d) (<u>eum</u>) pedem dextrum trahere.	d) *he is dragging his right foot.*

Nuntius dixit	*The messenger said*
<u>sē</u> quaesivisse	*that he had asked*
(question) cuius natiōnis esset	*what people he belonged to.*
(and that) <u>eum</u> *respondisse* nescioquid	*that he had made some(kind of) reply*
(abl. manner) turbātō sonō et vōce confūsa.	*with a disturbing sound and confused voice.*
(and that) <u>sē</u> nōn intellegere linguam eius	*that he did not understand his language*
(and that) <u>eum</u> nec Graecum esse nec Rōmānum	*that he was not Greek nor Roman nor of*
nec ūllīus gentis nōtae.	*any known race.*

Tum Iuppiter *iubet*	*Then Jupiter orders*
Herculem...	*Hercules...*
<u>quī</u>........errāverat	*who...had wandered*
et (<u>quī</u>) omnēs natiōnēs nōvisse vidēbātur	*and (who) seemed to know all nations*
īre et quaerere	*to go and to ask*
quōrum hominum esset.	*what peoples he belonged to.*

<u>Hercules</u>	*Hercules,*
<u>quī</u> nōn omnia mōnstra timuerit	*who (characteristic) was unafraid of every monster,*
<u>vidēns</u> hunc,	*seeing this person*
......turbatus est.	*......was troubled*
(hic homō) Herculī	*(This person) to Hercules,*
diligenter videntī	*as he was looking carefully*
vīsus est esse quasi homō.	*seemed to be, as it were, a human being.*

Accessit ergō et quaesīvit Graecē	*He approached, therefore, and asked in Greek*
(quod facillimum fuit Graecō)	*(which was a very easy thing for a Greek)*
cuius natiōnis esset.	*what nation he belonged to.*

<u>Claudius</u>,	*Claudius*
<u>gaudēns</u> esse illīc philologōs hominēs,	*rejoicing that literary people are there*
spērat	*hopes*
futūrum esse historiīs suīs locum.	*that there will be a place for his histories.*

Ergō et ipse...*respondit*	*Therefore he too replied*
(Homēricō versū)	*(in Homeric verse)*
Caesārem <u>sē</u> esse.	*that he was Caesar.*

Legenda 6b. Although the first sentence in this passage contains an indirect question, the paragraph contains many simple or compound sentences and direct questions.

Dīc nōbīs	*Tell us*
quālem deum velis.	*what kind of god you would like.*
Epicūrēus deus nōn potest esse.	*He cannot be an Epicurean god.*
Dolet enim nec sibi nec aliīs.	*For he does not grieve for himself or for others*
Stōicus?	*A Stoic?*
Quōmodo potest rotundus esse,	*How can he be round,*
ut dīcit Varrō?	*as Varro says?* [apposition]
Est nescioquid in illō Stōicī dēī,	*There is something of a Stoic god in him,*
iam videō;	*now I see;*
nec cor nec caput habet.	*he has neither heart nor head.*
Sī...(Sāturnālicius prīnceps)	*If...((this) Saturnalian emperor)*

ā Sāturnō petīvisset *hoc beneficium*	*had asked for this benefit from Saturnus,*
cuius mēnsem tōtum annum celebrāvit,	*whose month he celebrated through the whole year,*
nōn recēpisset *illud,*	*he would not have received it,*
nēdum ab Iove,	*not even from Jupiter,*
quem damnāvit incestī.	*whom he charged with incest.*

Iānus pater multa disertē dixit.	*Father Janus spoke many things eloquently*
quod in forō vīvēbat	*because he lived in the Forum.*
Dīxit	*He said*
"Ōlim magna rēs erat deus fierī.	*"Once it was an important thing to be made a god.*
Iam fāmam mīmum fēcistis.	*Now you have made a mockery of this fame.*
Ergō…	*Therefore…*
(nē videar in persōnam, nōn in rem, dīcere sententiam) [purpose clause]	*(Lest I seem to speak my opinion against the person, not against the situation)*
post hunc diem nēmō mortālis deus fīat."	*after this day let no mortal become a god."*

The final paragraph consists of two long periodic sentences, in keeping with the legal-istic bent of the god who is a money-lender:

Diespiter, quī nummāriolus fuerat,	*Diespiter, who had been a money-lender,*
cēnset haec.	*makes the following judgement:*
"Claudius (*contingit…et praecedit*):	*Claudius (is related to….and surpasses)*
et dīvum Augustum sanguine contingit	*he is related to deified Augustus by blood*
nec minus dīvam Augustam aviam suam,	*and no less his grandmother the deified Augusta,*
quam ipse deam esse iussit,	*whom he himself ordered to be a goddess,*
longēque omnēs mortālēs sapientiā praecēdit.	*and far surpasses all mortals in wisdom.*

Sitque ē rēpūblicā	*It would be good for the republic*
sī ūnus nostrum cum Rōmulō possit ferventiā rapa vorāre.	*if one of us could devour boiled turnips with Romulus.*
Cēnseō igitur	*Therefore I judge*
dīvum Claudium deum esse faciendum	*that Claudius must be made a god*
(ex hōc diē)	*(from this day)*
ita ut ante eum quī factus sit	*in such a way as the person who was made (a god) [qui/factus est] before him [ante eum] (i.e., before Claudius)*
(optimō iūre)	*(in keeping with the law)*
eamque rem ad metamorphōsēs Ovidiī esse adiciendam."	*and that this event must be added to Ovid's **Metamorphoses***

E. DERIVATIONS

	Meaning
aliās	g. an assumed name
alibi	p. elsewhere
antebellum	i. prewar
cui bonō	l. whom does it benefit?
cuius bonō	t. whose benefit?
deō volente	v. if God is willing
dēsiderātum	q. something wanted or needed
et al. (et aliī)	n. and others
exeunt omnēs	a. they all depart
exit	f. the place where one departs (s/he departs)
ex post factō	s. retrospectively
in locō parentis	b. replacing a parent
loc. cit. (in locō citātō)	h. in the place cited
nihil sub sōle novum	d. nothing new under the sun
nocturne	c. a musical piece appropriate to the evening

nōlō contendere	j.	refusal to plead guilty but acceptance of punishment
pacific	e.	calm
per capita	m.	for each person
q.e.d. (quod erat dēmōnstrātum)	u.	which has already been proven
suburban	k.	outside the city
suī generis	r.	of its own kind
vīvā vōce	o.	orally

XII
Fourth Declension; Indefinite Pronouns; Irregular Verb: Ferō; Cum-Clauses

A. Fourth Declension Nouns and Indefinite Pronouns

Fourth declension nouns are characterized by the **-u-** throughout the endings, except for the dative and ablative plural.

Most fourth declension nouns are masculine, but there are some neuter and feminine nouns in this declension.

A great many fourth declension nouns come from the perfect passive participles of verbs.

Indefinite pronouns and adjectives are, for the most part, formed from the relative pronoun **quī** or the interrogative pronouns **quis**.

A.1. Translate and decline the following phrases in the singular and plural:

a. **exitus quisque**   translation _____

	Singular	*Plural*
Nom.	_____	_____
Gen.	_____	_____
Dat.	_____	_____
Acc.	_____	_____
Abl.	_____	_____

b. **quaecumque domus**   translation _____

	Singular	*Plural*
Nom.	_____	_____

Gen. _____ _____

Dat. _____ _____

Acc. _____ _____

Abl. _____ _____

c. **quoddam cornū crescēns**   translation _____

	Singular	*Plural*
Nom.	_____	_____
Gen.	_____	_____
Dat.	_____	_____
Acc.	_____	_____
Abl.	_____	_____

d. **aliquī cursus**   translation _____

	Singular	*Plural*
Nom.	_____	_____
Gen.	_____	_____
Dat.	_____	_____
Acc.	_____	_____
Abl.	_____	_____

e. **quīvīs ortus**   translation _____

	Singular	*Plural*
Nom.	_____	_____
Gen.	_____	_____
Dat.	_____	_____
Acc.	_____	_____
Abl.	_____	_____

A.2. Translate the following phrases as ablative absolute:

1. Manū magnā veniente _____

2. Quādam manū urbem sublātūrā _____

3. manū tuā tentā _____

4. domō suā cadente _____

5. domō eōrum cadente _____

6. domo tuā magnā _____

7. versū longō lectō _____

8. versibus longīs lectīs _____

9. versibus longīs _____

10. poētā versūs longōs legente _____

11. poētā versūs longōs lectūrō _____

12. versibus longīs legendīs   _____

13. versibus longīs memorātīs   _____

14. Hercule serpentem tollente   _____

15. serpente illātō   _____

16. serpente sublātō   _____

17. serpente iactātō   _____

18. cornū raptō   _____

19. cornū crescente   _____

20. cornibus lūnae crescentibus   _____

21. arbore crescere nōn potente   _____

B. Ferō and its Compounds

B.1. Write synopses, including infinitives and participles, of the following compounds of **ferō**, as indicated.

a. **offerō,** 1st person plural

Principal Parts: _____ , _____ , _____ , _____ , translation: _____

Active Voice

	Indicative	Translation	Subjunctive
Pres.	_____	_____	_____
Imperf.	_____	_____	_____
Fut.	_____	_____	N/A
Perf.	_____	_____	_____
Plpf.	_____	_____	_____
Fut. Perf.	_____	_____	N/A

Passive Voice

	Indicative	Translation	Subjunctive
Pres.	_____	_____	_____
Imperf.	_____	_____	_____
Fut.	_____	_____	N/A
Perf.	_____	_____	_____
Plpf.	_____	_____	_____
Fut. Perf.	_____	_____	N/A

Infinitives

	Active	Translation	Passive	Translation
Pres.	_____	_____	_____	_____
Perf.	_____	_____	_____	_____
Future	_____	_____	N/A	N/A

Participles

	Active	Translation	Passive	Translation
Pres.	_____	_____	N/A	N/A
Perf.	N/A	N/A	_____	_____
Future	_____	_____	_____	_____

b. auferō, 2nd person singular

Principal Parts: _____ , _____ , _____ , _____ , translation: _____

Active Voice

	Indicative	Translation	Subjunctive
Pres.	_____	_____	_____
Imperf.	_____	_____	_____
Fut.	_____	_____	N/A
Perf.	_____	_____	_____
Plpf.	_____	_____	_____
Fut. Perf.	_____	_____	N/A

Passive Voice

	Indicative	Translation	Subjunctive
Pres.	_____	_____	_____
Imperf.	_____	_____	_____
Fut.	_____	_____	N/A
Perf.	_____	_____	_____
Plpf.	_____	_____	_____
Fut. Perf.	_____	_____	N/A

Infinitives

	Active	Translation	Passive	Translation
Pres.	_____	_____	_____	_____
Perf.	_____	_____	_____	_____
Future	_____	_____	N/A	N/A

Participles

	Active	Translation	Passive	Translation
Pres.	_____	_____	N/A	N/A
Perf.	N/A	N/A	_____	_____
Future	_____	_____	_____	_____

c. afferō, 3rd person singular

Principal Parts: _____ , _____ , _____ , _____ , translation: _____

Active Voice

	Indicative	Translation	Subjunctive
Pres.	_____	_____	_____
Imperf.	_____	_____	_____
Fut.	_____	_____	N/A
Perf.	_____	_____	_____
Plpf.	_____	_____	_____
Fut. Perf.	_____	_____	N/A

Passive Voice

	Indicative	Translation	Subjunctive
Pres.	_____	_____	_____
Imperf.	_____	_____	_____
Fut.	_____	_____	N/A
Perf.	_____	_____	_____
Plpf.	_____	_____	_____
Fut. Perf.	_____	_____	N/A

Infinitives

	Active	Translation	Passive	Translation
Pres.	_____	_____	_____	_____
Perf.	_____	_____	_____	_____
Future	_____	_____	N/A	N/A

Participles

	Active	Translation	Passive	Translation
Pres.	_____	_____	N/A	N/A
Perf.	N/A	N/A	_____	_____
Future	_____	_____	_____	_____

d. **sufferō,** 3rd person plural

Principal Parts: _____ , _____ , _____ , _____ , translation: _____

Active Voice

	Indicative	Translation	Subjunctive
Pres.	_____	_____	_____
Imperf.	_____	_____	_____
Fut.	_____	_____	N/A
Perf.	_____	_____	_____
Plpf.	_____	_____	_____
Fut. Perf.	_____	_____	N/A

Passive Voice

	Indicative	Translation	Subjunctive
Pres.	_____	_____	_____
Imperf.	_____	_____	_____
Fut.	_____	_____	N/A
Perf.	_____	_____	_____
Plpf.	_____	_____	_____
Fut. Perf.	_____	_____	N/A

Infinitives

	Active	Translation	Passive	Translation
Pres.	_____	_____	_____	_____
Perf.	_____	_____	_____	_____
Future	_____	_____	N/A	N/A

Participles

	Active	Translation	Passive	Translation
Pres.	_____	_____	N/A	N/A
Perf.	N/A	N/A	_____	_____
Future	_____	_____	_____	_____

C. Prepositional Prefixes

By learning to recognize compounded words in Latin, you will greatly increase your vocabulary (in English as well as Latin). The following summary of prepositional prefixes will be helpful in this regard.

a) **ad**, meaning *to, towards*, shows motion toward someone or something, and governs the accusative case. As a prefix, it occurs in the following ways:

i. before a vowel, it is unchanged. **addō**, *I add;* **adeō**, *I go towards.*

ii. before a consonant it is sometimes changed, and at other times unchanged.

Unchanged	Meaning	Changed	Meaning
adsum	*I am present*	**accēdō**	*I approach*
adveniō	*I am coming*	**accipiō**	*I accept*
advertō	*I am turning toward*	**afficiō**	*I influence, affect*
adferō	*I bring (to)*	**afferō**	*I bring (to)*
adtulī	*I brought (to)*	**attulī**	*I brought (to)*
adlātus	*brought (to)*	**allātus**	*brought (to)*

Observe that in the words in the second column, the **-d** of *ad* has been changed to duplicate the consonant that begins the root word. The variations in spelling make no difference in the meaning of the word.

b) **ā, ab, abs,** meaning *from, by*, shows separation from or agent, and governs the ablative case. As a prefix, it occurs in the following ways:

i. **ab** + vowel: unchanged. **abeō, abīre, abesse.**

ii. **ab** + consonant changes to **au: aufferō.**

or entire prefix adds **-s,** becoming **abs: abstulī.**

iii. **ab** added unchanged before consonant: **absum, absēns, ablātus.**

iv. **ā** + consonant, **āvertō, āmittō.**

c) **cum**

  i. becomes **com-** or **con-: commemorō, commendō, committō, compōnō, conferō, concēdō, conficiō, coniugium, constituō, contineō, convertō, convīvō.**

  ii. or **-m** or **-n** becomes the duplicate of the first consonant: **collātus, colligō, committō** (as above).

  iii. or **-m-** blends with first vowel at the beginning of the root word: **cōgō.**

The prepositions **dis** (as opposed to **dē**), **ex, in, ob, sub** have similarly protean characteristics when used as prefixes. Make careful note of their meanings, and look through the Latin-English Vocabulary List (p. 373-393), identifying how these prefixes change the meaning of the basic word to which they are attached.

Note also that some of these prepositions, in the new compound, will govern a case different from *or in addition to* that which the uncompounded word governs, e.g.,

ferre + accus.	**Herculēs auxilium tulit.**
	Hercules brought aid.
inferre + accus. + dat.	**Herculēs auxilium mihi intulit.**
	Hercules brought aid to me (or inflicted aid upon me).
offerre + accus. + dat.	**Herculēs auxilium mihi obtulit.**
	Hercules offered aid to me.

Notice also that **conferre** and **referre**, when used with the reflexive pronoun, is close in meaning to **īre** and to **cēdere.**

C.1. Identify the preposition and the first principal part of each verb **root.**

	Preposition	Verb	Meaning
absēns			
abstulit			
acceptus			
accessus			
accidit			
accommodātiō			
additus			
adiectus			
advocātus			
affectus			
affert			
allātus			
animadversus			
appetītus			
attulimus			
attulit			
aufert			
āversus			
coactus			

176

cognitiō
           _____

collatus

conditus

confectus

confers

coniectus

conventus

dēfers

differs

effert

rettulī

sublātus

D. Diagramming Sentences

D.1. Diagram passage 2, p. 228.
D.2. Diagram passage 5, p. 231-232.

E. Translation:

ARIADNE AND BACCHUS

Special Vocabulary:

Ariadna, -ae, *f.*	Ariadne
Bacchus, -ī, *m.*	Bacchus, god of wine
corōna, -ae, *f.*	crown
Crēta, -ae, *f.*	Crete, an island in the Mediterranean Sea
Thēseus, -ī, *m.*	Thēseus
Mīnōtaurus, -ī, *m.*	Mīnōtaur (a beast that was half-man, half-bull)
insula, -ae, *f.*	island
Naxus, -ī, *m.*	an island in the Aegean Sea
Vēr, Vēris, *n.*	springtime
tēla, -ae, *f.*	thread
dormiō, -īre, -īvī, -ītus	to sleep

1. Animum tuum ad hanc fābulam verte, tē amābō! Ad hanc fābulam animadverte!

2. In caelō sunt multa sīdera. Alia sīdera animālia esse videntur, alia ad fābulās deōrum hominumque clārōrum referunt.

3. Quoddam sīdus clārum "corōna" nōmine dīcitur, cum ad fābulam dē Thēseō, Ariadnā, et deō Bacchō referat.

4. Ariadna erat fīlia rēgis Crētae, id est, insulae in quā Mīnōtaurus, mōnstrum quī et bōs et vir fuisse crēditur, vīvēbat.

5. Ōlim iuvenis pulcher, Thēseus nōmine, Crētam sē contulit ut Mīnōtaurum interficeret.

6. Cum Ariadna illum iuvenem vīdit, magnam illius amōrem sēnsit.

7. Multīs aliīs iuvenibus ā Mīnōtaurō interfectīs, Ariadna huic adfutūra esse cōnstituit.

8. Theseō, domum Mīnōtaurī ineuntī, tēlam dedit ut exitum invenīret.

9. Mīnōtaurō interfectō, cum Crētae rex nōluisset, Thēseus tamen cum Ariadnā ex insulā discessit.

10. Thēseus cum nautīs suīs in insulā, Naxō nōmine, ūnam noctem agere constituit.

11. Cum Ariadna dormiēbat, Thēseus cum nautīs sē abstulit.

12. Cum Ariadna sē sōlam in insulā esse, sine amīcīs, sine fīliō, sine parentibus invēnit, dolōrem sibi sēnsit, Thēseōque nocēre voluisset.

13. Ea deōs vocābat cum, ab aliā parte insulae, deus Bacchus ad eius vōcis sonum trahēbātur.

14. Sīcut Ariadna Thēseum ōlim amāverat, nunc Bacchus illīus fēminae amōre incendit.

15. Nuptiīs Ariadnae Bacchīque confectīs, Bacchus eius corōnam ēiēcit in caelum, quō nunc omne Vēr in caelō fulget.

Key, Chapter XII

A.1.

Decline the following phrases in the singular and plural:

a. **exitus quisque,** *each departure* or *each exit*

	Singular	Plural
Nom.	exitus quisque	exitūs quīque
Gen.	exitūs cuiusque	exituum quōrumque
Dat.	exituī cuique	exitibus quibusque
Acc.	exitum quemque	exitūs quōsque
Abl.	exitū quōque	exitibus quibusque

b. **quaecumque domus,** *what(so)ever home*

	Singular	Plural
Nom.	quaecumque domus	quaecumque domūs
Gen.	cuiuscumque domūs	quārumcumque domuum
Dat.	cuicumque domuī	quibuscumque domibus
Acc.	quamcumque domum	quaecumque domūs
Abl.	quācumque domū	quibuscumque domibus

c. **quoddam cornū crescēns,** *a certain growing horn*

	Singular	Plural
Nom.	quoddam cornū crescēns	quaedam cornua crescentia
Gen.	cuiusdam cornūs crescentis	quōrundam cornuum crescentium
Dat.	cuidam cornū crescentī	quibusdam cornibus crescentibus
Acc.	quoddam cornū crescentem	quaedam cornua crescentia
Abl.	quōdam cornū crescentī	quibusdam cornibus crescentibus

d. **aliquī cursus,** *any journey*

	Singular	Plural
Nom.	aliquī cursus	aliquī cursūs
Gen.	alicuius cursūs	aliquōrum cursuum
Dat.	alicuī cursuī	aliquibus cursibus
Acc.	aliquem cursum	aliquōs cursūs
Abl.	aliquō cursū	aliquibus cursibus

e. **quīvīs ortus,** *whatever origin, beginning, rising*

	Singular	Plural
Nom.	quīvīs ortus	quīvīs ortūs
Gen.	cuiusvīs ortūs	quōrumvīs ortuum
Dat.	cuivīs ortuī	quibusvīs ortibus
Acc.	quemvīs ortum	quōsvīs ortūs
Abl.	quōvīs ortū	quibusvīs ortibus

A.2.

1. **Manū magnā veniente,** since a large band of men (is, was) coming
2. **Quādam manū urbem sublātūrā,** although/because/when a certain band of men (is, was) about to destroy the city
3. **manū tuā tentā,** when your hand has been held
4. **domō suā cadente,** since their own house (is, was) falling
5. **domō eōrum cadente,** since their home (is, was) falling
6. **domo tuā magnā,** since your home is large
7. **versū longō lectō,** when the long line of verse (has, had) been read
8. **versibus longīs lectīs,** when the long lines of verse (have, had) been read
9. **versibus longīs,** since the lines of verse (are, were) long
10. **poētā versūs longōs legente,** when the poet (is, was) reading the long lines of verse

11. **poētā versūs longōs lectūrō,** when the poet (is, was, will be) about to read the long lines of verse
12. **versibus longīs legendīs,** since the long lines of verse (must, had) to be read
13. **versibus longīs memorātīs,** when the long lines of verse (have, had) been recalled
14. **Hercule serpentem tollente,** with Hercules destroying the serpent
15. **serpente illātō,** when the serpent (has, had) been (inflicted, brought in)
16. **serpente sublātō,** when the serpent (has, had) been (raised, destroyed)
17. **serpente iactātō,** when the serpent (has, had) been hurled
18. **cornū raptō,** the horn having been seized
19. **cornū crescente,** with the horn growing
20. **cornibus lūnae crescentibus,** when the horns of the moon (are, were) waxing (increasing)
21. **arbore crescere nōn potente,** since the tree (is, was) not able to grow

B.1. FERŌ AND ITS COMPOUNDS

a. **offerō,** 1st person singular
Principal Parts: offerō, offerre, obtulī, oblātus *(present, show, offer)*

Active Voice

	Indicative	Translation	Subjunctive
Pres.	offerimus	we offer	offerāmus
Imperf.	offerēbāmus	we were offering	offerēmus
Fut.	offerēmus	we will offer	———
Perf.	obtulimus	we offered	obtulerīmus
Pluperf.	obtulerāmus	we had offered	obtulissēmus
FPerf.	obtulerimus	we will have offered	———

Passive Voice

	Indicative	Translation	Subjunctive
Pres.	offerimur	we are being offered	offerāmur
Imperf.	offerēbāmur	we were being offered	offerrēmus
Fut.	offerēmur	we will be offered	———
Perf.	oblātī sumus	we have been offered	oblātī erīmus
Pluperf.	oblātī erāmus	we had been offered	oblātī essēmus
FPerf.	oblātī erimus	we will have been offered	———

Infinitives

	Active	Translation	Passive	Translation
Pres.	offerre	to offer	offerrī	to be offerred
Perf.	obtulisse	to have offered	oblātus esse	to have been offerred
Future	oblātūrus esse	to be about to offer	———	———

Participles

	Active	Translation	Passive	Translation
Pres.	offerēns	offering	———	———
Perf.	———	———	oblātus	having been offered
Future	oblātūrus	about to offer	offerendus	about to be offered

b. **auferō,** 2nd person singular
Principal Parts: auferō, auferre, abstulī, ablātus *(remove, take away)*

Active Voice

	Indicative	Translation	Subjunctive
Pres.	aufers	you remove	auferās
Imperf.	auferēbas	you were removing	auferrēs
Fut.	auferēs	you will remove	———
Perf.	abstulistī	you removed	abstulerīs
Pluper.	abstulerās	you had removed	abstulissēs
FPerf.	abstuleris	you will have removed	———

Passive Voice

	Indicative	*Translation*	*Subjunctive*
Pres.	auferris	you are being removed	auferāmur
Imperf.	auferēbāris	you were being removed	auferrēmus
Fut.	auferēris	you will be removed	———
Perf.	ablātus es	you have been removed	ablātus erīs
Pluper.	ablātus erās	you had been removed	ablātus essēs
FPerf.	ablātus eris	you will have been removed	———

Infinitives

	Active	*Translation*	*Passive*	*Translation*
Pres.	auferre	to remove	auferrī	to be removed
Perf.	abstulisse	to have removed	ablātus esse	to have been removed
Future	ablātūrus esse	to be about to remove	———	———

Participles

	Active	*Translation*	*Passive*	*Translation*
Pres.	auferēns	removing	———	———
Perf.	———	———	ablātus	having been removed
Future	ablātūrus	about to remove	auferendus	about to be removed

c. **afferō,** 3rd person singular
Principal Parts: afferō, afferre, attulī, allātus *(to bring, report)*

Active Voice

	Indicative	*Translation*	*Subjunctive*
Pres.	affert	he brings	afferat
Imperf.	afferēbat	he was bringing	afferret
Fut.	afferēt	he will bring	———
Perf.	attulit	he brought	attulerit
Pluper.	attulerat	he had brought	attulisset
FPerf.	attulerit	he will have brought	———

Passive Voice

	Indicative	*Translation*	*Subjunctive*
Pres.	affertur	he is being brought	afferātur
Imperf.	afferēbātur	he was being brought	afferrētur
Fut.	afferētur	he will be brought	———
Perf.	allātus est	he has been brought	allātus erit
Pluper.	allātus erāt	he had been brought	allātus esset
FPerf.	allātus erit	he will have been brought	———

Infinitives

	Active	*Translation*	*Passive*	*Translation*
Pres.	afferre	to bring	afferrī	to be brought
Perf.	attulisse	to have brought	allātus esse	to have been brought
Future	allātūrus esse	to be about to bring	———	———

Participles

	Active	*Translation*	*Passive*	*Translation*
Pres.	afferēns	bringing	———	———
Perf.	———	———	allātus	having been brought
Future	allātūrus	about to bring	afferendus	about to be brought

d. **sufferō**, 3rd person plural
Principal Parts: sufferō, sufferre, sustulī, sublātus *(support, endure, suffer)*

	Indicative	Active Voice Translation	Subjunctive
Pres.	sufferimus	we support	sufferāmus
Imperf.	sufferēbāmus	we were supporting	sufferrēmus
Fut.	sufferēmus	we will support	———
Perf.	sustulimus	we supported	sustulerīmus
Pluper.	sustulerāmus	we had supported	sustulissēmus
FPerf.	sustulerimus	we will have supported	———

	Indicative	Passive Voice Translation	Subjunctive
Pres.	sufferimur	we are being supported	sufferāmur
Imperf.	sufferēbāmur	we were being supported	sufferrēmur
Fut.	sufferēmur	we will be supported	———
Perf.	sublātī sumus	we have been supported	sublātī erīmus
Pluper.	sublātī erāmus	we had been supported	sublātī essēmus
FPerf.	sublātī erimus	we will have been supported	———

C.1.

	Preposition	Verb	Meaning
absēns	ab	sum	absent
abstulit	ab	ferō (auferō)	he removed
acceptus	ad	capiō	received, welcomed
accessus	ad	cēdō	approached
accidit	ad	cadō	it happens
accommodātiō	ad	commodō	accommodation
additus	ad	dō	added
adiectus	ad	iaciō	added
advocātus	ad	vocāre	lawyer or witness, "summoned to"
affectus	ad	faciō	influenced or (noun) mood, disposition
affert	ad	ferō	he reports, brings
allātus	ad	ferō	reported, brought
animadversus	ad	vertō	he pays attention, or turns the mind toward
appetītus	ad	petō	attacked, or (noun) hunger
attulimus	ad	ferō	we reported, brought near
attulit	ad	ferō	he reported
aufert	ab	ferō	he is taking away
āversus	ab	vertō	turned away
coactus	cum	agō	compelled, forced
cognitiō	cum	noscō	recognition, understanding
collatus	cum	ferō	compared
conditus	cum	dō	founded, built
confectus	cum	faciō	completed
confers	cum	ferō	you compare
coniectus	cum	iaciō	thrown together, united
conventus	cum	veniō	agreed
dēfers	dē	ferō	you bring down, deliver
differs	dis	ferō	you disperse, you postpone
effert	ex	ferō	he proclaims, publishes, carries out
rettulī	re	ferō	I reported, brought back
sublātus	sub	ferō or tollō	supported, suffered or elevated, destroyed

D. Diagramming Sentences

D.1.

Passage 2, p. 228. This passage is a single question, written in meter (dactylic hexameter). The poet has suggested that the the emperor will become a god after his death, and is discussing which realm he will rule over after his deification.

Anne	**tē**	**addēs** *Can it be that you will add yourself*

nōvum sīdus	**tardīs mensibus**
a new star	*to the late months of the year*
(direct object)	
(in apposition to **tē***)*	

quā viā	**locus**	**panditur?**
where (by which path)	*a place*	*is opening*

inter Erīgone Chelāsque sequentēs	*Between Virgo and the pursuing claws*

(ardēns Scorpius ipse	**iam**	**bracchia** contrahit	*plūs* iustā parte caelī relīquit
burning Scorpio himself	*now*	*is drawing*	
		together his arms, (and)	*has left more than (plūs + abl.) a*
			a fair part of the sky

D.2.

Passage 5, pp. 231-232.

Spirituālēs substantiae ...agunt *The immaterial substances...... act*
       (subject) **in corporālia**   *upon the body*
           mediantibus caelestibus corporibus   *with heavenly bodies*
                                      acting as intermediaries (abl. abs.)

sed [Spirituālēs substantiae] ...agunt   *but they act*
    (implied subject) **in intellectum**   *upon the intellect*
        immediatē (adverb).   *directly.*
[Spirituālēs substantiae]   **voluntātem hūmānum**   **mūtāre nōn possunt.**
    (implied subject)   (direct object)   (main verb with complement)
                                      They cannot change human will.

Dīcendum est (plus indirect statement)   *It must be said*
    multitūdinem ...dūcī passiōnibus   *that the multitude is led by passions*
    (subject) (passive verb) (abl. instrument)
        quae [passiōnes] mōtūs sint...*which are movements*
        quās corpora caelestia imprimere possint
                      which can influence heavenly bodies.

autem   *However*
Paucī sunt sapientēs   *There are a few wise people*
      quī...passiōnibus resistant.   *who resist passions*
        huius modī   *of this sort.*
Et ergō   *And therefore*
astrologī   **vēra praedīcere possunt**   *astrologers are able to predict the truth*
            ut in plūribus   *as in the majority of cases*
            et maximē in commūnī   *and especially in a general sense.*

autem   *However*
nōn in speciālī vēra praedīcere possunt   *they cannot predice the truth in a particular case*
      quia nihil...prōhibet   *because nothing prevents*
          aliquem hominem....passiōnibus resistere   *that any man resist his passions*
              per līberum arbitrium   *through free will.*

Unde	*Whence*
ipsī astrologī dīcunt	*astrologers themselves say*
sapientem hominem astrīs dominārī	*the wise person is ruler over the stars*
inquantum scilicet	*inasmuch as, certainly,*
[sapientem] dominārī suīs passiōnibus	*he is ruler over his own passions.*

E. TRANSLATION: ARIADNE AND BACCHUS

1. Turn your mind to this story, please! Pay attention to this story!
2. In the sky there are many constellations. Some constellations seem to be animals, others refer to tales of gods and famous people.
3. A certain bright consellation is called "Corona" by name, since it refers to the story about Theseus, Ariadne, and the god Bacchus.
4. Ariadne was the daughter of the king of Crete, that is, the island on which the Minotaur, a monster who is believed to have been both a bull and a man, lived.
5. Once a handsome young man, Theseus by name, came to Crete to kill the Minotaur.
6. When Ariadne saw that young man, she felt a great love for him.
7. Since many other young men had been killed by the Minotaur, Ariadne decided that she would assist this one.
8. She gave a thread to Theseus when he was entering the home of the Minotaur so that he would find the way out.
9. After the Minotaur had been killed, although the king of Crete was against it, Theseus nevertheless departed from the island with Ariadne.
10. Theseus decided to spend one night on the island named Naxus with his sailors.
11. While Ariadne was sleeping, Theseus and his sailors departed.
12. When Ariadne perceived that she was alone on the island, without friends, without a brother, without parents, she felt sorry for herself and she wanted to hurt Theseus.
13. She was calling on the Gods when, from another part of the island, the god Bacchus was being drawn to the sound of her voice.
14. Now Bacchus was inflamed with love for that woman, just as Ariadne formerly loved Theseus.
15. When the marriage of Ariadne and Bacchus was completed, Bacchus threw her crown into the sky, where now it is bright in the sky, every Spring.

XIII
Comparative and Superlative Adjectives and Adverbs; Indirect Commands

A. Positive, Comparative and Superlative Degrees in English

In English, as in Latin, adjectives and adverbs change their forms to show a greater degree of the quality named in the simple word (the positive degree). English compares adjectives and adverbs two ways, 1) by adding -er, and 2) by using *more* . It indicates the superlative degree 1) by adding -est, and 2) by using *most*.

	Positive	*Comparative*	*Superlative*
adjective	hot	hotter	hottest
	eager	more eager	most eager
adverb	hotly	more hotly	most hotly
	often	oftener, more often	oftenest, most often

COMPARATIVE AND SUPERLATIVE DEGREE OF LATIN ADJECTIVES AND ADVERBS

Latin adds **-ior** (m. and f.) or **-ius** (n.) to the stem of the adjective to form the comparative, and **-issimus, a, um** to form the superlative. The exceptions are adjectives whose stems end in **-er**, which add **-rimus, -a, -um** to the stem, and the six adjectives ending in **-lis** (listed on p. 245 of *Traditio*) and their compounds, which add **-limus, -a, -um** in the superlative.

A.1. Change the following adjectives and adverbs to the positive and superlative degrees, retaining the case and number of the original, and translate each new form:

Adjectives:

Positive	*Comparative*	*Translation*	*Superlative*	*Translation*
aptus	_____	_____	_____	_____
bellā	_____	_____	_____	_____
cārus	_____	_____	_____	_____
crūdēlis	_____	_____	_____	_____

184

difficilem _____ _____ _____ _____

dissimilia _____ _____ _____ _____

dīversus _____ _____ _____ _____

facilia _____ _____ _____ _____

formōsōrum _____ _____ _____ _____

gracilium _____ _____ _____ _____

grave _____ _____ _____ _____

humile _____ _____ _____ _____

levibus _____ _____ _____ _____

similis _____ _____ _____ _____

tristis _____ _____ _____ _____

vīcīnus _____ _____ _____ _____

apertus _____ _____ _____ _____

dēficiēns _____ _____ _____ _____

Adverbs:

saepe _____ _____ _____ _____

fortiter _____ _____ _____ _____

cupidē _____ _____ _____ _____

potenter _____ _____ _____ _____

diū _____ _____ _____ _____

sapienter _____ _____ _____ _____

A.2. Translate the following phrases:

1. Ille senex fēlicior est quam hic.

2. Ille fēlicior hōc est.

3. Quam fēlicissima erit.

4. Saepe pōne ante oculōs ōsissima facta puellae.

5. Num quid sit ōsius quam facta puellae nōn iam amātae?

6. Cupīdō ingentior in mē crescit.

7. Haec cupīdō ingentior est quam illa.

8. Est ingentior illā.

9. Est ingentissima.

10. Est quam ingentissima.

11. Tē manum meam dēficientem tentūram esse spērō.

12. Manibus meīs dēficientiōribus vocāberis.

13. Haec manus dēficientior est illā.

14. Manū dēficientissimā tē vocābō.

B. Jussive Noun Clauses (Indirect Commands)

In English, as in Latin, any clause that functions in a sentence as a noun is a *noun clause*, also known as a *substantive clause*, since *substantive* refers to something—a noun, an infinitive, a clause—that is *functioning as a noun*. This means it can be the subject or object of a verb, or can function in some of the other ways a noun can function. In English, noun clauses are often introduced by *that, what, who, whoever, whatever, why,* and *when,* and they are usually subjects or objects.

a) Noun clause as *direct object*:

> Ariadne realized *that she had been abandoned.*

> He never expected *that he would be punished.*

> The hunter did not realize *that the bear was his own mother.*

b) Noun clause as *subject*:

> *That Theseus had departed* did not immediately occur to her.

> *That Ceres would punish him* was not anticipated by Erysichthon.

> *That the hunter would kill his own mother* was not permitted.

c) Noun clause as *object of preposition*:

> She wanted revenge <u>for</u> *what Theseus had done to her.*

> The nymphs asked Ceres to punish Erysichthon
>> <u>for</u> *what had been done to the tree.*

d) Noun clause set *in apposition* to another noun:

> The centaur gave her this <u>promise</u>,
>> [namely] *that the cloak would restore Hercules' love.*

> Theseus forgot his father's <u>request</u>,
>> [namely]*that he change the sails on his ship* .

In Latin, the examples in a) would be expressed by indirect statement, and the examples in c) could be expressed by the declined form of a neuter word such as **id** or **illud** elaborated by a relative clause, for example:

> ...eī *(for that thing)* quod Theseus fēcerat *(which Theseus had done).*
> ...illī *(for that thing)* quod arborī factum erat *(which had been done to the tree).*

The examples in b) and the first example in d) would be expressed by *subjective* and *objective* (as opposed to *jussive*) noun clauses, which you will learn about in Chapter XVII.

The second example in d) would be expressed by a *jussive noun clause.* This kind of noun clause conveys a command or request for action that is either stated or implied. Its Latin form looks like a regular purpose clause: it is introduced by **ut** or, for a negative command, by **nē**. The difference between a purpose clause and a jussive noun clause comes in part from the verb that introduces the clause, but not entirely, since these verbs (e.g., **monēre, quaerere, petere, dīcere, cōgere, rogāre,** etc.) can also introduce a number of other constructions. The sense of what accompanies or follows these verbs has to be taken into consideration. For example, when there is an accusative form in the main clause, is it in anticipation of the subject of the subordinated clause:

> *Hoc tibi dīxī ut auxilium darēs.*
> I told you this (direct object) so that you would give aid. (purpose)

> *Tibi dīxī ut auxilium darēs.*
> I told you to give aid. (indirect command)

> *Tibi dīxī te auxilium dare.*
> I said to you that you were giving aid. (indirect statement)

Nōs monēs ut hoc faciāmus. (or) *Monēs ut hoc faciāmus.*
You advise us to do this thing. (indirect command)

Monēs nōs hoc facere.
You advise that we are doing this thing. (indirect statement)

B.1. Translate the following sentences and indicate whether the subordinate clause shows purpose, indirect command, indirect question, or indirect statement.

1. Auxilium ferēmus ut ille senex fēlicior sit.

2. Pār auxilium utrīque fers nē ūnus fēlicior sit quam alius.

3. Nē ūnus aliō felicior sit, auxilium utrīque lātum est.

4. Quam fēlicissimus sit ut bonam vītam agat.

5. Quaesīvit quae facta puellae tuae ōderis.

6. Scīs quae facta ōssisima sint.

7. Monuit ut saepe ante oculōs facta puellae ōsissima pōnerēs.

8. Quaesīvit quid esset ōsius quam facta puellae nōn iam amātae.

9. Haec fac nē ingentior cupīdō in tē crescat.

10. Tibi dīc quae cupīdō ingentior sit quam illa.

11. Vōbīs imperāte ut humiliōrēs sītis illīs.

12. Vōs monēmus nē humiliōrēs sītis.

13. Petīvit ut quam decorissima mūnera ferrentur.

14. Ā tē quaerō ut manum meam dēficientem tollās.

15. Imperābō ut vocēris.

16. Ōrāvērunt nē arborī nocēret.

17. Nymphae Erysichthonī suādēre nē arborem tolleret nōn poterant.

B.2. Translate the following sentences into good English. Notice that the even-numbered sentences are indirect commands:

1. Quam fēlicissimus sum.

2. Mē monuit ut quam fēlicissimus essem.

3. Lacrimās saepe dēpōne et rīdē.

4. Suādēs mihi ut lacrimās saepe dēpōneam et rīdeam.

5. Accipe opus quod canās.

6. Cupīdō mihi imperavit ut acciperem opus quod canerem.

7. Ante oculōs omnia eius vitia dispōne.

8. Magister tē monēbit ut ante oculōs omnia eius vitia dispōneās.

9. Quid sit senectūs nescite.

10. Amīcī ā nōbīs petunt ut quid sit senectūs nesciāmus.

188

C. Derivations

Identify the distinctions between the following pairs of English words by identifying their Latin roots and then providing the meaning (below) which comes closest to the Latin elements at the heart of each pair of words.

	Latin Root	Latin Prefix	English Meaning
effect			
affect			
except			
accept			
persuade			
dissuade			
demand			
command			
imposition			
proposition			
deposition			
disposition			
exponent			
deponent			
cognate			
agnate			
perfect			
confect			

Meanings:

a. to deter by advice
b. something presented for consideration
c. to accomplish something
d. one who explains
e. prepare from ingredients
f. to impress in mind or feeling
g. physical or mental inclination
h. a particular detail
i. a male relation on the father's side
j. convince someone of something
k. to leave out
l. an extraordinary burden
m. to claim as a right
n. removal from office
o. related in origin
p. to direct with authority
q. bring to completion
r. appearance to the mind or eye
s. to take something with approval
t. one who testifies under oath in writing

D. Translation:

Special Vocabulary

nōn aliter	not otherwise, in the same way
anguis, -is, *m.*	snake, serpent
concurrō, -ere, concurrī, concursus	run together, meet in conflict
contendō, -ere, contendī, contentus	engage in a contest,
cūnae, -ārum *f. pl.*	cradle
digitus, -ī *m.*	finger
dum + subjunctive	provided that
duo (indeclinable)	two
fīgō, -ere, fīxī, fīxus	fix, fasten, drive in
harēna, -ae *f.*	sand
humus, -ī *m.*	the ground, the soil
infringō, -ere, infrēgī, infractus	break off
oblīquus, -a, -um	slanting sideways
ōs, ōris, *n.*	face, mouth
pectus, pectoris, *n.*	chest
pecus, pecoris, n.	farm animals, especially cattle and sheep
pretium, -ī *n.*	reward, price
prōnus, -a, -um	inclined forward, prone
pugna, -ae, *f.*	battle, contest
pugnus, -ī, *m.*	the fist, boxing
regnum, -ī, *n.*	kingdom, realm
revellō, -ere, revellī, revulsus	pluck or tear off
sōlācium, -ī, *n.*	consolation, comfort
taurus, -ī, *m.*	bull
turpis, -e	disgusting, disgraceful
uxōrem domum dūcere	to marry (to lead home as wife)
viridis, -e	green (the color of a river)

ACHELOUS AND THE ORIGIN OF THE CORNUCOPIA

Quisque fluvius suum deum habet. Dī fluviōrum duo cornua in capite semper gerunt. Ūnus autem hōrum deōrum, Achelous nōmine, ūnum sōlum cornū gerit. Alterum āmīsit cum ille deus Herculēsque, Dēianīram uxōrem domum dūcere petentēs, contenderent.

Achelous, cōgitāns turpius esse sī deus mortālī cēderet —nam Herculēs nōndum deus erat— ōrātiōne gravissimō dēclāmāvit hīs et aliīs dictīs,

"Rēgem mē cernis aquārum
cursibus oblīquīs inter tua regna fluentem."

Herculēs autem saevius respondit, "Tū linguā vince, dum ego pugnīs superem." Itaque deus fluviī viridem vestem dē corpore ēiēcit bracchiaque opposuit manūsque et membra pugnae parāvit. Tōtō pectore prōnus et digitōs digitīs et frontem fronte premēbant. Nōn aliter fortēs concurrunt taurī cum, pretium pugnae, pulchra petitur uxor. Spectant timentque pecora, nescia quem maneat tantī victōria regnī.

Diū premēbant sed denique terra genū deī pressa est et harēnās ōre momordit. Ergō formam suam in anguem mūtāvit, sed Herculēs deum mūtātum rīsit et dixit, "Cūnārum labor est anguēs superāre meārum." Tum deum in taurī formam mūtātum traxit dēpressaque dūra cornua humō figit. Deō in harēnā iactātō, Herculēs manū dexterā cornū capit infrēgitque et ā fronte revellit.

Nymphae hoc cornū, pomīs fēlicibus et odōrō flōre implētum, Deae Bonae Copiae obtulērunt. Achelous victus dēclāmāvit, "Nōn tam turpe vincī fuit, quam contendisse decōrum est, magnaque dat nōbīs sōlācia victor."

(after Ovid, Metamorphoses, *9.4-93)*

Key, Chapter XIII

A.1.

Adjectives:

Positive	Comparative	Translation	Superlative	Translation
aptus	aptior	more suitable	aptissimus	most suitable
bellā	belliōre	more beautiful	bellissima	most beautiful
cārus	cārior	dearer	cārissimus	dearest
crūdēlis	crūdēlior	crueler	crūdēlissimus	cruelest
difficilem	difficiliōrem	more difficult	difficillimum	most difficult
dissimilia	dissimiliōra	more different	dissimillimum	most different
dīversus	dīversior	more contrary	dīversissimus	most contrary
facilia	faciliōra	easier (pl. *n.*)	facillima	easiest
formōsōrum	formōsiōrum	more beautiful	formōsissimōrum	most beautiful
gracilium	graciliōrum	slenderer	gracillimōrum	slenderest
grave	gravius	heavier	gravissimum	heaviest
humile	humilius	more humble	humillimum	most humble
levibus	leviōribus	lighter	levissimīs	lightest
similis	similior	more similar	simillimus	most similar
tristis	tristior	sadder	tristissimus	saddest
vīcīnus	vīcīnior	nearer	vīcīnissimus	nearest
apertus	apertior	more open	apertissimus	most open
dēficiēns	dēficientior	more lacking	dēficientissimus	most lacking

Adverbs:

saepe	saepius	more often	saepissimē	most often
fortiter	fortius	more bravely	fortissimē	most bravely
cupidē	cupidius	more desirously	cupidissimē	most desirously
potenter	potentius	more powerfully	potentissimē	most powerfully
diū	diūtius	for a longer time	diūtissimē	for the longest time
sapienter	sapientius	more wisely	sapientissimē	most wisely

A.2.

1. That old man is happier than this one.
2. That one is happier than this one.
3. She will be as happy as possible.
4. Often place the girl's most hated deeds before (*your*) eyes.
5. Surely nothing is more hateful than the deeds of a girl (*who is*) no longer loved, is it? (**num** anticipates the answer "no"; **nōn iam** = no longer)
6. A greater desire is growing in me.
7. This desire is greater than that one.
8. It (*the desire*) is greater than that one.
9. It is very great.
10. It is as great as possible.
11. I hope that you will hold my failing hand.
12. You will be summoned by my rather (*too*) failing (*weak*) hands.
13. This hand is weaker than that one.
14. I will summon you with a very weak hand.

B.1.

1. We shall bring aid so that that old man will be happier.   (purpose)
2. You are bringing equal aid to both so that one person will not be happier than the other one. (purpose)
3. So that one will not be happier than the other, aid was brought to each of them.   (purpose)
4. Let him be as happy as possible so that he may lead a good life.   (purpose)
5. He asked what deeds of your girl you despise.   (ind. question)
6. You know what deeds are most hateful.   (indirect question)

7. He advised that you often place the girl's most hated deeds before (*your*) eyes. (ind. command)
8. He asked what was more hateful than the deeds of a girl no longer loved. (indirect question)
9. Do these things so that a greater desire will not grow in you. (purpose)
10. Tell yourself what desire is greater than that one. (indirect question)
11. Order yourselves to be more humble than those (*people*). (indirect command)
12. We advise you not to be too humble. (indirect command)
13. He asked that gifts as proper as possible be brought. (indirect command)
14. I ask you to lift up my weakening hand. (indirect command)
15. I will order that you be summoned. (indirect command)
16. They implored that he not harm the tree. (indirect command)
17. The Nymphs were not able to persuade Erysichthon not to destroy the tree. (indirect command)

B.2.

1. I am as happy as possible.
2. He advised me to be as happy as possible.
3. Often set aside (*your*) tears and laugh.
4. You urge me to set aside (*my*) tears often and laugh.
5. Accept the kind of work (*song*) you may sing. (**quod canās**; relative clause of characteristic)
6. Cupid ordered me to accept the kind of work (*song*) I may sing.
7. Arrange (*place*) all her faults before (*your*) eyes.
8. The teacher will advise you to arrange (*place*) all her faults before (*your*) eyes.
9. Know not what old age is. (i.e., *make a point of not knowing…*)
10. (*Our*) friends ask us to know not what old age is.

C. DERIVATIONS

	Latin Root	Latin Prefix	English Meaning
effect	faciō	ex	c
affect	faciō	ad	f
except	capiō	ex	k
accept	capiō	ad	s
persuade	suādeō	per	j
dissuade	suādeō	dis	a
demand	mandō	dē	m
command	mandō	cum	p
imposition	pōnō	in	l
proposition	pōnō	prō	b
deposition	pōnō	dē	n
disposition	pōnō	dis	g
exponent	pōnō	ex	d
deponent	pōnō	dē	t
cognate	noscō	cum	o
agnate	noscō	ad	i
perfect	faciō	per	q
confect	faciō	cum	e

D. ACHELOUS AND THE ORIGIN OF THE CORNUCOPIA

Each river has its own deity/god. These river gods always wear two horns on their head(s). One of these gods, however, Achelous by name, wears only one horn. He lost the other one when the god and Hercules, seeking to marry Deianira, fought (contended in battle).

Achelous, thinking it was rather shameful if a god should yield to a mortal—for Hercules was not yet a god— declaimed (made a speech) in a very weighty speech with these and other words,

"You behold me, king of rivers (waters)
flowing cross-wise (with cross-wise flow) among your realms."

Hercules, however, responded rather cruelly, "Conquer with your tongue, provided I win with my fists." And so the god of the river cast off his green cloak from his body and set his arms and hands in opposition and prepared his limbs for battle. They pressed down with the entire chest, fingers with fingers and forehead with forehead. In the same way mighty bulls clash when a beautiful spouse, the reward of the battle, is sought. The herds watch and are fearful, not knowing which one the victory over so great a kingdom awaits. (i.e., who will win so great a kingdom).

For a long time they struggled (pressed) but finally the earth was pressed by the knee of the god and he bit the dust ("he bit the sand with his mouth"). Therefore he changed his shape into a serpent, but Hercules laughed at the changed god and said, "Conquering serpents is the labor of my cradle!" Then he dragged the god (now) changed into the shape of a bull and he planted the god's horns, (which had been)pushed down into the soil. Once the god was thrown on the sand, Hercules takes the horn with his right hand and breaks it and tears it from his forehead.

The nymphs offered this horn, filled with wonderful fruits and scented flower(s), to the goddess, **Bona Copia** ("good abundance"). Achelous, defeated, declaimed, "It was not so shameful to be defeated as it is proper (and seemly) to have fought, and the victor (being who he is) gives me ("us") great solace."

XIV
Fifth Declension; Fīō; Gerunds, Gerundives, and Supines

A. Fifth Declension

A.1. Translate and decline the following phrases:

a. illa rēs gravis

b. diēs clarus īdem

c. quaedem spēs

d. spēs crescēns

e. rēs crescēns

A.2. Translate the following forms of **fīō, fierī, factus sum** into English, and then change them to the subjunctive, retaining the person and tense of the original.

	Translation	*Subjunctive*
fīs		
fīēbās		
factus es		
factus erat		
factī sunt		
facta es		
fīmus		
factī sumus		
fīunt		
fīēbant		

A.3. Translate the following into Latin, using as many of the following words as is appropriate: **rēs, spēs, diēs, fierī**

1. Rome has become a republic.

2. Your (s.) hopes have become my hopes.

3. The situation must not be made more difficult.

4. The day grows long without you.

5. Day became night, and night became day.

6. Don't lose your inheritance.

7. I hope that you won't lose your hopes or your inheritance or your state.

8. This has become such a great thing!

9. I hope the long days will not become too difficult for us.

B. Gerunds vs. Participles

In English, a gerund is a verbal *noun*, in the active voice, which ends in *-ing*. It occurs only in the singular:

> *Learning* Latin is not difficult.   (*Learning* is the subject of *is*.)
>
> *Seeing* is *believing*.   (*Seeing* is the subject, and *believing* is the predicate.)
>
> *Thinking* correctly is not always easy.   (*Thinking* is the subject.)
>
> *Thinking* pleases me.   (*Thinking* is the subject.)

The gerund in English should not be confused with the present active participle, which also ends in "*-ing*". Participles, in English and in Latin, are always verbal *adjectives*: In the following examples, *learning, seeing, believing, and thinking* are functioning not as gerunds (verbal nouns) even though they end in *-ing*, but as *adjectives* which modify the underlined name:

> <u>Augustine,</u> *while learning* Latin, enjoyed the story of the fall of Troy.
>
> *Seeing* Dido in this condition, <u>Aeneas</u> feel great sorrow.
>
> <u>Aeneas,</u> *believing* she did not understand, tried to explain.
>
> *Thinking* she would benefit Hercules, <u>Deianira</u> instead inflicted harm.

In these examples, *learning* describes Augustine, *seeing* and *believing* describe Aeneas, and *thinking* describes Deianira, whereas in the previous examples these same words are used as (verbal) nouns.

The gerunds in the examples above are the subject of the finite verb in the sentence. English gerunds can be found in all the declined functions common to other nouns:

	(Latin case equivalent)
He is fond *of learning*.	(objective genitive)
For enjoying life, nothing is greater than this!	(dative of reference)
I have dedicated myself *to enjoying* life.	(indirect object)
We all need *learning*.	(direct object)
Learn to do *by doing*.	(ablative of means)

In Latin, too, the gerund is a verbal noun. The gender of the Latin gerund is neuter. It occurs only in the active voice and is always singular. It is not found in the nominative case, however, as it is in English. Instead of a gerund in the nominative case, Latin uses the infinitive where English would use a gerund for the subject of a finite verb. When used in the place of the nominative form of the gerund, the infinitive is known as a "substantive infinitive", that is, an infinitive functioning as a noun. The gender of the substantive infinitive is also neuter.

Substantive Infinitive in place of Nominative case:

Discere linguam Latīnam nōn est difficile.	*Learning* Latin is not difficult.
Vidēre est *crēdere.*	*Seeing* is *believing.*
Rectē *cōgitāre* nōn est semper facile.	*Thinking* correctly is not always easy.

Declined cases (Gerunds):

Gen.	Amōrem *docendī* habet.	He has a love of (for) teaching. (objective gen.)
Dat.	*Docendō* crēdet.	He believes in teaching.
Acc.	Ad *docendum* veniet. (ad + *acc.*)	She will come to teach (for the purpose of teaching).
Abl.	*Docendō* Latīnam, ipse doctus fiet.	By teaching Latin, he himself will become educated.

Gerundives

You have learned that that the future *passive* participle is formed by adding **-nd-** plus the 1st and 2nd declension endings, **us, a, um** to the present stem of the verb: **docendus, a, um; videndus, a, um; credendus, a, um**. The future passive participle is called the *"gerundive"*, because, as the English signifies, in appearance it "resembles a gerund." But there the similarity ends. Whereas the gerund is a noun, the gerundive is an adjective; while the gerund is active in meaning, the gerundive is passive in meaning.

The gerundive, then, is a verbal adjective, passive in meaning, and always agrees with the noun it modifies in case, number, and gender: **docendus, a, um**, about to be taught, **videndus, a, um**, about to be seen, **credendus, a, um**, about to be believed. Its meaning can also have the sense of "deserving to be/worthy of being" (taught, seen, believed). The gerundive, or future passive participle, is an adjective of the first and second declension and therefore uses only the endings of those declensions.

When a gerund takes an object, Latin frequently replaces it with a gerundive phrase:

gerund + object	*will tend to be replaced by:*	
diēs fēlīcēs spērandī	diērum fēlīcium spērandōrum	*of hoping for happy days*
verba tua audiendō	verbībus tuīs audiendīs	*by hearing your words*
rem publicam servandō	rē publicā servandā	*by saving the state*

Expressions of Purpose

Gerunds and Gerundive phrases (often referred to simply as "Gerundives") are often prefaced by the preposition *ad* (which always governs the accusative case) to show purpose:

Vēnī ad laudandum.	I came to praise.	(gerund)
Vēnī ad spēs tuās audiendās.	I came to hear your hopes.	(gerundive)
Veniet ad rem pūblicam servandam.	He will come to save the republic.	(gerundive)

Purpose is also expressed by the genitive of the gerund or gerundive followed by the ablative of **causā** or **gratiā** ("for the sake of")

Vēnī laudandī gratiā.	I came to praise. (gerund)
Vēnī verbōrum tuōrum audiendōrum causā.	I came to hear your words. (gerundive)
Veniet reī pūblicae servandae causā.	He will come to save the republic. (gerundive)

B.1. Translate the following sentences into English:

1. Domum rediendī cupīdus sum.

2. Domum rediendō patrī placēbō.

3. Domō abīre mihi nōn placet.

4. Diem natālem rūrī agendō, Sulpicia diem molestum ēgit.

5. Medicāmen celerrimē bibendō, vītam quam longissimam agēs.

6. Vītam quam longissimam agendī causā, medicāmen celeriter bibit.

7. Oscula dandī causā puellam meam vocābō.

8. Iste dōna accipiendī causā hīc vēnit.

9. Hercules, bovēs inveniendī causā, ad spēluncam adīvit.

10. Deianira, vīrēs amōrī reddendī causā, ad Herculem vestem mīsit.

B.2. Translate the following phrases into Latin, using a gerund and the vocabulary of chapters 13 and 14 where possible:

1. By influencing my mother

2. For the sake of warning our friends

3. For the sake of distinguishing one thing from another

4. Art for the sake of art

5. Disclosing the truth is difficult.

6. Taking pleasure in the difficulties of others is not good.

7. Hating people is not a good thing.

8. By laughing you will save the day.

9. I told you (*pl*) these things to persuade you.

10. She raised her hands to pray.

11. By mixing his words with tears, he persuaded us.

Cases of Gerunds and Gerundives: Summary

1. Nominative case:

A substantive infinitive serves as the nominative form of a gerund:

> **Iam *placēre* est omnis tua cūra.**
>
> Now *pleasing* (*to be pleasing*) is all your concern.

2. Genitive case.

The genitive of the Gerund or Gerundive is used with nouns or adjectives. As with regular nouns and substantive adjectives, the genitive shows a *relationship between two nouns (or substantive adjectives)*, most often as an *objective* genitive:

> **Polyphēmus *placendī* cūram sēnsit.**   (gerund)
>
> Polyphemus felt a concern *for pleasing*.

> **Polyphēmus *hominum placendōrum* cūram sēnsit.** (gerundive)
>
> Polyphemus felt a concern *for pleasing people*.

> **Tuus modus *vīvendī* mihi nōn placet.**   (gerund)
>
> Your manner *of living* does not please me.

The genitive of the gerund or gerundive followed by *causā* or *gratiā* indicates purpose:

> **Polyphēmus *placendī causā* multa dōna tulit.** (gerund)
>
> Polyphemus brought many gifts *in order to/for the sake of pleasing*.

Polyphēmus *puellae placendae causā* multa dōna tulit. (gerundive)
Polyphemus brought many gifts in order to/for the sake of pleasing the girl.

3. Dative case.

The Dative of the Gerund or Gerundive is used in a few expressions after verbs:

a. After verbal expressions that govern the dative case:

> **Diem dīxit *agrō colendō*.** (gerundive)
> He appointed the day *for cultivating the field.*

> ***Cantandō* operam dedit.** (gerund)
> He worked *at singing* (directed his efforts *to singing*).

b. After adjectives, especially those which indicate fitness or adaptability:

> **Nōn erat *nubendō* aptus.** (gerund)
> He was not suitable *for marrying.*

> **Polyphēmus nōn erat *Galatēae nubendae* aptus.** (gerundive)
> Polyphemus was not suitable *to marry Galataea.*

4. Accusative case.

The most common occurrence of the gerund or gerundive in the accusative case is with the preposition **ad**, to indicate Purpose. Note that the preposition **ad** always governs the accusative case, pointing to a direction; this direction can consist of a place, a time, a person, or an intention:

a. Place:

***ad urbem* vēnit.**	He came *to/toward/near the city.*
***ad meridiem* sē contulit.**	He went [he took himself] *toward the south/southward* .

b. Time:

***ad nōnam hōram* mānsit.**	He waited *until the ninth hour.*

c. Person:

***ad eōs* vēnit.**	He came *to them/toward them.*

d. Intention:

***ad petendam pacem* vēnit.**	He came *to seek peace.* (gerundive)
***ad placendum* cantāvit.**	He sang *to please.* (gerund)

Thus the accusative of the Gerund and Gerundive, when used after the preposition **ad** comes to denote the *Intention* or *Purpose* of the subject of the main verb in the clause.

5. Ablative Case.

The Ablative of the Gerund and Gerundive is used

a. To express *manner, means, cause, etc.*:

> ***cantandō* amōrem ostendit.**   (Means)
> He shows his love *by singing.*

> ***dōnīs dandīs* Galatēam vincere optat.**   (Means)
> He hopes to win Galatea *by giving gifts.*

b. After comparatives:

> **Nihil *dōnīs dandīs* est facilius.**
> Nothing is easier *than giving gifts.*

c. After the prepositions **ab, de, ex, in.**

> ***In cantandō* vītam agit.**
> He consumes his life/ spends his time *in singing.*

197

C. The Supine

The Supine is a verbal noun of the fourth declension, which occurs only in the accusative or ablative case, singular. Although it is formed from the fourth principal part of the verb (perfect passive participle), it translates in the active voice.

a. Supine in the Accusative case.

The Supine ending in **-um** is used after verbs of motion to express purpose. It may take an object, but more often does not:

> **Polyphēmus** *cantātum* **vēnit.**
> Polyphemus came *to sing.*

> **Vēnit** *quaesītum* **Galatēam.**
> He came *to look for /to seek* Galatea.

b. Supine in the Ablative case.

The Supine ending in **-ū** is used with a few adjectives and with the nouns **fās**, **nefā**s, and **opus** to indicate an action in reference to which the quality is asserted.

> **Polyphēmus erat mōnstrum nōn modo** *vīsū* **sed etiam** *audītū* **turpe.**
> Polyphemus was a monster not only ugly [**turpis, -e**] *to see* but even *to hear.*

C.1. Exercises: Translate the following:

1. Hoc est facile factū.

2. Cantāre est facile factū.

3. Vēnī cantātum.

4. Eāmus cantōrem clārum audītem. (**cantor, -ōris,** *m.* singer)

5. Eāmus Rōmam cantōrem cantantem audītum.

6. Eāmus ad cantōrem audiendum. Eāmus ut cantōrem audiāmus.

7. Difficile audītū erat. Difficilius cantōrem vīsū erat.

8. Multī hominēs vēnērunt ad clāmandum. Vēnērunt ut clāmārent. Vēnērunt clāmātum.

9. Nōs nōn clāmātum sed audītum venimus.

10. Opus est haec compositū. Fās est haec compositū.

11. Nefās aliīs invīsū. Nefās est hoc dubitātū.

12. Erat difficilius tacēre quam clāmāre.

13. Canis dominum cernēns gaudēbat. Canī erat difficile tacitū. Opus erat clāmātū.

14. Nihil est suāvius vīsū quam faciēs tua.

15. Quā rē opus erat iter factū?

16. Iter fēcit ut copiās in aliīs terrīs pervidēret. Iter fēcit ad copiās pervidendās. Iter fēcit copiārum pervidendārum causā.

17. Opus erat iter facere ad rem pūblicam servandam. Opus erat iter facere ut rēs pūblica servārētur.

Key, Chapter XIV

A. Fifth Declension

A.1.

a. *that serious matter*
illa rēs gravis
illīus reī gravis
illī reī gravī
illam rem gravem
illā rē gravī

illī rēs gravēs
illārum rērum gravium
illīs rēbus gravibus
illās rēs gravīs
illīs rēbus gravibus

b. *the same bright (famous) day*
diēs clārus īdem
diēī clārī eiusdem
diēī clārō ēīdem
diem clārum eundem
diē clārō eōdem

diēs clārī eidem
diērum clārōrum eōrundem
diēbus clārīs eīsdem
diēs clārōs eōsdem
diēbus clārīs eīsdem

c. *a certain hope*
quaedem spēs
cuiusdem speī
cuidem speī
quandem spem
quādem spē

quaedem spēs
quārundem spērum
quibusdem spēbus
quāsdem spēs
quibusdem spēbus

d. *increasing (growing) hope*
spēs crescēns
speī crescentis
speī crescentī
spem crescentem
spē crescentī

spēs crescentēs
spērum crescentium
spēbus crescentibus
spēs crescentīs
spēbus crescentibus

e. *increasing (growing) matter/situation*
rēs crescēns
reī crescentis
reī crescentī
rem crescentem
rē crescentī

rēs crescentēs
rērum crescentium
rēbus crescentibus
rēs crescentīs
rēbus crescentibus

A.2.

	Translation	Subjunctive
fīs	you are becoming or being made	fīās
fīēbās	you were becoming	fierēs
factus es	you became or have been made	factus sīs
factus est	he became or has been made	factus sit
factī sunt	they have become or been made	factī sint
facta es	you (fem.) have become or been made	facta sīs
fīmus	we are becoming or being made	fīāmus
factī sumus	we have become or been made	factī sīmus
fiunt	they are becoming or being made	fiant
fīēbant	they were becoming or being made	fierent

A.3.

1. Rōma rēs publica facta est.
2. Spēs tuae meae factae sunt.
3. Rēs difficilior nōn facienda est.
4. Diēs sine tē longa fit.
5. Diēs nox facta est, et nox diēs.
6. Nē rem tuam amitte. (*or* Nōlī rem tuam āmittere.)
7. Spērō tē nec spēs nec rem nec cīvitātem tuam āmissūram esse.
8. Haec rēs tanta facta est! (or Tanta facta est haec rēs!)
9. Spērō diēs longās nōbīs difficiliōrēs nōn faciendās esse.

B.1.

1. I am eager to return home. (literally, I am desirous of returning home: objective genitive)
2. I shall please father by returning home. (ablative of means)
3. Leaving home does not please me. (**abīre** is the subject of **placet**.)
4. By spending her birthday in the countryside, Sulpicia spent an annoying day.
5. By drinking the medicine (antidote) very quickly, you will live as long a life as possible.
6. In order to live as long a life as possible, he drank the antidote quickly.
7. I shall summon my girlfriend in order to give (her) kisses.
8. That man came here for the purpose of receiving gifts.
9. Hercules, in order to find his cattle, went toward the cave.
10. Deianira, for the purpose of restoring strength to love, sent the cloak to Hercules.

B.2.

1. Matrem meam afficiendō
2. Amīcos nostrōs monendī causā
3. Aliud ab aliō cernendī causā
4. Ars artis gratiā
5. Difficile est vērītātem aperīre.
6. Difficultātibus aliōrum gaudēre nōn bonum est.
7. Hominēs ōdisse nōn bonum est.
8. Rīdendō diem servābis.
9. Haec vōbīs dixī ad vōs suādendōs. (vōbīs suādendī causā)
10. Manūs ad ōrandum (ōrandī causā) sustulit.
11. Verba cum lacrimīs miscendō, nōbīs persuāsit.

C.1.

1. This is easy to do.
2. Singing is easy to do.
3. I came to sing. (for the purpose of singing)
4. Let us go to hear the famous singer.
5. Let us go to Rome to hear the singer singing.
6. Let us go to hear the singer. (gerundive) Let us go to hear the singer. (purpose clause)
7. It was difficult to hear. It was more difficult to see the singer.
8. Many men came to shout. (gerund) They came to shout. (purpose clause) They came to shout. (supine).
9. We came not to shout but to listen.
10. It is necessary to compare these things. It right to compare these things.
11. It is wrong to envy (**invidēre**) others. It is wrong to doubt this.
12. It was more difficult to be silent than to shout out.
13. The dog, seeing his master, was rejoicing. It was difficult for the dog to be silent. There was a need to shout.
14. Nothing is sweeter to see than your face.
15. Why (because of what thing) was it necessary to make the journey?
16. He made the journey to look over the troops in foreign (other) lands. He made the journey to review the troops. (**ad** + gerundive) He made the journey to review the troops. (genitive of gerundive + **causā**).
17. It was necessary to make the journey to save the republic. (**ad** + gerundive) It was necessary to make the journey so that the republic would be saved. (purpose clause, passive voice).

XV
Irregular Comparative and Superlative Adjectives and Adverbs; Intransitive Verbs; Review of the Dative Case

A. Irregular Comparative and Superlative Adjectives and Adverbs

A.1. Identify the Latin positive, comparative or superlative adjective which is the origin of each of the following English words:

English Word	Positive Degree	Comparative Degree	Superlative Degree
		Latin Origin	
major	_____	_____	_____
minuscule	_____	_____	_____
pejorative	_____	_____	_____
prior	_____	_____	_____
optimist	_____	_____	_____
pessimist	_____	_____	_____
facilitate	_____	_____	_____
plurality	_____	_____	_____
sum	_____	_____	_____

similitude	_____	_____	_____
aptitude	_____	_____	_____
infinitely	_____	_____	_____
maximum	_____	_____	_____
minimum	_____	_____	_____
graceful	_____	_____	_____
prime	_____	_____	_____

A.2. Translate the following phrases into Latin and decline them in the singular or plural, as directed:

1. more art (singular only)

2. less money (singular)

3. more things (**rēs**) (plural only)

A.3. Translate the following phrases into Latin:

1. worse times

2. more badly

3. more and more

4. for better or for worse

5. Can anything be better than the best?

6. Believe that the worst things can happen.

7. Forgive them, for they do not know what they do.

8. You have harmed the worst possible person.

9. If it pleases you, it pleases me.

10. Your sweet words have persuaded me to forgive you.

11. Save yourself (pl.) if you can.

12. By saving yourself (s.), you will serve your country well.

13. Whom will you serve?

14. Whose servant are you?

15. The servant saved the master.

16. The servant served the master.

17. The child obeyed the father.

18. The father spared the child.

B. Integrated Exercises

B.1. Translate the following into good English:

1. Tuus fīlius minor est.

2. Tuus fīlius minor est meō fīliō.

3. Quam minimus est. Quam maximus est.

4. In hāc fābula sunt plūra verba quam in illā.

5. Haec fābula longissima est.

6. Haec fābula longior est.

7. Haec fābula longior illā est.

8. Iste homō novissimus esse vidēbātur.

9. Novē dīcere vidētur.

10. Novius dīcere vidētur.

11. Novissimē dīcere vīsus est.

12. Studēre litterīs optimīs maximā cum cūrā volō.

13. Optimus discipulus esse voluit.

14. Optimus omnium discipulōrum esse māluit.

15. Pēior mē discipulus esse nōlet.

16. Pēius mē agere nōn vult.

17. Quis est omnium discipulōrum optima?

18. Omnēs discipulī meliōrēs sē clārissimōrum hominum simillimōs futūrōs esse putant .

19. Quis est quī nōn quam maxima agere velit?

20. Tityre, tū mē fēlīcior esse vidēris. (**Tityrus, -ī**, *m*, proper name)

21. Quemadmodum tū fēlix esse potes?

22. Num quis tē umquam fēlīcior esse possit?

23. Tū quam fēlīcissimus esse vidēris.

24. Putō tē fēlīciorem mē esse.

25. Iter Rōmam, quae urbs maxima est, fēcī.

26. Rōma māior quam nostra urbs est.

27. Scīsne urbem māiōrem Rōmā?

28. Est urbs ad quam plūrimī iter faciunt.

29. Est urbs ad quam plūrimī iter faciant.

30. Est urbs ad quam plūrimī iter facere velint.

31. Est māior meliorque aliīs urbibus.

32. Iter prīmum Rōmam hōc annō multī facient.

33. Iter Rōmam magis quam Athēnās facere volō.

34. Iter prius Rōmam quam Athēnās facere mālō.

35. Iter Rōmam omnibus faciendum est.

36. Plūrēs artēs Rōmae quam in nostrā urbe exercentur.

37. Quō magis quam Rōmae artēs gravissimae exercentur?

38. Athēnīsne aut Rōmae sunt exercitae artēs gravius?

39. Parvae sunt tuae cūrae. Tuae cūrae sunt minimae.

40. Tū dē minimīs cūrās.

41. Lēgēs nostrae dē maximīs, nōn dē minimīs cūrant.

42. Dē minimīs nōn cūrat Lex.

43. Senātus lēgēs nostrās, deī iūra nostra faciunt.

44. Iūs et Lex sunt rēs gravissimae.

45. Homō deīs cārior est quam sibi.

46. Mēns sāna in corpore sāno tibi placeat.

47. Mēns sāna in corpore sāno magis divitiīs tibi placeat.

48. Ego minus quam aliī dē iūribus civilibus nōvī.

C. Dative Case:

C.1. Translate the following sentences into Latin, using at least one of the following verbs:

crēdere, fāvēre, ignoscere, imperāre, nocēre, parcere, parēre, placēre, servīre, studēre, suādēre.

1. Trust me! I trust you more than you trust me.

2. We believed that they were willing to obey all the laws.

3. We advise you to be fair to all and to favor no one.

4. He was favorably inclined toward those he trusted.

5. We persuaded him to favor only those whom he trusted.

6. Don't be too eager to please them. (too, *adv.* **nimis**)

7. He stood before us warning us to beware of the dog.

8. It is better to forgive mistakes, and to spare all those who are not going to harm us.

9. It is wiser to harm your enemies and forgive your friends.

10. How many masters can we serve at one time?

Key, Chapter XV

A.1.

	Positive Degree	Comparative Degree	Superlative Degree
major	magnus, -a, -um	māior, māius	maximus, -a, -um
minuscule	parvus, -a, -um	minor, minus	minimus, -a, -um
pejorative	malus, -a, -um	peior, peius	pessimus, -a, -um
prior	[prae, pro]	prior, prius	prīmus, -a, -um
optimist	bonus, -a, -um	melior, melius	optimus, -a, -um
pessimist	malus, -a, -um	peior, peius	pessimus, -a, -um
facilitate	facilis, -e	facilior, facilius	facillimus, -a, -um
plurality	multus, -a, -um	plus (noun)	plurimus, -a, -um
sum	superus, -a, -um	superior, superius	summus, -a, -um
similitude	similis, -e	similior, similius	simillimus, -a, -um
aptitude	aptus, -a, -um	aptior, aptius	aptissimus, -a, -um
infinitely	infīnitus, -a, -um,	infīnītior, infīnītius	infīnītissimus, -a, -um
maximum	magnus, -a, -um	maior, maius	maximus, -a, -um
minimum	parvus, -a, -um	minor, minus	minimus, -a, -um
graceful	gracilis, -e	gracilior, gracilius	gracillimus, -a, -um
prime	[prae, pro]	prior, prius	prīmus, -a, -um

A.2.

1. plūs artis, plūris artis, [plūrī artis], plūs artis, plūre artis.
2. minus pecūniae, minōris pecūniae, minōrī pecūniae, minus pecūniae, minōre pecūniae.
3. rēs plūrēs, rērum plūrium, rēbus plūribus, rēs plūrēs, rēbus plūribus.

A.3.

1. tempora pēiōra
2. pēius
3. magis magisque
4. aut meliōrī aut pēiōrī
5. Num quid melius quam optimum (*or* melius optimō) sit?
6. Crēdē (*or* Crēdite) pessima fierī posse.
7. Eīs ignosce, nam nesciunt quid faciant.
8. Quam pessimō hominī nocuistī.
9. Sī tibi placet, mihi placet.
10. Tua verba dulcia mihi ut tibi ignoscerem persuāsērunt.
11. Vōs servāte sī potestis.
12. Tē servandō (tē servāns), nōbīs bene serviēs. (*or* tē servandō, gerundive)
13. Cui serviēs?
14. Cui servīs? (*or* cuius servus es?)
15. Servus dominam servāvit.
16. Servus dominō servīvit (*or* serviēbat).
17. Puer patrī parēbat (*or* paruit).
18. Pater puerō pepercit.

B.1.

1. Your son is rather small.
2. Your son is smaller than my son.
3. He is as small as possible. He is as large as possible.
4. There are more words in this story than in that one.
5. This story is very long.
6. This story is rather (*or* too) long.
7. This story is longer than that one.
8. That man seemed to be very strange.
9. He seems to speak strangely.

10. He seems to speak rather strangely (*or*, too strangely).
11. He seemed to speak very strangely.
12. I want to study the best literature with great care (*or*, very carefully).
13. He wanted to be the best student.
14. He preferred to be the best of all the students.
15. He will be unwilling to be a worse student than me.
16. He is unwilling to act worse than me.
17. Who is the best (f.) of all the students (both m. and f.)?
18. All the better students think that they will be most similar to (like) very famous people.
19. Who is there who is not willing to do the best things possible? (rel. clause of characteristic)
20. Tityrus, you seem to be happier than me.
21. How can you be happy?
22. Could anyone ever be happier (luckier) than you? (deliberative subjunctive)
23. You seem to be as happy as possible.
24. I think that you are happier than I am.
25. I travelled (made a journey) to Rome, which is the largest city.
26. Rome is larger than our city.
27. Do you know a city larger than Rome?
28. It is the city to which the most people travel.
29. It is the kind of city to which the most people travel.
30. It is the kind of city to which most people would want to travel.
31. It is larger and better than other cities.
32. Many people will make (their) first trip to Rome this year. (within this year)
33. I want to go to Rome more than to Athens.
34. I prefer to make a trip to Rome more than to Athens.
35. Everyone must visit (make a trip to) Rome.
36. More arts are practiced at Rome than in our city.
37. Where are the most important arts practiced more than at Rome?
38. Are the arts practiced more seriously at Athens or at Rome?
39. Your concerns are small. Your concerns are very small
30. You are concerned about very small things.
41. Our laws are concerned with very big things, not with very small things.
42. The Law is not concerned with very trivial things.
43. The senate makes our laws, the gods make our rights.
44. Right and Law are very important things.
45. Man is dearer to the gods than to himself.
46. Let a sound mind in a sound body be pleasing to you.
47. Let a sound mind in a sound body please you more than wealth.
48. I know less than others (do) about the civil laws.

C.1.

1. Mihi crēdite! Tibi crēdō magis quam mihi crēdis.
2. Crēdidimus eōs lēgibus parēre velle. (indirect statement)
3. Tē monēmus ut omnibus aequus sīs neminīque faveās. (indirect command)
4. Eīs quibus crēdidit fāvit (or, favēbat).
5. Eī suāsimus (or, persuāsimus) ut eīs sōlīs quibus crēdēret favēret. (indirect command, containing a relative clause of characterisitic).
6. Nē eīs nimis placēre studeās.
7. Nōs monēns ut canem cavērēmus praestitit.
8. Melius est errōribus ignoscere et omnibus quī nōbīs nōn nocitūrī sint parcere.
9. Sapientius est hostibus nocēre amīcīsque ignoscere.
10. Quot dominīs ūnō tempore servīre possumus?

XVI
Deponent Verbs; Optative Mood; Verbs of Fearing or Prevention; Ablative Case Summary

A. Deponent Verbs

A.1. Write complete synopses of the following verbs in the person and number indicated, and translate the indicative form:

1.   **sequor** (3rd person sing.)

principal parts: _____, _____, _____,

meaning: _____

	Indicative	*Translation*	*Subjunctive*
pres.	_____	_____	_____
imperf.	_____	_____	_____
fut.	_____	_____	N/A
perf.	_____	_____	_____
plpf.	_____	_____	_____
fut. perf.	_____	_____	N/A

	imperative (sing. + pl.)	*translation*
	_____	_____

	infinitives	translation
pres.	_____	_____
perf.	_____	_____
fut. perf. active	_____	_____

	participles	translation
pres.	_____	_____
perf.	_____	_____
fut. perf. active	_____	_____
fut. perf. passive	_____	_____

2. **gradior** (1st person sing)

principal parts: _____, _____, _____,

meaning: _____

	Indicative	Translation	Subjunctive
pres.	_____	_____	_____
imperf.	_____	_____	_____
fut.	_____	_____	N/A
perf.	_____	_____	_____
plpf.	_____	_____	_____
fut. perf.	_____	_____	N/A

	imperative (sing. + pl.)	translation
	_____	_____

	infinitives	translation
pres.	_____	_____
perf.	_____	_____
fut. perf. active	_____	_____

	participles	translation
pres.	_____	_____
perf.	_____	_____
fut. perf. active	_____	_____
fut. perf. passive	_____	_____

3. **morior** (2nd person sing.)

principal parts: _____, _____, _____,

meaning: _____

	Indicative	Translation	Subjunctive
pres.	_____	_____	_____
imperf.	_____	_____	_____
fut.	_____	_____	N/A
perf.	_____	_____	_____
plpf.	_____	_____	_____
fut. perf.	_____	_____	N/A

	imperative (sing. + pl.)	translation
	_____	_____

	infinitives	translation
pres.	_____	_____
perf.	_____	_____
fut. perf. active	_____	_____

	participles	translation
pres.	_____	_____
perf.	_____	_____
fut. perf. active	_____	_____
fut. perf. passive	_____	_____

4.   **moror** (3rd person pl.)

principal parts: _____, _____, _____,

meaning: _____

	Indicative	Translation	Subjunctive
pres.	_____	_____	_____
imperf.	_____	_____	_____
fut.	_____	_____	N/A
perf.	_____	_____	_____
plpf.	_____	_____	_____
fut. perf.	_____	_____	N/A

	imperative (sing. + pl.)	translation
	_____	_____

	infinitives	translation
pres.	_____	_____
perf.	_____	_____
fut. perf. active	_____	_____

	participles	translation
pres.	_____	_____
perf.	_____	_____
fut. perf. active	_____	_____
fut. perf. passive	_____	_____

5. **patior** (1st person pl.)

principal parts: _____, _____, _____,

meaning: _____

	Indicative	Translation	Subjunctive
pres.	_____	_____	_____
imperf.	_____	_____	_____
fut.	_____	_____	N/A
perf.	_____	_____	_____
plpf.	_____	_____	_____
fut. perf.	_____	_____	N/A

	imperative (sing. + pl.)	translation
	_____	_____

	infinitives	translation
pres.	_____	_____
perf.	_____	_____
fut. perf. active	_____	_____

	participles	translation
pres.	_____	_____
perf.	_____	_____
fut. perf. active	_____	_____
fut. perf. passive	_____	_____

6. **utor** (2nd person pl.)

principal parts: _____, _____, _____,

meaning: _____

	Indicative	Translation	Subjunctive
pres.	_____	_____	_____
imperf.	_____	_____	_____
fut.	_____	_____	N/A

perf.	_____	_____	_____
plpf.	_____	_____	_____
fut. perf.	_____	_____	N/A

	imperative (sing. + pl.)	*translation*
	_____	_____

	infinitives	*translation*
pres.	_____	_____
perf.	_____	_____
fut. perf. active	_____	_____

	participles	*translation*
pres.	_____	_____
perf.	_____	_____
fut. perf. active	_____	_____
fut. perf. passive	_____	_____

A.2. Translate the following deponent verbs, and then change them to the tenses indicated, retaining the original mood, person, and number of the verb given. On the lines below the new forms, write their translations.

Present	*Translation*	*Imperfect*	*Future*	*Perfect*	*Pluperfect*
conātur	_____	_____	_____	_____	_____
		_____	_____	_____	_____
conāris	_____	_____	_____	_____	_____
		_____	_____	_____	_____
coner	_____	_____	_____	_____	_____
		_____	_____	_____	_____
ingreditur	_____	_____	_____	_____	_____
		_____	_____	_____	_____
aggrediātur	_____	_____	_____	_____	_____
		_____	_____	_____	_____
ēgrediantur	_____	_____	_____	_____	_____
		_____	_____	_____	_____
gradiuntur	_____	_____	_____	_____	_____
		_____	_____	_____	_____
hortāmur	_____	_____	_____	_____	_____
		_____	_____	_____	_____
hortēmur	_____	_____	_____	_____	_____
		_____	_____	_____	_____

Present	Translation	Imperfect	Future	Perfect	Pluperfect
loqueris	_____	_____	_____	_____	_____
	_____	_____	_____	_____	_____
loquāris	_____	_____	_____	_____	_____
	_____	_____	_____	_____	_____
mīrēmur	_____	_____	_____	_____	_____
	_____	_____	_____	_____	_____
mīrāmur	_____	_____	_____	_____	_____
	_____	_____	_____	_____	_____
moriāmur	_____	_____	_____	_____	_____
	_____	_____	_____	_____	_____
sequiminī	_____	_____	_____	_____	_____
	_____	_____	_____	_____	_____
ūtere (indic.)	_____	_____	_____	_____	_____
	_____	_____	_____	_____	_____
fruuntur	_____	_____	_____	_____	_____
	_____	_____	_____	_____	_____
fruantur	_____	_____	_____	_____	_____
	_____	_____	_____	_____	_____

B. Derivations

B.1. Identify the stem of the Latin verb which is the origin of each of the following English words.

Example.

English word	gradient (noun)

Latin stem	_Principal parts of Latin verb_	_Meaning of Latin verb_
gradiēns (pres. p.)	gradior, gradī, gressus sum	take steps, walk, go

Meaning — a rising or descending surface (a slope), or the degree of rising or descending

(Note: pres.p. = present participle; perf.p. = perfect participle; pres.inf. = present infinitive)

English word & Meaning	_Latin stem_	_Principal parts of Latin verb_	_Meaning of Latin verb_
access	_____	_____	_____
meaning:	_____		
accident	_____	_____	_____
meaning:	_____		
advent	_____	_____	_____
meaning:	_____		
adverse	_____	_____	_____
meaning:	_____		

advertisement _____ _____ _____

meaning: _____

aggressive _____ _____ _____

meaning: _____

colloquy _____ _____ _____

meaning: _____

commorant _____ _____ _____

meaning: _____

commorient _____ _____ _____

meaning: _____

conative _____ _____ _____

meaning: _____

conjuration _____ _____ _____

meaning: _____

consecutive _____ _____ _____

meaning: _____

consequence _____ _____ _____

meaning: _____

destitute _____ _____ _____

meaning: _____

deterrent _____ _____ _____

meaning: _____

egress _____ _____ _____

meaning: _____

elocution _____ _____ _____

meaning: _____

execute _____ _____ _____

meaning: _____

exhortation _____ _____ _____

meaning: _____

ferriferous _____ _____ _____

meaning: _____

fixation _____ _____ _____

meaning: _____

fruit _____ _____ _____

meaning: _____

impede _____ _____ _____

meaning: _____

English word & Meaning	Latin stem	Principal parts of Latin verb	Meaning of Latin verb
impedimenta			
meaning:			
impeditive			
meaning:			
interlocutory			
meaning:			
miracle			
meaning:			
mirror			
meaning:			
mortuary			
meaning:			
nascent			
meaning:			
natal			
meaning:			
nation			
meaning:			
native			
meaning:			
nature			
meaning:			
obsequious			
meaning:			
passion			
meaning:			
passive			
meaning:			
patient			
meaning:			
progress			
meaning:			
prosecute			
meaning:			
prohibition			
meaning:			

reveal

meaning: _____

reverence

meaning: _____

sequence

meaning: _____

solisequious

meaning: _____

use

meaning: _____

utilize

meaning: _____

veil

meaning: _____

velar

meaning: _____

velate

meaning: _____

vulnerable

meaning: _____

C. Verbs of Fearing

C.1. Translate the following phrases into good English:

1. Cavē nimis loquentēs. (**nimis**, adv., excessively)
2. Hīs locūtīs, Sibylla puerum prōhibuit quīn plūra peteret.
3. Puer tenērī nōn potest quīn plūra petat.
4. Sibyllae verba puerum nē plūra petat impediunt.
5. Puer plūra petere dubitat.
6. Dubitatne Sibylla eī respondēre?
7. Nōn dubitat Sibylla quīn puer nimis loquentēs fugere dēbeat.
8. Lucrētia, honōris causā moritūra, virum vocāvit. (**Lucrētia, -ae,** f. proper name)
9. Vir eius et virī amīcī domum Lucrētiae aggressī sunt.
10. Lucrētiae, virtūte optimā fēminae, mēns ā dolōre ad mortem trānsierat.
11. Domum aggredientēs, virī rēs pessimās veritī sunt.
12. Prō rē pūblicā, prō omnibus fēminīs optimīs, nē hoc facere dubitētis.
13. Virum et amīcos terruit. Nēminī erant vīrēs illīus pārēs.
14. Nēmō illam dēterrēre potuit quīn morerētur.

15. Lucrētia nōn morābitur.

16. Moriēturne Lucrētia manū suā dextrā?

17. Lucrētiā passā, rēs pūblica Rōmāna facta est.

18. Populus Rōmānus rēgēs nōn iam passus est, Lucrētiā mortuā.

19. Rex ultimus ūnius virī, Luciī Brūtī nōmine, manū est occasus.

20. Rēs pūblica Marcī Brūtī manū dextrā occāsa est.

21. Temporibus longē remōtīs, Brūtōrum manū occasī sunt.

22. Aliī crēdidērunt et Lucium et Marcum Brutum rem pūblicam et servāvisse et servīvisse.

23. Ob quaedam signa Caesar diū morātus est.

24. Ob quaedam signā nōn dubium erat quīn moritūrus esset.

25. Ūtinam nē Caesar perīsset! Vereor nē Caesar peritūrus sit.

26. Caesāre mortuō, Sōl Rōmam miserātus est. (**miseror, -ārī,** feel pity for)

27. Sōl Rōmam mīrārī vidētur. Rōmānōs multīs mōnstrīs monet.

28. Cum caput suum vēlāvit, ut Rōmānī noctem aeternam timuērunt!

29. Multa mīranda vīsa sunt, capite Sōlis vēlātō.

30. Vereor nē forte mē domum secūtūrī sint.

D. Translation

D.1. Translate the following into Latin, using the verbs indicated:

1. They tried (**cōnor**) to help her by swearing that they would pursue (**sequor**) her enemy.

2. Enjoy (**fruor**, 2nd person pl.) as many good things as possible.

3. Try (**cōnor**, 2nd person sing.) to enjoy (**ūtor**) a life that is noble.

4. They dread (**vereor**) the arrival of the enemy.

5. Fearing (**metuō**) the enemy would soon attack (**aggredior**), they abandoned (**destituō**) their homes and their lands.

6. Some people abandoned their homes, and some lingered longer than seemed wise.

7. "Go to (**aggredior**) your homes and die there if you (s.) wish!", he said (**loquor**).

8. We will try to prevent your (s.) suffering (**patior**) such vicious things (**scelerātus, a, um**) as we have suffered.

9. When the sun was about to rise, the leader proceeded toward the ships, and the sailors followed.

10. The faithful servant hesitated for as long as possible, but finally placed the flame under the pyre.

11. He doubted whether he ought to place the flame under the pyre.

12. He walks with me and he talks with me.

Key, Chapter XVI

A.1.

1.   sequor (3rd person sing.)
principal parts: **sequor, sequī, secūtus sum**
meaning: follow, pursue

	Indicative	Translation	Subjunctive
pres.	sequitur	he follows	sequātur
imperf.	sequēbatur	he was following	sequerētur
fut.	sequētur	he will follow	
perf.	secūtus est	he has followed	secūtus sit
plpf.	secūtus erat	he had followed	secūtus esset
fut. perf.	secūtus erit	he will have followed	

	imperative	translation
	sequere, sequiminī	follow, pursue

	infinitives	translation
pres.	sequī	to follow
perf.	secūtus esse	to have followed
fut.perf. active	secūtūrus esse	to be about to follow

	participles	translation
pres.	sequēns, sequentis	following
perf.	secūtus, -a, -um	having followed
fut. perf. active	secūtūrus, -a, -um	about to follow
fut. perf. passive	sequendus, -a, -um	to be followed

2.   gradior (1st person sing.)
principal parts: **gradior, gradī, gressus sum**
meaning: walk, go

	Indicative	Translation	Subjunctive
pres.	gradior	I go	gradiar
imperf.	gradiēbar	I was going	graderer
fut.	gradiar	I shall go	
perf.	gressus sum	I have gone	gressus sim
plpf.	gressus eram	I had gone	gressus essem
fut.perf.	gressus erō	I shall have gone	

	imperative	translation
	gradere, gradiminī	go!

	infinitives	translation
pres.	gradī	to go
perf.	gressus esse	to have gone
fut. perf. active	gressūrus esse	to be about to go

	participles	translation
pres.	gradiēns, gradientis	going
perf.	gressus, -a, -um	having gone
fut. perf. active	gressūrus, -a, -um	about to go
fut. perf. passive	gradiendus, -a, -um	(usually translated as impersonal verb, e.g., gradiendum est — walking must be done)

3.   morior (2nd person sing.)
principal parts: **morior, morī, mortuus sum**
meaning: die

	Indicative	Translation	Subjunctive
pres.	moreris	You are dying	moriāris
imperf.	moriēbāris	You were dying	morerēris

fut.	morięris	You will die	
perf.	mortuus es	You have died	mortuus sīs
plpf.	mortuus erās	You had died	mortuus essēs
fut. perf.	mortuus eris	You will have died	

| *imperative* | | *translation* |
| morere, moriminī | die! |

infinitives		*translation*
pres.	morī	to die
perf.	mortuus esse	to have died (to be dead)
fut. perf. active	moritūrus esse	to be about to die

participles		*translation*
pres.	moriēns, morientis	dying
perf.	mortuus, -a, -um	having died
fut. perf. active	moritūrus, -a, -um	about to die
fut. perf. passive	moriendus, -a, -um	(usually translated as impersonal verb, e.g., moriendum est — dying must be done)

4. moror (3rd person pl.)
principal parts: **moror, morārī, morātus sum**
meaning: delay

	Indicative	*Translation*	*Subjunctive*
pres.	morantur	They delay	morēntur
imperf.	morābantur	They were delaying	morārentur
fut.	morābuntur	They will delay	
perf.	morātī sunt	They have delayed	morātī sint
plpf.	morātī erant	They had delayed	morātī essent
fut. perf.	morātī erunt	They will have delayed	

| *imperative* | | *translation* |
| morāre, morāminī | Delay! |

infinitives		*translation*
pres.	morārī	to delay
perf.	morātus esse	to have delayed
fut. perf. active	morātūrus esse	to be about to delay

participles		*translation*
pres.	morāns, morantis	delaying
perf.	morātus, -a, -um	having delayed
fut. perf. active	morātūrus, -a, -um	about to delay
fut. perf. passive	morandus, -a, -um	to be delayed

5. patior (1st person pl.)
principal parts: patior, patī, passus sum
meaning: suffer, endure

	Indicative	*Translation*	*Subjunctive*
pres.	patimur	I am suffering	patiāmur
imperf.	patiēbāmur	I was suffering	paterēmur
fut.	patiēmur	I shall suffer	
perf.	passī sumus	I have suffered	passī sīmus
plpf.	passī erāmus	I had suffered	passī essēmus
fut. perf.	passī erimus	I shall have suffered	

| *imperative* | | *translation* |
| patere, patiminī | suffer! |

infinitives		*translation*
pres.	patī	to suffer
perf.	passus esse	to have suffered
fut. perf. active	passūrus esse	to be about to suffer

	participles	*translation*
pres.	patiēns, patientis	suffering
perf.	passus, -a, -um	having suffered
fut. perf. active	passūrus, -a, -um	about to suffer
fut. perf. passive	patiendus, -a, -um	to be suffered, endured

6. **utor** (2nd person pl.)

principal parts: **ūtor, ūtī, ūsus sum**

meaning: use, enjoy

	Indicative	*Translation*	*Subjunctive*
pres.	ūtiminī	you are using	ūtāminī
imperf.	ūtēbāminī	you were using	ūterēminī
fut.	ūtēminī	you will use	
perf.	ūsī estis	you have used	ūsī sītis
plpf.	ūsī erātis	you had used	ūsī essētis
fut. perf.	ūsī eritis	I shall have used	

	imperative	*translation*
	ūtere, ūtiminī	use!

	infinitives	*translation*
pres.	ūtī	to use
perf.	ūsus esse	to have used
fut. perf. active	ūsūrus esse	to be about to use

	participles	*translation*
pres.	ūtēns, ūtentis	using
perf.	ūsus, -a, -um	having used
fut. perf. active	ūsūrus, -a, -um	about to use
fut. perf. passive	ūtendus, -a, -um	to be used

A.2.

Present	Translation	Imperfect	Future	Pefect	Pluperfect
cōnātur	he tries, is trying	cōnābātur he was trying	cōnābitur will try	cōnātus est has tried	cōnātus erat had tried
cōnāris,	you try, are trying	cōnābāris you were trying	cōnāberis will have tried	cōnātus es ———	cōnātus erās had tried
cōner	subjunctive: let me try	cōnārer	———	cōnātus sim	cōnātus essem
ingreditur	he is entering	ingrediēbātur he was entering	ingrediētur will enter	ingressus est has entered	ingressus erat had entered
aggrediātur	subjunctive: let him approach	aggrederētur	———	aggressus sit	aggressus esset
ēgrediantur	subjunctive: let them depart	ēgrederentur	———	ēgressī sint	ēgressī essent
gradiuntur	they are going	gradiēbantur they were going	gradientur will go	gressī sunt have gone	gressī erant had gone
hortāmur	we are urging/encouraging	hortābāmur we were urging	hortābimur will urge	hortātī sumus have urged	hortātī erāmus had urged
hortēmur	subjunctive: let us encourage	hortārēmur	———	hortātī sīmus	hortātī essēmus
loqueris	you are speaking	loquēbāris you were speaking	loquēris will speak	locūtus es have spoken	locūtus erās had spoken
loquāris	subjunctive: speak!	loquerēris	———	locūtus sīs	locūtus essēs
mīrēmur	subjunctive: let us admire	mīrārēmur	———	mīrātī sīmus	mīrātī essēmus

mīrāmur we admire	**mīrābāmur** we were admiring	**mīrābimur** will admire	**mīrātī sumus** have admired	**mīrātī erāmus** had admired
moriāmur subjunctive: let us die	**morerēmur**	———	**mortuī sīmus**	**mortuī essēmus**
sequiminī you are following or follow	**sequēbāminī** you were following	**sequēminī** will follow	**secutī estis** have followed	**secūtī erātis.** had followed
ūtere you are using	**ūtēbāre** you were using	**utēre** ———	**ūsus es** have used	**ūsus erās** had used
fruuntur they are enjoying	**fruēbantur** they were enjoying	**fruentur** will enjoy	**fructī sunt** have enjoyed	**fructī erant** had enjoyed
fruantur subjunctive: let them enjoy	**fruerentur** ———	———	**fructī sint** ———	**fructī essent** ———

B. DERIVATIONS

B.1.

(Note: *pres. p.* = present participle; *perf. p.* = perfect participle; *pres. inf.* = present infinitive)

English word & Meaning	Latin stem	Principle parts of Latin verb	Meaning of Latin verb
access *a way or means of approach*	**cessus** *(perf. p.)*	**ad; cēdō, -ere, cessī, cessus**	go (to), approach
accident *unexpected mishap*	**cadēns** *(pres. p.)*	**ad; cadō, -ere, cecidī, cāsus**	fall (to)
advent *the coming, arrival*	**ventus** *(perf. p.)*	**ad; veniō, -īre, vēnī, ventus**	come (to)
adverse *antagonistic, opposing*	**versus** *(perf. p.)*	**ad; vertō, -ere, verti, versus**	turn toward, against
advertisement *a public notice*	**vertere** *(pres. inf.)*	**ad; vertō, -ere, verti, versus**	turn (toward)
aggressive *making the first attack, energetic*	**gressus** *(perf. p.)*	**ad; gradior, gradī, gressus**	go (toward, against)
colloquy *a speaking together*	**loquī** *(pres. inf.)*	**cum; loquor, loquī, locūtus**	speak (with)
commorant *dwelling, resident*	**morāns** *(pres. p.)*	**cum; moror, morārī, morātus**	delay, loiter (with)
commorient *dying at the same time*	**moriēns** *(pres. p.)*	**cum; morior, morī, mortuus**	die (with)
conative *pertaining to that portion of mental life having to do with trying or attempting*	**cōnātus** *(perf. p.)*	**cōnor; cōnārī, cōnātus**	try, attempt
conjuration *an incantation*	**coniūrātus** *(perf. p.)*	**cum; iūrō, āre, āvī, ātus**	take an oath (with)
consecutive *following in order*	**secūtus** *(perf. p.)*	**cum; sequor, sequī, secūtus**	follow (with)
consequence *an effect or result*	**sequēns** *(pres. p.)*	**cum; sequor, sequī, secūtus**	follow (with)
destitute *lacking the means of subsistence*	**dēstitūtus** *(perf. p.)*	**dēstituō, -ere, dēstituī, dēstitūtus**	abandon
deterrent *discouraging through fear*	**dēterrēns** *(pres. p.)*	**dē; terreō, -ēre, -uī, -itus**	frighten (from)

egress *exit*	**gressus** *(perf. p.)*	ex; gradior, gradī, gressus	go (from)
elocution *manner of speaking or reading in public*	**locūtus** *(perf. p.)*	ex; loquor, loquī, locūtus	speak (out, from)
execute *to follow out, to fulfill*	**secūtus** *(perf. p.)*	ex; sequor, sequī, secūtus	follow (from)
exhortation *utterance or address containing urgent advice*	**hortātus** *(perf. p.)*	ex; hortor, -ārī, -ātus	urge, encourage
ferriferous *bearing or containing iron*	**ferre** *(pres. inf.)*	ferrum, -ī, n.; ferō, ferre, tulī, lātus	bear, carry (iron)
fixation *act of making firm (fixing), or state of being fixed*	**fīxus** *(perf. p.)*	fīgō, -ere, fīxī, fīxus	drive in, pierce
fructify *to bear fruit*	**fructus** *(perf. p.)*	fruor, fruī, fructus	have the enjoyment of
impede *to hinder*	**impedīre** *(pres. inf.)*	impediō, -īre, -īvī, -ītus	hinder
impeditive *tending to hinder*	**impedītus** *(perf. p.)*	impediō, -īre, -īvī, -ītus	hinder
impedimenta *physical defects (pl.) or obstacles*	**impedīre** *(pres. inf.)*	impediō, -īre, -īvī, -ītus	hinder
ingredient *something that enters as an element into the mixture*	**gradiēns** *(pres. p.)*	in; gradior, gradī, gressus	go (into)
interlocutory (noun) *a discussion*	**locūtus** *(perf. p.)*	inter; loquor, loquī, locūtus	speak (among)
miracle *an event the defies the laws of science*	**mīrarī** *(pres. inf.)*	mīror, -ārī, -ātus	marvel at, admire
mirror *a looking glass*	**mirārī** *(pres. inf.)*	mīror, -ārī, -ātus	marvel at, admire
mortuary *a place where dead people are kept*	**mortuus** *(perf. p.)*	morior, morī, mortuus	die
nascent *coming into being*	**nascēns** *(pres. p.)*	nascor, nascī, nātus	be born
natal *connected with birth, dating from birth*	**nātus** *(perf. p.)*	nascor, nascī, nātus	be born
nation *an historically developed community, usually with a territory, common language, etc.*	**nātus** *(p. part.)*	nascor, nascī, nātus	be born
native *inborn, not acquired*	**nātus** *(perf. p.)*	nascor, nascī, nātus	be born
nature *essential, inborn character of a person or thing*	**nātus** *(perf. p.)*	nascor, nascī, nātus	be born

222

obsequious *excessively willing to serve or obey*	**sequī** *(pres. inf.)*	**ob; sequor, sequī, secūtus**	follow (toward, be-cause of)
passion (originally) *suffering, agony; extreme emotion*	**passus** *(perf. p.)*	**patior, patī, passus**	suffer, endure
passive *not active, receiving impressions from outside agents*	**passus** *(perf. p.)*	**patior, patī, passus**	suffer, endure
patient *enduring, long-suffering*	**patiēns** *(pres. p.)*	**patior, patī, passus**	suffer, endure
progress *forward movement*	**gressus** *(perf. p.)*	**prō, gradior, gradī, gressus**	go (forward)
prosecute *follow or pursue for the purpose of accomplishing something*	**secūtus** *(perf. p.)*	**prō; sequor, sequī, secūtus**	follow (in behalf of)
prohibition *an order or law forbidding something*	**prōhibitus** *(perf. p.)*	**prōhibeō, -ēre, -uī, -itus**	prevent, deter
reveal *disclose, draw away the curtain*	**velāre** *(pres. inf.)*	**re-; velāre, -āvī, -ātus**	cover, wrap up (negated by **re-**)
reverence *a feeling of awe, respect*	**verēns** *(pres. p.)*	**re-; vereor, -ērī, veritus**	feel awe of, fear (intensified by **re-**)
sequence *a succession or series of things, following in a certain order*	**sequēns** *(pres. p.)*	**sequor, sequī, secūtus**	follow
solisequious *follows the sun*	**sequī** *(pres. inf.)*	**sōl, -is; sequor, sequī, secūtus**	follow (the sun)
use *the act of using or the power to make use of*	**ūsus** *(perf. p.)*	**ūtor, ūtī, ūsus**	use, enjoy
utilize *make use of*	**ūtī** *(pres. inf.)*	**ūtor, ūtī, ūsus**	use, enjoy
veil *cover*	**vēlāre** *(pres.inf.)*	**velāre, -āvī, ātus**	cover, wrap up
velar *relating to the soft palate in the mouth*	**vēlāre** *(pres. inf.)*	**velāre, -āvī, ātus**	cover, wrap up
velate *having a veil or covering*	**vēlātus** *(perf. p.)*	**velāre, -āvī, -ātus**	cover, wrap up
vulnerable *capable of being hurt*	**vulnerāre** *(pres. inf.)*	**vulnerō, -āre, -āvī, -ātus**	wound, injure

C. Verbs of Fearing

1. Beware of people who talk too much.
2. When she had said these things, the Sibyl prevented the boy from asking more (things).
3. The boy cannot be restrained from asking more.
4. The Sibyl's words prevent the boy from asking more.
5. The boy hesitates to ask more.
6. Does the Sibyl hesitate to respond to him?
7. The Sibyl does not doubt that the boy ought to avoid people who talk too much.

8. Lucretia, doomed to die/about to die/ determined to die for honor's sake, summoned her husband.
9. Her husband and friends of her husband approached the home of Lucretia.
10. The mind of Lucretia, a woman of outstanding virtue, went from grief to death.
11. As they were approaching the house, the men feared very bad things.
12. For the sake of the Republic, for all honorable (the best) women, don't hesitate to do this.
13. She terrified (her) husband and (his) friends. No one had strength equal to that person.
14. No one was able to prevent her from dying.
15. Lucretia will not delay.
16. Will Lucretia die by her own right hand?
17. Because Lucretia had suffered, the Roman republic came into being.
18. The Roman people no longer endured kings, after Lucretia had died.
19. The last king perished at the hand of one man, Lucius Brutus by name.
20. The republic perished at the right hand of Marcus Brutus.
21. In times far removed, they perished at the hands of the Bruti (Brutuses).
22. Some people believed that both Lucius and Marcus Brutus saved and served the republic.
23. On account of certain signs, Caesar delayed for a long time.
24. On account of certain signs, there was no doubt that he would perish.
25. I wish that Caesar had not perished! I fear that Caesar will perish.
26. When Caesar had died, the Sun felt pity for Rome.
27. The Sun seems to admire Rome. He warns Romans with many omens.
28. When he veiled his head, how Romans feared eternal night!
29. Many marvels (things deserving to be marvelled at) were seen, when the Sun's head was covered.
30. I fear they may by chance follow me home.

D. Translation

1. Iūrandō sē hostem secūtūrōs esse eī auxilium dare cōnātī sunt.
2. Quam optimīs fruiminī.
3. Vītā nōbilī ūtī cōnāre.
4. Adventum hostis verentur.
5. Metuentēs nē hostis mox aggressūrī sint, et domūs et agrōs destituērunt.
6. Aliī domūs destituērunt, aliī diūtius quam sapiēns visum est morātī sunt.
7. "Domum aggrediminī ibique moriminī, sī tibi placet," locūtus est.
8. Prōhibēre nē tam scelerāta patiāris quam nōs passī sumus cōnābimur.
9. Sōle oritūrō, dux navēs aggressus est, nautaeque secūtī sunt.
10. Servus fidēlis quam diūtissimē dubitābat, sed tum flammam sub pyrā locāvit.
11. Dubitāvit nē flammam sub pyrā pōnere dēbēret.
12. Mēcum graditur loquiturque.

XVII
Roman Numbers; Noun Clauses; Definitive and Descriptive Conjunctions

A. Roman Numerals

A.1. Write out the following numbers in Roman numerals, in the Latin Cardinal, and in the Latin Ordinal:

	Roman Numeral	Latin Cardinal	Latin Ordinal
1. Two			
2. Three			
3. Ten			
4. Twenty-one			
5. Twenty-two			
6. Twenty-three			
7. Twenty-five			
8. Fifty-two			
9. Fifty-six			
10. One hundred and nine			
11. One hundred and eight			
12. One hundred and seven			
13. Two hundred and six			
14. Two hundred and five			
15. Three hundred and twenty-one			

16. Five hundred and fifty _____ _____ _____

17. One thousand _____ _____ _____

18. Two thousand _____ _____ _____

A.2. Translate the following into Latin. (See also Appendix E, pp. 366-367)

1. One, two, three, four, please open up the door.

2. Five, six, seven, eight, what great things do you anticipate? (*to hope for, expect,* **sperō, -are**)

3. When I was twenty-one, a wise man gave me stern advice. (literally, "of twenty-one (descriptive gen.) of years" (partitive gen.) **natus eram.**)

4. Now I am twenty-two, and I know too late that he advised me very truthfully.

5. Sing a song about twenty-four birds. (*song,* **carmen, carminis,** *n.; bird,* **avis, avis,** *m.*)

6. In this picture, she is the third person from the left. (**pictūra, -ae,** *f.*)

7. The three men hurried to Lucretia.

8. Two of these men became the first consuls of Rome.

9. The third man gave help to the fourth, fifth, and sixth men.

10. Give me two thousand and twenty nine kisses. (*kiss,* **basium, basiī,** *n.*)

11. On one occasion (once), the girls sang one-by-one.

12. Twice the girls sang in pairs (in groups of two).

13. Three times the men and women sang in groups of three.

14. In the tenth year, ten slaves at a time were set free.

B. Noun Clauses and Impersonal Verbs.

B.1. Translate the following into Latin:

1. Three times she tried to raise herself, and three times she grew weary.

2. It follows (logically) that each year follows the previous one, and ten years quickly becomes twenty.

3. You may proceed, if it pleases you.

4. We can make you depart.

5. You made me love you.

6. It pleased us that they were present. (*to be present,* **adsum, adesse**)

7. Pity me if this is true!

8. Romans never felt regret for the location of their city. (*location, site,* **locus, -ī,** *m.*)

9. It happened that Rome was placed beside a river. (*to place, establish,* **locō, -āre**)

10. The mother confessed she had no idea what the two infants' fate would be.

11. The two abandoned infants happened to be found by a she-wolf (*she-wolf,* **lupa, -ae,** *f.*)

C. Definitive/Descriptive Conjunctions

"when":	**quandō, ubi, postquam** + indicative (indicates time when)
	cum + indicative ("whenever")
	cum + subjunctive (circumstantial)
"before":	**antequam, priusquam**
"while", "until":	**dōnec, dum** + indicative (limits the time)
	dōnec, dum + subjunctive (anticipated limit)
	dummodo, modo ut + subjunctive (provided that)
	sī modo + subjunctive (if at least)
"since" or "because":	**quoniam, quandō, quod, quia:** + indicative (simple fact)
	quod, quia: + subjunctive (alleged reason)
	cum: + subjunctive (cause)

C.1. Choose what seems the most appropriate conjunction for the underlined words, and then translate the entire sentence into Latin:

1. <u>When</u> a she-wolf was passing (**praetereō**) that spot, she discovered the two abandoned infants.

2. <u>Whenever</u> I went to the forum, that person followed me and tried to converse with me.

3. <u>Whenever</u> I can, I go to the forum.

4. I went to the forum once <u>when</u> I was a child.

5. <u>After</u> she heard them, she saw them beside the river.

6. She heard the infants <u>before</u> she discovered them.

7. <u>Before</u> I ran to the forum, he approached to converse with me.

8. I left the forum <u>before</u> he began to speak with me.

9. Although she heard them, she did not see them <u>until</u> she went to drink.

10. The she-wolf protected the infants <u>until</u> the shepherd found them. (*shepherd*, **pastor, -ōris,** *m.*)

11. That child often used to go to the forum <u>until</u> his parents made him stay home.(*often, adv.* **saepe**)

12. We waited in the forum <u>until</u> Caesar came.

13. He did not see me <u>until</u> I went to the forum.

14. He wants to linger in the forum <u>until</u> he sees the sun set.

15. <u>While</u> I was going to the forum, I saw a hundred-year old woman.

16. <u>As long as</u> you linger in the forum, you will never find what you are looking for.

Key, Chapter XVII

A.1.

		Roman Numeral	Latin Cardinal	Latin Ordinal
1.	Two	II	duo, duae, duo	secundus, -a, -um
2.	Three	III	trēs, tria	tertius, -a, -um
3.	Ten	X	decem	decimus, -a, -um
4.	Twenty-one	XXI	vīgintī ūnus	vīcēsimus (-a, -um) prīmus (-a, -um)
5.	Twenty-two	XXII	vīgintī duo	vīcēsimus secundus
6.	Twenty-three	XXIII	vīgintī trēs	vīcēsimus tertius
7.	Twenty-five	XXV	vīgintī quīnque	vīcēsimus quīntus
8.	Fifty-two	LII	quīnquāginta duo	quīnquāgēsimus secundus
9.	Fifty-six	LVI	quīnquāginta sex	quīnquāgēsimus sextus
10.	One hundred and nine	CIX	centum novem	centēsimus nōnus
11.	One hundred and eight	CVIII	centum octō	centēsimus octāvus
12.	One hundred and seven	CVII	centum septem	centēsimus septimus
13.	Two hundred and six	CCVI	ducentī, -ae, -a sex	ducentēsimus sextus
14.	Two hundred and five	CCV	ducentī quīnque	ducentēsimus quīntus
15.	Three hundred and twenty-one	CCCXXI	trecentī vīgintī ūnus	trecentēsimī vīcēsimus prīmus
16.	Five hundred and fifty	DL	quīngentī quīnquāgentā	quīngentēsimus quīnquāgēsimus
17.	One thousand	M	mīlle	mīllēsimus
18.	Two thousand	MM	duo mīlia	duomīllēsimus

A.2.

1. Ūnum, duo, trēs, quāttuor, tē amābō, iānuam aperte.
2. Quīnque, sex, septem, octō, quās magnās rēs spērātis?
3. Dum vīgintī et unīus annōrum nātus erām, sapiēns cōnsilium sevērum mihi dedit.
4. Nunc vīgintī et duo annōrum nātus sum et eum sapientem mē vērissimē hortātum esse tardius nōvī.
5. Carmen dē vīgintī (et) quāttuor avium cane. (canite)
6. In hāc pictūrā, ea est ab laevā (manū) tertia persōna.
7. Trēs virī ad Lucrētiam cucurrit.
8. Duo dē his tribus prīmī cōnsulēs Rōmae factī sunt.
9. Tertius vir auxilium quartō, quīntō, sextōque virō dedit.
10. Da mī (mihi) duo mīlia et vīgintī nōna basiōrum.
11. Puellae singulae semel cantāvērunt.
12. Puellae bīnae bis cantārunt. (cantāvērunt)
13. Virī fēminaeque ternī ter cantāvēre. (cantāvērunt)
14. Decimō annō, dēnī servī līberatī sunt.

B.1.

1. Ter sē tollere cōnāta est, terque taeduit.
2. Sequitur ut quisque annus priōrem sequātur, decemque annī celeriter vīgintī fiant.
3. Licet ut prōgrediāris, sī tibi placet. (Licet te prōgredī, sī tibi placet.)
4. Licet nōs efficere (facere) ut ēgrediāris. (or, efficere (facere) ut ēgrediāris possumus.)
5. Fecistī (effecistī)ut tē amārem.
6. Ut eōs adessent nōbīs placuit.
7. Mē miserēre sī hoc vērum sit.
8. Numquam Rōmānōs locī urbis paenituit.
9. Factum est ut Rōma locāta esset ad fluvium.
10. Māter sē nescīvisse quid fātum infantium duōrum fore (futūrum esse) fāta est.
11. Factum est ut duo infantēs dēstitūtī ā lupā inventī essent.

C.1.

1. **cum-circumstantial** (+ imperfect subj.) Cum lupa illum locum praeterīrent, duōs infantēs dēstitūtōs invēnit.
2. **cum-whenever** (+ indic.) Cum ad forum aggrediēbar (accēdēbam, adībam), ille homō mē secūtus est mēcumque loquī cōnātus est.
3. **cum-whenever** (+ indic.) Ad forum adeō cum possum.
4. **cum-circumstantial** (+ perfect subj.) Ad forum adīvī (aggressus sum, accessī) ūnō tempore cum puer (puella) fuerim.
5. **postquam** (+ indic.) Post eōs audīvit quam ad fluvium vīdit. (or, Eōs audīvit postquam vīdit.)
6. **priusquam** (+ indic.) Infantēs audīvit priusquam eōs invēnit. (or, Prius...audīvit quam...invēnit.)
7. **antequam** (+ indic.) Antequam (Priusquam) ad forum cucurrī, aggressus est ut mēcum loquerētur.
8. **priusquam** (+ perfect subj., showing anticipation) Prius ē forō ēgressus sum quam mēcum loquī coeperit. (or, Ē forō ēgressus sum priusquam mēcum loquī coeperit.)
9. **cum-circumstantial** (+ subj.) Cum audīvisset, eōs tamen nōn vīdit dum accesserit ad bibendum (bibendī causā, or, ut biberet).
10. **dum** (+ indic.) Lupa infantēs servāvit dum pastor eōs invēnit. (Note that **invēnit** is indicative. Subjunctive here would imply that the wolf anticipated the shepherd coming and finding them.)
11. **dōnec, dum** (+ indic.) Ille puer ad forum saepe adībat dum parentēs fēcērunt ut domī mānserit.
12. **dōnec** (+ imperfect subj., showing anticipation) In forō morābāmur dōnec Caesar venīret.
13. **dōnec** (+ indic.) Nōn mē vīdit dōnec ad forum vēnī.
14. **dum** (+ present subj., showing anticipation) In forō morārī vult dum sōlis occasum videat.
15. **dum** (+ indic.) Dum ad forum adībam, centum annōrum fēminam vīdī.
16. **dum** (+ present subj., showing anticipated limit of time) Dum in forō morēris, numquam id quod petis inveniēs.

XVIII
Alternate Latin Forms; Accusative Case; Genitive Case

A. Alternate forms:

1. **-re = -ris** (2nd person singular, passive ending)
2. **-ēre = ērunt**
3. **fore = futūrum esse**
4. **forem, forēs, foret, etc. = essem, essēs, esset, etc.**
5. accusative **īs = ēs** (ī-stem nouns only)
6. syncope = omission of vowels, including **-v-**, between consonants.
7. historical infinitive = imperfect indicative in meaning.
8. future imperative:

	active		*passive*	
person	S.	Pl.	S.	Pl.
2nd	-tō	-tōte	-tor	—
3rd	-tō	-ntō	-tor	-ntor

A.1. Substitute the appropriate alternate forms for the words underlined, and then translate each sentence into good English:

1. Mē nōvistīne?

2. Nōlō tē nōvisse.

3. Aliī mē nuptiās facere coēgērunt.

4. Aliī fēcērunt ut nuptiās fēcerim.

5. Cōgitat audāciam meam futūram esse mihi remediō malōrum meōrum.

6. Noctēs diēsque rogāvit quid sua fortūna futūra esset.

7. Loquendō ēloquentiae artēs nōvērunt.

8. Sī ēloquentiam discēs, in Cicerōnis vestigiīs sequēris.

9. Ita studēte ut sapientiā impleāris.

10. Hās fābulās aliī trādidērunt.

11. Omnēs cīvēs dūcere vīs. Tū autem nōn dūcēs sed dūcēris.

12. Nōn cīvēs verēbar, sed nē cīvēs istī ducī malō crēderent.

13. Fīnēs nostrās aggredī coepērunt.

14. Ab Augustō fīnēs imperiī Rōmānī auctae sunt.

15. Hercule ēgrediente, bovēs sonum sonuērunt.

16. Bovēs ēgredientēs aliōs bovēs dēstituere dubitāvērunt.

A.2. Translate the following phrases, all of which contain alternate forms, into English, and indicate what the regular forms would be:

1. Servā vestem meam ut Herculis amōrem tueāre. (**tueor, tuērī, tūtus sum,** *safeguard*)

2. Dōna centaurī nōn Herculem servārunt.

3. Ēgredere ex urbe.

4. Sequere mē Rōmam.

5. Morāre mēcum hīc in forō.

6. Ūtere vītā tuā.

7. Metuō ut vītā tuā ūtāre.

8. Faciam ut vītā tuā ūtāre.

9. Sī tam somnia mihi quam tibi forent, numquam dormīrem.

10. Nēmō scīvit quis post Caesārem cōnsul foret.

11. Metuō nē tū mē sequāre.

12. Loquere mēcum.

13. Sī cum istā loquāre, marsuppium tuum cavēre sapiēns sit.

14. Illī quī dixēre, "Verbum satis sit sapientī," vērē dixēre.

B. Accusative and Genitive Constructions:

B.1. Indicate what use of the accusative or genitive case is needed for the underlined word, and then translate the entire sentence into Latin:

1. The horse neighed.

2. There was a loud noise in the city.

3. Whenever I dream such a dream, I write it in my book.

4. I have lived my life as well as possible.

5. Hannibal swore an oath to destroy Rome.

6. Your purse smells of silver and gold.

7. My father taught <u>me</u> <u>important things</u> when I was a child.

8. My friends called <u>me</u> <u>all kinds of</u> <u>names</u>.

9. Oh, my dear <u>father</u>! He was so good to me!

10. We came to ask <u>you</u> <u>for peace</u>. (**poscō, -ere,** *to ask, request*)

11. He asked <u>the Sibyl</u> <u>for advice</u>. (**poscō, -ere**)

12. I pity <u>you</u> your <u>sorrow</u>. (**dolor, dolōris,** *m.*)

13. <u>Who</u> would be ashamed of such a <u>father</u>?

14. My <u>neighbor's</u> house is so close I can touch it with my hand. (**vicīnus, -ī,** *m., neighbor*
     vicīnus, -a, -um, *close, near*)

15. <u>In order to see</u> my neighbor, I have to go away.

16. Part <u>of me</u> wants to go away, but love <u>of Rome</u> makes me want to linger.

17. Part <u>of him</u> wanted to go away, but <u>his</u> love <u>of Rome</u> made him want to stay.

18. Rome is a city <u>of many people</u> and <u>customs</u>.

19. Such boldness will be a your remedy <u>for trouble</u>.

Key, Chapter XVIII

A.1.

1.	**nōstīne**	Do you know me?
2.	**nōsse**	I don't want to know you.
3.	**coēgēre**	Others compelled me to marry.
4.	**fēcēre**	Others brought about my marriage. (i.e., brought it about that I married.)
5.	**fore**	He thinks my boldness will be a remedy for me (double dative) for my problems.
6.	**noctīs, fore**	Through nights and days he asked what his fortune would be.
7.	**artīs, nōrunt**	They learned the art of eloquence by speaking.
8.	**sequēre**	If you learn eloquence, you will follow in Cicero's footsteps.
9.	**impleāre**	Study in such a way that you may be filled with wisdom.
10.	**trādidēre**	Others have handed down these stories.
11.	**omnīs cīvīs, dūcēre**	You want to lead all the citizens; you, however, will not lead but will be led.
12.	**cīvīs**	I did not fear the citizens but that the citizens would believe that wicked general.
13.	**fīnīs, coepēre**	They began to attack our borders/territory.
14.	(no change, since this is nom. case)	The boundaries of the Roman empire were increased by Augustus.
15.	**sonuēre**	When Hercules was leaving, the cattle lowed (made their characteristic sound).
16.	**dubitāvēre**	The departing cattle hesitated to abandon the other cattle.

A.2.

1.	**tueāris**	Save my garment in order to safeguard Hercules' love.
2.	**servāvērunt**	The centaur's gifts did not save Hercules.
3.	**ēgrederis**	You are leaving the city. (or, with no change, imperative: Go from the city)
4.	**sequeris**	You are following me to Rome. (or, with no change, imperative: Follow me to Rome)
5.	**morāris**	You are lingering here in the forum with me. (or, with no change, imperative: Linger here in the forum with me.)
6.	**ūteris**	You are enjoying your life. (or, with no change, imperative: Enjoy your life.)
7.	**ūtāris**	I fear you are not enjoying your life.
8.	**ūtāris**	I will make you enjoy your life.
9.	**futūra essent**	If I were having dreams such as yours, I would never sleep.
10.	**futūrus esset**	No one knew who would be consul after Caesar.
11.	**sequāris**	I am afraid that you may follow me.
12.	**loqueris**	You are speaking with me. (or, with no change, imperative: speak with me.)
13.	**loquāris**	If you should speak with that woman, it would be wise to be cautious about your purse.
14.	**dixērunt**	Those who said, "A word to the wise is sufficient" spoke truthfully.

B.1.

1. Equus sonum sonuit. (cognate accus.)
2. In urbe magnum sonitum est. (accus. of inner object)
3. Cum tantum somnium somniō, id in librō meō scrībo. (cognate accus.)
4. Vītam meam quam optimē vīxī. (cognate accus.)
5. Hannibal iūs iūrāvit ut Rōmam sublātūrus esset. (cognate accus.)
6. Marsuppium tuum argentum aurumque olet. (cognate accus.)
7. Pater meum mē puerum rēs magnās docuit. (double accus.)
8. Amīcī meī mē nōmina omnis generis appellābant. (**omnis generis**, descriptive gen., **mē, nōmina**, cognate accus.)
9. Ō, meum cārum patrem! Is erat tam bonus mihi! (accus. of exclamation)
10. Vēnimus ut vōs pacem poscerēmus. (double accus.)
11. Sibyllam cōnsilium poposcit. (double accus.)
12. Mē miseret tuī doloris. (direct object; objective gen.)
13. Quem tantī patris puderet? (direct object; objective gen.)
14. Domus vicīnī meī est tam vicīnus ut manū tangere possim. (possessive gen.)

15. Vicīnī videndī causā, mihi ēgrediendum est. (egredī dēbeō). (gen. of purpose)
16. Pars meī abīre vult, sed amor Rōmae efficit ut morārī velim. (partitive gen.)
17. Pars eius abīre voluit (volēbat), sed eius amor Rōmae effēcit (efficiēbat) ut morārī vellet. (partitive gen., subjective gen.)
18. Rōma est urbs multōrum hominum mōrumque. (descriptive gen.)
19. Tanta audācia erit tibi remediō malōrum. (objective gen.)